Understanding Greek Tragic Theatre

This new edition will be a great resource 'and an enjoyable read' for anyone interested in Greek tragic theatre. As both scholar and actor/director, Rush Rehm knows the right questions to ask, and his answers are richly informative and thought-provoking.

Professor Pat Easterling, *University of Cambridge, UK*

Understanding Greek Tragic Theatre, a revised edition of *Greek Tragic Theatre*, is intended for those interested in how Greek tragedy works. By analysing the way the plays were performed in fifth-century Athens, Rush Rehm encourages classicists, actors, and directors to approach Greek tragedy by considering its original context.

Emphasizing the political nature of tragedy as a theatre of, by, and for the *polis*, Rehm characterizes Athens as a *performance culture*, one in which the theatre stood alongside other public forums as a place to confront matters of import and moment. In treating the various social, religious, and practical aspects of tragic production, he shows how these elements promoted a vision of the theatre as integral to the life of the city – a theatre whose focus was on the audience.

The second half of the book examines four exemplary plays, Aeschylus' *Oresteia* trilogy, Sophocles' *Oedipus Tyrannus*, and Euripides' *Suppliant Women* and *Ion*. Without ignoring the scholarly tradition, Rehm focuses on how each tragedy unfolds in performance, generating different relationships between the characters (and chorus) on stage and the audience in the theatre.

Rush Rehm is Professor of Classics and Theater and Performance Studies at Stanford University, USA. He is also a freelance actor and director, and Artistic Director of Stanford Repertory Theater.

Understanding Greek Tragic Theatre

Second Edition

Rush Rehm

Routledge
Taylor & Francis Group

LONDON AND NEW YORK

Second edition published 2017
by Routledge
2 Park Square, Milton Park, Abingdon, Oxon OX14 4RN

and by Routledge
711 Third Avenue, New York, NY 10017

Routledge is an imprint of the Taylor & Francis Group, an informa business

First edition published by Routledge 1992

British Library Cataloguing-in-Publication Data
A catalogue record for this book is available from the British Library

Library of Congress Cataloging-in-Publication Data
Names: Rehm, Rush, author.
Title: Understanding Greek tragic theatre / Rush Rehm.
Other titles: Greek tragic theatre
Description: Abingdon ; New York : Routledge, 2016. | Series:
Understanding
the Ancient World | Includes bibliographical references and index.
Identifiers: LCCN 2016001824| ISBN 9781138812611 (hardback : alk.
paper) |
ISBN 9781138812628 (pbk. : alk. paper) | ISBN 9781315748696 (ebook)
Subjects: LCSH: Greek drama (Tragedy)--History and criticism. | Political
plays, Greek--History and criticism. | Theater--Greece--History--To 500.
Classification: LCC PA3131 .R38 2016 | DDC 882/.010916--dc23
LC record available at http://lccn.loc.gov/2016001824

ISBN: 978-1-138-81261-1 (hbk)
ISBN: 978-1-138-81262-8 (pbk)
ISBN: 978-1-315-74869-6 (ebk)

Typeset in Sabon
by GreenGate Publishing Services, Tonbridge, Kent

Contents

Plates

My thanks to the Deutsches Archaeologishes Institut-Athen for permission to reproduce Plates 1 and 3; to the American School of Classical Studies at Athens: Agora Excavations for permission to reproduce Plate 2; to Mr Christian Schieckel (who created the model) and the Deutsches Theatermuseum, München (Foto Klaus Broszat) for permission to reproduce Plate 5; and to Hans Rupprecht Goette of the Deutsches Archaeologishes Institut-Berlin for providing me with his drawing of the early theatre of Dionysus (Plate 4), and for his generosity and collegiality in sharing with me his deep knowledge of the early theatre of Dionysus in Athens.

Preface

... Trying to find a frame in which to fit

Large things that progress bundles out of sight:

Grief, awe, terror, transcendent light.

(Chris Wallace-Crabbe[1])

This book is a revision of *Greek Tragic Theatre*, originally published in 1992 in the Theatre Production Studies series edited by the great John Russell Brown. John and the series have passed away, but Greek tragedy remains. *Understanding Greek Tragic Theatre* brings the earlier volume up to date.

Greek tragedy continues to attract the attention of students, scholars, and theatre artists, and the plays are performed across the globe.[2] I confess that I find most modern productions and adaptations disappointing, for the simple reason that, far too often, they fail to do justice to the material. The translations sound stilted or un-theatrical, and the adaptations range so far from the original, or strain so hard for contemporary relevance, that the plays lose their powerful strangeness. What have we gained if we convert Greek tragedy into a musical, a soap opera, a talking heads TV drama, an agitprop diatribe, or an avant-garde piece for a privileged elite?

Greek tragedy can generate an unforgettable theatrical experience, all the more astounding for speaking across centuries of cultural and historical difference. In such moments of rediscovery, something of the complex simplicity of Greek tragedy finds us out – the dance of the language, the agonizing passion of the characters, the surge of the chorus, the sound of a mythic name evoking its story of pain and insight.

Enthusiasms such as these are important in drawing us into the theatre, but they don't get us very far once we are there. For the challenge of the stage, as the Greeks well knew, is to wed ideas and insights to their concrete realization, incarnating words and actions in performance, giving the tale to be told a specific shape before a particular audience. With that in mind, this book addresses the question of how Greek tragedy *worked*, focusing on what the plays do rather than what can be extracted from them. My hope is that the reader – student, classicist, playgoer, theatre practitioner – catches some sense of the excitement of engaging Greek tragedy on its own terms, and comes away with a better idea of how its theatrical challenges can be met by understanding how they once were.

Part I emphasizes the political culture that produced Athenian tragedy, in the sense that it was a theatre of, by and for the *polis* ('city'), the social institution that bound Greeks together as a human community. In this light, I discuss Athens as a *performance culture*, one in which the theatre stood alongside other public forums as a place to confront matters of import and moment.[3] This poses a radical challenge to the contemporary view of thea-tre as entertainment, or as the artistic plaything for anyone who wants to have a go at it. Individual chapters follow on specific aspects of fifth-century tragic performance: the festival context, participation in and responsibility for dramatic production, the constraints and opportunities presented by the Athenian theatre of Dionysus, and important conventions of tragic staging. I show how the generic elements of production cohered around a vision of the theatre as integral to the life of the city – a theatre, in short, whose focus was on the audience.

In Part II, I examine four exemplary tragedies – in the case of the *Oresteia*, a connected trilogy – as they might have been realized in their original per-formance. My choice of the *Oresteia* and *Oedipus Tyrannus* may appear unadventurous, but the towering status of these works has tended to inhibit scholars from approaching them as plays enacted before an audience. Two tragedies by Euripides are probably too few, given the range of his work and the fact that much more of it has survived. By examining *Suppliant Women* and *Ion* (rarely produced on the modern stage), I treat two Euripidean plays of genius but quite different in form and content.

While not ignoring the critical tradition, my discussion of individual tragedies focuses on how each unfolds in performance, generating different relationships between the characters (and chorus) on-stage and the audi-ence in the theatre.[4] Such a sequential approach runs the risk of alienating those readers closely familiar with the texts, but a certain amount of 're-telling' is unavoidable if we are to engage imaginatively in the dynamics of performance.

By following the path that each play lays out, I shift perspectives between that of a director staging a production and that of an audience helping to make the production come to life. The audience is a virtual one, 'we', although I do differentiate fifth-century spectators (not a monolithic body) from their modern counterparts when issues of cultural and historical speci-ficity are paramount. As Adrian Poole reminds us, 'the power of Greek tragedy to outlive the local conditions of its original production depends on the quality of the challenge which it once offered to those local conditions'.[5]

The book avoids any general comments about the differences between the three great tragedians, concentrating instead on the dramatic and imaginative integrity of the particular play under discussion. Generalizations about the nature of Aeschylean and Sophoclean tragedy are particularly dangerous, given that our sample is so small. On the basis of Sophocles' seven extant plays, can we confidently pronounce the nature of the more than a hundred others that we have lost? Let us simply admit that the fifth century was a time of extraordinary theatrical production, and appreciate that all three playwrights were innovators, theatrical experimentalists, beneficiaries of the tradition from which they drew even as they challenged and reshaped it.

Notes

1 From 'Sonnets to the Left', in *I'm Deadly Serious*, Oxford, Oxford University Press, 1988, p. 27.
2 On modern productions and adaptations of tragedy, see *The Oxford Handbook of Greek Drama in the Americas*, eds K. Bosher, F. Macintosh, J. McConnell, and P. Rankine, Oxford, Oxford University Press, 2015; *Agamemnon in Performance, 458 BC to AD 2004*, eds F. Macintosh, P. Michelakis, E. Hall, and O. Taplin, Oxford, Oxford University Press, 2005, *Dionysus Since 69: Greek Tragedy at the Dawn of the Third Millennium*, eds E. Hall, F. Macintosh, and A. Wrigley, Oxford, Oxford University Press, 2004; and K.V. Hartigan, *Greek Tragedy on the American Stage: Ancient Drama in the Commercial Theater, 1882–1994*, Westport, CT, Greenwood Press, 1995.
3 Performance culture now seems like a cliché in scholarship on fifth-century Athens, but such was not the case when *Greek Tragic Theatre* first appeared 25 years ago.
4 I use the term 'on-stage' to mean 'in sight of the audience'; it does not imply that the performer stood on a raised stage.
5 A. Poole, *Tragedy, Shakespeare and the Greek Example*, Oxford, Blackwell, 1987, p. 12.

Acknowledgements

To acknowledge fully, and with full grace, the many people who have influenced my approach to Greek tragedy and its theatrical life is impossible. I am indebted to the long tradition of classical scholarship reflected (in a limited way) in the Notes, with special thanks to R.D. Murray, George Gellie, D.W. Conacher, Martin Esslin, Liviu Cieulei, William Arrowsmith, and Zeph Stewart (all deceased); W.R. Connor, Marsh McCall, Mark Edwards, Bonna Wescoat, Richard Patterson, Cynthia Patterson, Andrea Nightingale, and Pat Easterling. I have had the good fortune to act in and direct many of the plays discussed here, and much of my understanding of Greek tragedy comes from these theatrical encounters. Special thanks to James McCaughey and the members of Melbourne's Greek Theatre Project, the Performance: *Iliad* company, Geoffrey Reeves, Courtney Walsh, and the artists of Stanford Repertory Theater.

A note on translations and editions

In discussing individual passages, I have followed (where possible) the lineation of the Loeb editions, published by Harvard University Press (Cambridge, MA and London).

AESCHYLUS, edited by A.H. Sommerstein

Aeschylus I:	*Persians, Seven Against Thebes, Prometheus Bound* (2008)
Aeschylus II:	*Agamemnon, Choephori, Eumenides* (2008)
Aeschylus III:	*Fragments* (2008)

SOPHOCLES, edited and translated by H. Lloyd-Jones

Sophocles I:	*Ajax, Electra, Oedipus Tyrannus* (1994)
Sophocles II:	*Antigone, Women of Trachis, Philoctetes, Oedipus at Colonus* (1994, corrected 1998)
Sophocles III:	*Fragments* (1996)

EURIPIDES, edited and translated by D. Kovacs

Euripides I:	*Cyclops, Alcestis, Medea* (1994)
Euripides II:	*Children of Heracles, Hippolytus, Andromache, Hecuba* (1995)
Euripides III:	*Suppliant Women, Electra, Heracles* (1998)
Euripides IV:	*Trojan Women, Iphigeneia Among the Taurians, Ion* (1999)
Euripides V:	*Helen, Phoenician Women, Orestes* (2002)
Euripides VI:	*Bacchae, Iphigeneia at Aulis, Rhesus* (2002)
Euripides VII:	*Fragments, Aegeus–Meleager*, ed. and trans. C. Collard and M. Cropp (2008)
Euripides VIII:	*Fragments, Oedipus–Chrysippus & Other Fragments*, ed. and trans. C. Collard and M. Cropp (2009)

Translations are my own. Those of Aeschylus' *Oresteia* can be found *in Aeschylus' Oresteia: A Theatre Version*, Melbourne, Hawthorn Press, 1978.

All dates are BC unless otherwise noted. The Athenian year ran (roughly) from June to June, which explains a date such as 508/7; the lower number is closer to our era.

Part I

The social and theatrical background

1 The performance culture of Athens

In the culture of fifth-century Athens, Greek tragic theatre represented one kind of performance among many, drawing its strength (and occasionally its material) from the greater and lesser public occasions that surrounded it. The areas of politics, law, religious festivals, athletic games, choral competitions, and poetic recitations shared with the theatre the idea of public performance, where one form of cultural expression commented on another. Important aspects of family life – including rites of passage of birth, puberty, marriage, and death – also 'went public' in a quasi-theatrical fashion. Gatherings for wine, food, and entertainment called *symposia* provided occasions for more private performance, especially music and solo poetry. Although barred from these drinking parties (unless present as musicians, dancers, or prostitutes), women sang and told stories when they worked at the loom, and their participation in various religious festivals and cult worship included the performance of choral songs and dances.

In almost every tragedy we find references to, and enactments of, these political, ritual and artistic practices, as if theatre acknowledged its debt to the other manifestations of Athenian performance culture. We may contrast the Elizabethan and Jacobean playwrights who use theatrical metaphors to explain life beyond the stage: Jacques' 'All the world's a stage / and all the men and women are merely players' in Shakespeare's *As You Like It*, or Macbeth's conclusion that 'Life's but a walking shadow, a poor player / who struts and frets his hour upon the stage / and then is heard no more'. Far from singling out the stage as a metaphor for life, Greek tragedy reflected a society imbued with a sense of *event*, of things said and done in the context of a conventional frame, so that participation entailed both a commitment to the moment and a critical distance from it. Today, for example, we perceive a great difference between participating in a ritual where issues of belief are paramount, and attending a theatrical performance where suspension of disbelief is required. Ancient Athenians seem to have viewed these events more as a continuum than as opposed attitudes to the world.

We can find no better example of the pervasiveness of performance in ancient Greece than the political system of participatory democracy by which Athenians governed themselves. At least once every month (but usually two, three, or even four times) the citizens of Athens (free-born males over 18) gathered on the hill called the Pnyx for the meeting of the Assembly.[1] Appealing to reason, emotion, tradition, and morality, Assembly speakers swayed the citizen body, much like actors in a large outdoor theatre. Anyone present was free to speak, although the size of the audience – 6,000 or more – made such a prospect daunting. In this egalitarian public gathering, rhetorical performance would be judged critically and knowledgeably, for the Assembly was *the* means of formulating state policy, determined year in and year out by simple majority vote.

The large concavity of the Pnyx established a relationship between the (changing) speakers and their audience that mirrored the relationship between actors and spectators at the theatre of Dionysus,[2] discussed in Chapter 4. The same situation applied in the smaller political forums, such as the Council (a group of 500 who set the agenda for the Assembly), the assemblies of local districts (*dêmoi*, henceforth 'demes'), and the meetings of kinship and neighbourhood organizations. For example, when the Athenians rebuilt their Council chamber at the end of the fifth century, they set the seating banks around the speaker's platform on the model of the seating area surrounding the orchestra in the theatre; reporting an act of sacrilege by anti-democratic elements that took place in that very chamber, Xenophon describes the forceful removal of the suppliants as if it were a scene in a Euripidean tragedy – only the actions were staged to terrify the Council members rather than a theatre audience.[3]

We get a sense of the eloquence and power of political speeches from Thucydides' *History*, an account of the Peloponnesian War fought between Athens and Sparta in the last third of the fifth century. The confrontation between opposing speakers in various Thucydidean debates has all the vitality and imaginative life of a dramatic scene, with the assembled citizenry as audience, alternately swept up in the rhetoric and reflecting critically on its ramifications. An even closer analogue to the verbal life of a Greek tragic performance took place in the Athenian law courts. After hearing speeches offered by the litigants, the jury (ranging from 100 to 1,500 jurors) reached its verdict by simple majority vote, taken without consultation.[4] As with the decisions of the Assembly that could be overturned at a subsequent meeting, the trial-by-jury process was ongoing and open-ended. The loser of a case one day could file a counter-charge the next and try his opponent before a different set of jurors, a process that fully acknowledged the autonomy and variability of any given audience.

Many law court speeches have survived, composed by professional writers for litigants to deliver, as there were no lawyers present at the trial. The legal system converted both plaintiff and defendant into actors interpreting their lines for the benefit of the jury-audience.[5] The speechwriter's task required establishing the good character of his client and attacking that of his opponent. Was this the kind of man who would harm the city? Would this sort of citizen do that sort of thing? Histrionics from the sublime to the ridiculous characterize these forensic displays – one minute a speaker claims that he has observed all the duties owed his dead forebears, and in the next he mounts an attack on the legitimacy of his opponent's mother.

The creation and interpretation of a 'character' for a single law court performance drew on, as it influenced, the comparable work of the dramatist in the theatre. As well as providing a bottomless source of material for Greek comedy, Athenian litigiousness left its mark on tragedy. Consider the genre's rich legal vocabulary and the frequency of 'courtroom scenes', ranging from the momentous trial of Orestes in Aeschylus' *Eumenides* to the arraignment of Polymnestor in Euripides' *Hecuba*, where the verdict is reached *after* the accused has been brutally punished.[6]

Athens offered countless other occasions for rhetorical and forensic display, reflecting the spontaneity and theatrical flair of her citizens. Athens was animate with debate and argument, where a community of interested (or simply curious) parties could form at any moment. Lectures by philosopher–teachers known as sophists became popular during the fifth century, and the rhetoricians captured the imagination and custom of the sons of the Athenian elite, who developed their skills in persuasive argument in order to influence political events. Informal debates in the agora (market place) were common fare, as we know from the Platonic dialogues where Socrates prods some arrogant soul into revealing he has no rational basis for his most cherished opinions. The dialogue structure that Socrates adopts owes much to the tragedies staged in Athens, although the philosopher remained suspicious of the relationship between speaker and audience, between performer and 'performed upon', that operated in the theatre and other public forums:

> Isn't it the public themselves who are sophists [educators] on a grand scale, and give a complete training to young and old, men and women, turning them into just the sort of people they want ... when they crowd into the seats in the assembly, or law courts, or theatre?[7]

The Athenian state devoted over a hundred days in the calendar year to public festivals, organized around religious cults sanctioned by the city. In recreating what these occasions were like, we should keep in mind the differences between pagan and modern attitudes towards religion. Sir Kenneth Dover reminds us that, 'to the ordinary Greek, festive and ceremonial occasions were the primary constituent of religion; theology came a very bad second'.[8] Unlike the political forums of the city, most civic festivals were open to everyone: men, women, slaves, children, resident aliens, visiting foreigners. There were exceptions – the exclusion of men from the all-women festivals associated with Demeter, for example – but generally speaking the city gathered in all its variety, providing both performers and audiences for the different events.

A basic ritual pattern characterized most festival worship, including many recognizable theatrical elements. A procession involving an array of participants made its way to the temple that housed the cult-image of the deity. The parade included priests wearing sacral robes, underlings who carried various ritual objects, attendants who led the beasts to be sacrificed, common folk who marched or simply watched as the others passed by. The Parthenon frieze gives a rich impression of what the grandest of these Athenian processions, the Panathenaia, was like.

Assembled before the altar outside the temple, the crowd then witnessed the performance of the sacrifice itself. Looking out from the altar steps over the gathered throng, the priest uttered prayers and formulae, and after a series of actions to signal the victim's consent, the dramatic moment arrived. The first animal was struck, the women raised a ritual cry, and the smoke of burnt flesh rose to the heavens. At large-scale festivals such as the City Dionysia and the Panathenaia, the ritual slaughter had less of a sacred character than one might suppose. An enormous number of victims were offered (an excessive 240 cattle at the City Dionysia in 333 BC).[9] It was customary that only the inedible parts of the animal were dedicated and burnt to the gods; the rest were cooked and distributed to the crowd in a city-sponsored feast. A similar practice was followed at local sacrifices and those made in private households, allowing the participants to enjoy meat that was far too expensive to be consumed on less than special occasions.

After the feast, the other festival events occurred, and these frequently included performances organized as contests. There were athletic events, instrumental competitions on the lyre and *aulos* (a reed instrument comparable to a clarinet), solo songs with the singer accompanying himself on the lyre, choral singing and dancing, and so on. Many of the songs and choral odes make reference to their actual performance, reminding us that they were rehearsed, sung, and danced under the direction of the poet as choirmaster and choreographer.[10] Although the contestants officially offered their performances to the divinity, their efforts were directed primarily to the tastes and interests of the people who gathered as celebrants to watch and listen, to judge and reward. This was certainly the case at the City Dionysia, the main festival where comedies and tragedies were performed, as we shall see in the following chapter.

In addition to the festivals in Athens, great pan-Hellenic (all-Greek) gatherings were celebrated at Olympia, Nemea, and Isthmia, renowned for their athletic competitions, and at Delphi, famed for contests in poetry and music. Athens sent an ambassador to each of these festivals, and her citizens entered the competitions as individuals – the ancient games lacked some of the nationalistic zeal that dominates the modern Olympic movement. Victories at these prestigious competitions could generate their *own* performances, for the victors would commission poets such as Pindar to compose victory-odes, called *epinicians*, that were sung and danced by a chorus in the victor's home town, and possibly on other public occasions as well. Other genres found their way into tragedy, as the playwrights incorporated contemporary elements into the mythic world of their plays, exemplifying the pervasive modality of performance in fifth-century Athens.

Leaving the enormous crowds of the pan-Hellenic games, let us briefly consider performances of a more intimate nature, the rituals of weddings and funerals. These rites played a central role in the life of the Greek family and constitute a recurring motif in Greek tragedy.[11] Neither ritual was conceived as a single event, but rather as an ongoing series of performed activities, offering the playwright a variety of possible points of reference. On their wedding day, an Athenian bride and groom were given (separately) a ritual bath, and then dressed in white with a crown or garland to mark the occasion. The evening began with a banquet offered by the bride's father, where the gathered company danced and sang wedding hymns, followed by a nocturnal procession as the groom conveyed the bride to her new home. If circumstances allowed, the journey was made by horse- or mule-cart, accompanied by torchbearers and friends who played music and sang. The groom's parents met the couple at the threshold of their new home, and during the night, the parties who accompanied the procession sang *epithalamia*, songs 'outside the marriage chamber'. In the morning more songs awakened the couple, who later received gifts in a ceremony that led to a final wedding banquet. We find references to these rites in almost every extant tragedy, from the nuptial bath that Polyxena will never enjoy in *Hecuba* to the wedding procession Admetus remembers in *Alcestis*, from the wedding hymn that Sophocles' Antigone sings en route to her 'burial', to the poisoned wedding gifts that convert Jason's new bride into her own nuptial torch in *Medea*.

At the other end of the ritual spectrum, funerals constituted a performance for and about the dead. The ritual tasks of preparing the corpse – washing, anointing, dressing, crowning, adorning with flowers, and covering it for burial – fell to the female members of the family. The body was laid out in the courtyard where mourners, dressed in black, paid their respects, and the women wailed dirges and other lamentations. When the time came for burial, the men led the funeral cortège while the women followed behind the bier, reciting the ritual lament, occasionally accompanied by professional musicians and dirge-singers. As with the wedding, no priest officiated the rites, for the family and friends of the deceased arranged and carried out the funeral. After the inhumation or cremation, the mourners sang a final dirge, poured offerings, and returned to their homes. That evening the funeral party held a banquet, where they delivered eulogies for the deceased and sang funeral hymns. As in the case of weddings, such theatrical elements as costuming, singing, dancing, and making speeches constituted a good part of Greek burial custom. We find death ritual throughout Greek tragedy – the lamentations and threnodies that resound in Aeschylus' *Persians*, the focus on burial in Sophocles' *Ajax* and *Antigone*, the procession of corpses in Euripides' *Suppliant Women*. Aspects of the funeral ritual occur so frequently that scholars once thought the earliest tragedy originated from laments at the gravesite.

Both the Athenian wedding and funeral rites were conceived as performances where the participants moved back and forth between the roles of actor and spectator, conjoining public and private worlds in a way that is hard for us to imagine. This is not to romanticize life in fifth-century Athens, where slavery was practised, where women had extremely limited opportunities, where living conditions frequently were primitive and disease was poorly understood. But in grappling with the performance culture out of which tragedy grew, we must realize that it operated very differently from our professional, pre-packaged society, where everything is marketed for consumers – from peanuts to side-arms, from sex to salvation, from care for the elderly to care for the dead. To be sure, Athenians bought and sold in their market place, the agora in the centre of the city, but as they haggled over prices they also talked of the Assembly, the latest case in the law courts, a nephew's initiation, the upcoming festivals, a friend's wedding, the theatre – events that took place within a short walk from the fish stalls, as we can see in the aerial photograph of the city (see Plate 1).

One such event deserves our closer attention, for it played an important role in the development of tragedy – the contests for reciting the great epic poems of Homer, the *Iliad* and *Odyssey*. Although unofficial performances of Homer went back many years, Athens included an official competition among rhapsodes in the Panathenaic festival sometime between 566 and 514 BC, with the odds on an earlier rather than a later date. Unlike other pre-tragic contests, epic recitation was not based on music, spectacle, or lyric poetry, but on the solo performance of a complex narrative. We learn from Plato that a rhapsode resembled an actor, interpreting from memory the lines of a great poet, combining the technical demands of verse and vocal production (the crowds were large) with the emotional expression and sympathy required to play several different roles in the course of his recitation.[12] Roughly two-thirds of the *Iliad* is in direct speech, and the rhapsodes must have varied their delivery, volume, and tone to convey the different characters and their response to changing situations. Although composed long before the first tragedy, the poems are highly dramatic, and the most compelling sections read like scenes written for the stage: the great quarrel between Agamemnon and Achilles in *Iliad* Book 1; the encounters in Book 6 between Hector and his mother Hecuba, his sister-in-law Helen, and his wife Andromache (a scene much admired by the tragedians); the great embassy in Book 9, where Odysseus, Phoenix, and Ajax try to persuade Achilles to rejoin the battle; the unprecedented encounter between Priam and Achilles in Book 24, where mortal enemies momentarily unite in the communality of grief.[13]

The oral and aural qualities of Homeric poems remind us of their intimate connection with performance. Eric Havelock points out that 'we read as texts what was originally composed orally, recited orally, heard acoustically, memorized acoustically, and taught acoustically in all communities of early Hellenic civilization'.[14] We get some sense of what oral

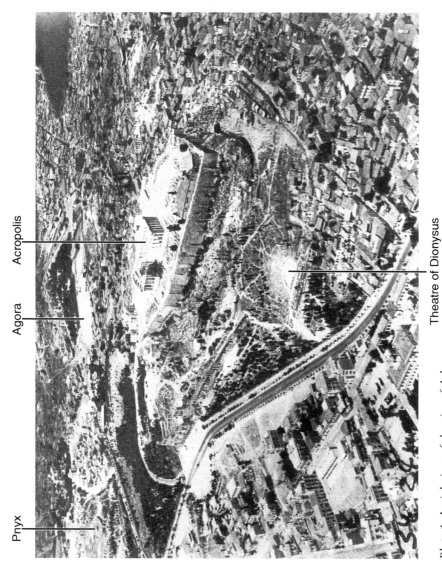

Pnyx

Agora

Acropolis

Theatre of Dionysus

Plate 1 Aerial view of the city of Athens.

performance might have been like, not only from Plato's account of the later rhapsodes, but also from the Homeric epics themselves. Odysseus impresses the Trojans by the stillness and control with which he delivers his speech, ancient evidence of the value of playing against audience expectations (*Il.* 3.216–20). Helen disguises her voice to mimic the wives of the Greek soldiers hidden in the Trojan horse so effectively that the men nearly betray their presence by answering (*Od.* 4.271–89). The bard Demodocus sings of the fall of Troy, and the unrecognized Odysseus responds so emotionally that he is forced to divulge his identity (*Od.* 8.485–9.20). In the later Homeric hymn to Apollo, the island girls of Delos imitate the speech of others so convincingly that 'each one would say that he himself was singing' (*h. Ap.* 149–64). The power of the spoken word to create a credible fiction of another's presence lies at the core of ancient theatrical performance, and Plato was surely right to call Homer 'the supreme master of tragic poetry'.[15]

The epic poems unfold not simply via speaking characters, but through the alternation of their direct speech with more conventional narration, a pattern similar to the shift between rhetoric (actors' speech) and lyric (choral song and dance) in Greek tragedy. In particular, epic narrative is distinguished by the presence of extended similes that introduce different perspectives on the action, drawing the audience into a new relationship with what went before and what is to come. The 'epic simile' may have had an impact on the placement and function of lyric sections in tragedy as that new genre developed, discussed in Chapter 5.

In addition to the epic's formal influence, it would be hard to exaggerate the importance of the Homeric poems on the spirit, sensibility, and ethos that gave rise to Greek tragedy. The *Iliad* and *Odyssey* provide, respectively, the prototypes for many plots and character types that appear in Attic tragedy and comedy. The Iliadic Hector, Achilles, Agamemnon, Priam, Helen, Hecuba, and Andromache are clearly the ancestors of the great heroes of tragedy, and the clever inventiveness of Odysseus in the *Odyssey* finds its counterpart in the comic heroes of Aristophanes. As for Homer's ethical and normative influence, Northrop Frye summarizes: 'It is hardly possible to overestimate the importance for Western literature of the *Iliad*'s demonstration that the fall of an enemy, no less than of a friend or leader, is tragic and not comic'.[16]

The recitations of Homeric epic brought home to sixth-century Athenians in general, and to the future tragedians in particular, the power of words to animate the dramatic imaginations of the audience until they join the performer–poet in creating living characters. The ability to draw an audience imaginatively and critically into this process is not the least of the 'slices' that the tragedians took from the 'banquet of Homer',[17] part of the ongoing feast offered by the performance culture of ancient Athens.

Notes

1 In fifth-century Athens, 'citizenship' meant something like 'belonging to the city' rather than our contemporary 'whoever can vote, rights-based' concept. Legally dependant on their male guardian (father, male relative, or husband), Athenian women could not hold public office, vote in the Assembly, fight in war, serve as jurors, or bring lawsuits. Nonetheless, membership in the Athenian *polis* was a double-stranded bond of men and women, inscribed in Pericles' Citizenship Law, which limited political activity to males over 18 who were the offspring of two Athenians. As 'politically non-active citizens', Athenian women could control property, serve as priestesses in religious cults (often by election), enrol as members of the deme and local phratry, and so on, making them 'privileged shareholders in the Athenian polis'. See C. Patterson, *Pericles' Citizenship Law of 451/50 BC*, New York: Arno Press, 1981, 151–74, and *The Family in Greek History*, Cambridge, MA, Harvard University Press, 1998, pp. 5–43, 125–29 (quotation at 129).

2 For the Pnyx, see K. Kourouniotes and H.A. Thompson, 'The Pnyx in Athens', *Hesperia*, 1932, vol. 1, pp. 96–107; and H.A. Thompson, 'The Pnyx in Models', *Hesperia* Supplement 19, 1982, pp. 134–38.

3 For the Council chamber, see W.A. McDonald, *The Political Meeting Places of the Greeks*, Baltimore, MD, Johns Hopkins University Press, 1943, pp. 172–73 and Plates 3 and 4; H.A. Thompson and R.E. Wycherley, *The Athenian Agora*, Vol. 14, Princeton, NJ, American School of Classical Studies, 1972, p. 34; and Xenophon, *Hellenica* 2.3.50–56.

4 For courtroom and legal practices, see A.L. Boegehold, *The Athenian Agora*, Vol. 28, *The Lawcourts at Athens: Sites, Buildings, Equipment, Procedure, and Testimonia*, Princeton, NJ, American School of Classical Studies, 1995; J. Ober, *Mass and Elite in Democratic Athens*, Princeton, NJ, Princeton University Press, 1989, pp. 141–48; and D.M. MacDowell, *The Law in Classical Athens*, Ithaca, NY, Cornell University Press, 1978, pp. 33–40.

5 MacDowell, op. cit., pp. 247–54.

6 R. Garner, *Law and Society in Classical Athens*, London, Croom Helm, 1987 (rpt. Routledge 2014), has a useful chapter on 'Law and Drama', but read his interpretations of individual tragedies with caution. The influence went both ways; see E. Hall, *The Theatrical Cast of Athens: Interactions Between Ancient Greek Drama and Society*, Oxford, Oxford University Press, 2006, pp. 353–92, and *Law and Drama in Ancient Greece*, eds E.M. Harris, D.F. Leão, and P.J. Rhodes, London, Duckworth, 2010.

7 Plato, *Republic*, 492a–b. A.W. Nightingale, *Genres in Dialogue: Plato and the Construct of Philosophy*, Cambridge, Cambridge University Press, 1995, pp. 60–92, explores Plato's use of Athenian tragedy as he constructs the new prose genre of philosophy.

8 K.J. Dover, *Aristophanic Comedy*, Berkeley, University of California Press, 1972, p. 33. For an excellent introduction, see J. Gould, 'On Making Sense of Greek Religion', in *Greek Religion and Society*, eds P.E. Easterling and J.V. Muir, Cambridge, Cambridge University Press, 1985, pp. 1–33. The number of holidays is not excessive; Greek society had no notion of the weekend and work-rhythms followed the agricultural season.

9 H.W. Parke, *Festivals of the Athenians*, Ithaca, NY, Cornell University Press, 1977, pp. 18–25 and 188–89, summarizes sacrificial practice. Officiating priests usually received a share of the carcasses (skins, hooves, etc.). Even the meat in the butchers' shops came from sacrificial victims; it was wasteful to slaughter animals on purely secular occasions.

10 J. Herington, *Poetry into Drama*, Berkeley, University of California Press, 1985, pp. 20–31, calls these passages 'lyric dramatizations of lyric'. See the discussion of choral self-reference in Chapter 5, below.

11 See R. Rehm, *Marriage to Death: The Conflation of Wedding and Funeral Rituals in Greek Tragedy*, Princeton, NJ, Princeton University Press, 1994; and R. Seaford, 'The Tragic Wedding', *Journal of Hellenic Studies* 107, 1987, pp. 106–30.

12 Plato, *Ion*, 530a–d, 535a–536b; Herington, op. cit., pp. 10–15, 51–52, 170–71; and J.M. González, *The Epic Rhapsode and His Craft*, Cambridge, MA, Harvard University Press, 2015, pp. 296–97, 663–66.

13 For dramatic qualities in Homeric epic and their influence on tragedy, see S.E. Bassett, *The Poetry of Homer*, Berkeley, University of California Press, 1938, pp. 57–80, and C.A. Trypanis, *The Homeric Epics*, Warminster, Aris & Phillips, 1977, pp. 59–64, 82–92.

14 E.A. Havelock, 'The Oral Composition of Greek Drama', in his *The Literate Revolution in Greece and Its Cultural Consequences*, Princeton, NJ, Princeton University Press, 1982, pp. 262–63. Scholars continue to question whether the Homeric epics were composed without benefit of writing, but the substance of Havelock's judgement remains valid.

15 Plato, *Theaetetus*, 152e; Herington, op. cit., pp. 213–15, collects ancient references to Homer's influence on tragedy.

16 N. Frye, *Anatomy of Criticism*, Princeton, NJ, Princeton University Press, 1957, p. 319.

17 As Aeschylus reportedly described his plays, in Athenaeus, *The Deipnosophists*, 8.347e.

2   The festival context

'There is much that is uncertain here.'

(Sir Arthur Pickard-Cambridge)

Formal dramatic productions in Athens took place as part of festivals dedicated to the god Dionysus, and we can understand how tragedy worked only by viewing the performances in their festival context. The association of tragedy with Dionysus leads inexorably to the problem of tragic origins. Although we have no simple answer to the question 'whence tragedy?' a brief review of the evidence will clear up some persistent misconceptions.[1] We then will examine the nature of Dionysiac worship, its relationship to tragedy, and trace out the organization and schedule of the greatest dramatic festival, the City (or Great) Dionysia, held every spring in Athens.

Explanations for the rise of tragedy and the incorporation of tragic performances into the life of Athens tend to focus on the following influences: contemporary ritual, including funeral lamentation, hero cults, and initiation rites; earlier forms of artistic performance, including song, dance, poetry, and Homeric recitation (discussed in the previous chapter); Dionysiac worship, ranging from folkdances linked with the harvest to a ritualized loss of self, from drunken revels to formal initiation into the Dionysiac mysteries; anthropological paradigms, such as the worship of a cyclical 'year-god' who suffers, dies, and comes back to life with the changing seasons; intellectual, spiritual, and creative energies cohering in a 'tragic' vision, epitomized in Nietzsche's brilliantly speculative *The Birth of Tragedy*; and political and cultural forces aimed at promoting civic loyalty, democratic ideology, and social cohesion.

Although little can be claimed with confidence, it seems that a combination of these influences – ritual, artistic, Dionysiac, folkloric, political – rather than any single element in isolation gave rise to Greek tragic theatre. The performance culture of ancient Athens included rural celebrations in honour of Dionysus, where the agricultural cycle of planting and harvesting played an important role, and we have evidence of Dionysiac worship in Greece dating back to the Bronze Age (1250 BC). Above all the god of wine (both its cultivation and enjoyment), Dionysus seems to have represented the 'sap' of life, a deity of natural, animate forces that were worth celebrating, but that also needed pacifying. Perhaps the intensity with which the Greeks felt the forces of nature led them to view Dionysus as the embodiment of contradictory tendencies, a fundamental paradox in the world, life-giving but potentially destructive. As a modern scholar puts it, 'More than any other Greek god, Dionysus lacks a consistent identity. Duality, contrast and reversal are his hallmark.'[2] If a numinous force lies behind the theatrical impulse, then most theatre artists would agree that the ever-changing Dionysus seems perfectly cast for the role.

The most notorious activity associated with the god was ritual maenadism. Unfortunately the horrific excesses depicted in Euripides' *Bacchae* have occluded what we know from other sources about the actual practice of this female cult. A far cry from anarchic frenzy, maenadism took place within fixed periods and defined regional locations, with the female celebrants organized in local congregations. Every two years the women gathered in specified mountainous areas (the Athenian congregation joined others on Mt Parnassus above Delphi). They dressed in special raiment (possibly animal skins), carried a thyrsos (a large fennel wand wreathed in ivy and vine-leaves topped by a pine cone), sacrificed to Dionysus, and performed ecstatic dances in his honour. We cannot know what the experience of maenadism was like, but its structured nature militates against the modern notion of mass hysteria and uncontrolled violence. Never popular in the fifth century, maenadic cult involved small groups of women who celebrated Dionysus in a strenuous but liberating way, translating physical exhaustion into spiritual well-being and merging their separate consciousnesses into that of the group.[3]

By leaving their homes and going to the mountains, activities associated with male hunters, the maenads participated in the kind of sexual role reversal found in other cults linked to Dionysus. For example, at the Oschophoria (a September festival celebrating the grape harvest), a sacrificial procession made its way from a temple of Dionysus in Athens to the seaside shrine of Athena Skiras, a cult of the goddess linked to the vintage. Two men, carrying grapes on the vine and dressed in female robes, led the procession. Hardly encouraged in everyday society, cross-dressing found its way into other festivals as part of their ritual licence, and the practice seems to have been associated with the transition of adolescent males into adults. In the case of the Oschophoria, the female clothing may have recalled a trick by which the Athenian hero Theseus smuggled in a pair of young warriors for two of the girls meant to be sacrificed to Minos (of Minotaur fame) on Crete.[4]

Costumes, masking, and disguise played a part in one of the oldest Athenian festivals for Dionysus, the Anthesteria.[5] Celebrating the opening of the new wine in the early spring, the festivities included a procession of Dionysus travelling in a ship-cart, accompanied by men dressed as satyrs. Wearing a large mask and lavish robes, the archon *basileus* ('king magistrate') impersonated the god. This annually elected officer oversaw the city's religious activities, including the Anthesteria. In the more formalized part of the festival, the archon's wife (*basilinna*, 'queen') celebrated a sacred marriage with this same 'Dionysus', the couple spending the night together in the archon's headquarters as a symbol of the fertility of the city. Athenians escorted the archon-in-disguise and his bride in a torchlight procession, an evening pageant similar to a normal wedding, albeit on a grander scale. Again we observe how the performance culture of Athens brought together domestic ritual and public festival, Dionysiac worship and play-acting, agricultural rites and civic identity.

The earliest pre-dramatic celebrations in honour of Dionysus were known as *komoi* ('revels'), the root of the word 'comedy'. Some of this carousing may have included a traditional refrain called the dithyramb, our earliest reference from a fragment of the seventh-century poet Archilochus: 'I know how to lead [*exarchai*] the fair song of [in honour of?] Lord Dionysus, / the dithyramb, when my wits are fused with wine.'[6] The poet seems to imply that he acted as the leader (*exarchos*) who sang an improvisation, followed by the conventional response from a group of revellers. We find a less festive parallel in the funeral lamentation for Hector, where women selected as leaders sing a dirge and then are joined in ritual wailing by the other female mourners (*Iliad* 24, 718–75).

Viewing the question of tragic origins from his fourth-century perspective, Aristotle credits those who 'led off' (*exarchontôn*) the dithyrambs – poets themselves? – with the key moment in the development of tragedy, when they stepped out of the group as proto-actors. From this early, improvised stage, dithyrambs gradually evolved into more formal compositions intended for choral performance. The mode was narrative rather than dramatic, focusing on a divine or heroic legend at least tangentially connected to Dionysus. Performances usually were accompanied by the *diaulos* (a double-*aulos*, akin to our oboe), an instrument used in many other contexts – accompanying rowing, choruses honouring Apollo, gymnastic exercise, epinician odes, female lamentation, as well as a solo instrument in musical competitions.[7] Along with tragedies and comedies, the City Dionysia eventually included dithyrambs, large choral performances of fifty men or fifty boys dressed in simple robes and without masks. Unlike the tragic and comic playwrights who were primarily Athenian, foreign poets dominated the contest dithyramb – Pindar of Thebes, Simonides and Bacchylides of Keos.

Inevitable questions arise. When were the first productions of *tragedy*, and at what point were tragic performances incorporated in the festival life of the city? The standard textbooks assert that the first tragic competitions at the City Dionysia took place in 534 BC and included plays by the tragedian Thespis. Then dithyrambs were added in 508, and comedies followed in 486. Based on a probable misreading of the Marmor Parium (an inscribed marble slab found on the island of Paros and shipped to London in 1627 AD), however, the conclusion that the tyrant Peisistratus instituted the Great Dionysia in 534 BC seems far from secure. To understand why, we need to consider some particulars of the festival itself.

The City Dionysia honoured Dionysus Eleuthereus, the cult of the god 'having to do with Eleutherae', a town with a sanctuary to Dionysus that lay on the border between Boeotia and Attica. At some point Athens annexed Eleutherae, and the cult-image of Dionysus Eleuthereus was moved to its new Athenian home, most likely *after* the overthrow of the Peisistratid tyranny in 510, and perhaps coinciding with the democratic reforms of Cleisthenes in 508–07.[8] The city re-enacted the incorporation of the god's cult every year prior to the start of the City Dionysia. Escorts removed the cult-statue from the temple just below the theatre of Dionysus and took it to a temple on the road to Eleutherae. That evening, after sacrifice and hymns, a torchlight procession carried the statue *back* to the temple, a symbolic re-creation of the god's arrival in Athens, as well as a reminder of the inclusion of the Boeotian town into Attica. The name Eleutherae resembles the Greek word for 'freedom', *eleutheria*, and Athenians may have considered the new cult ideal for celebrating their own political liberation and democratic reforms.

More evidence comes from an inscription called 'the Fasti' that lists the victories in the festival, beginning with *komoi* to Dionysus, then adding tragedies, and finally comedies. Although the inscription is fragmentary and requires restoration, scholars generally agree that the record for tragedies goes back only to 501 BC. Those who link the first tragic performances with the legendary playwright Thespis, the tyrant Peisistratus, and the year 534 BC, argue that the Fasti refers to a *reorganization* of the City Dionysia. However, it seems that 501 BC is a more reasonable date for the initial incorporation of tragedy into the festival. As the Fasti indicates, earlier performances consisted of *komoi* (eventually leading to competitions in the dithyramb) and then branched out to include tragedies. By 488–87 (the date seems secure from the inscription), the festival expanded to include comedies.

If this interpretation is correct, then tragic performances linked to Thespis must have been part of older, non-civic celebrations honouring Dionysus. Apparently hailing from the rural Attic deme of Ikaria, the semi-legendary Thespis was said to perform on a farm wagon. Similarly, the etymological connection between tragedy and 'goat song' (*tragos* + *aoidê*) may imply that early competitions offered a goat as prize, befitting a rural context. It stands to reason that some such dramatic prototype preceded the inclusion of state-sponsored tragedies at the Great Dionysia, a festival of singular importance in the cultural and political life of fifth-century Athens.

The City Dionysia took place in the Attic month of Elaphebolion ('deer-shooter', an epithet of the goddess Artemis) middle to late March, which coincided with the opening of the sailing season. This schedule allowed foreigners to visit Athens more easily; overland journeys were arduous and slow, making travel by sea the preferred method even between points on the mainland. Farmers would have gathered the last reluctant olive in the Attic countryside in February, and the barley and wheat crop would not be ready to harvest until late May. In addition to fitting into a break in the agricultural season, the timing of the City Dionysia enabled tragedies and comedies to have a particularly strong political impact. The annual election of the ten *stratêgoi* (military commanders chosen by tribe) followed soon after the festival, as did the Assembly meetings that would decide on military campaigns and initiatives for peace, if the Athenians were (as so often) at war.

Although precise correlation between festival days and specific events is difficult to determine, the following order was probably in place until the outbreak of the Peloponnesian War in 431 required changes in the schedule.[9] After the torchlight procession of the cult-statue (discussed above) but before the first day of the festival, the *proagôn* ('pre-contest') took place, but we do not know where. The competing playwrights and actors (without masks or costumes) mounted a wooden platform and introduced the plays they would be performing over the next few days. These theatrical 'teasers' took a more formal tone with the construction of Pericles' Odeion (c. 444 BC) just to the east of the theatre, a roofed 'music hall' that housed the *proagôn* as well as musical competitions for Athens' other great civic festival, the Panathenaia, held in midsummer.

The City Dionysia began officially on the Tenth Elaphebolion. A law prohibited any Assembly meeting or commencement of legal proceedings on that day, and prisoners were released on bail. A grand procession (*pompê*) wound its way (the exact route is unclear) through the agora and around to the south slope of the Acropolis and the temple of Dionysus just below the theatre. Men and women bore various ritual vessels and offerings for the god, resident aliens wore scarlet robes, citizens carried leather wineskins (for what reason we do not know), the *chorêgoi* (citizen-producers) of the various performances dressed in gorgeous robes to mark their status, and other participants bore phalloi in honour of Dionysus. Typical of most Dionysiac cult, everyone was included – there were no prohibitions against women, children, foreigners, or slaves – and it seems reasonable to assume that the same applied to attending the performances.[10]

We get a sense of the excitement of the onlookers during the *pompê* from a passage in Euripides' *Bacchae:*

> Those in the road, those in the road, make way!
> Who stays inside? Come out! and on all lips
> let there be good words, holy words. Our custom
> for Dionysus, I will sing always for the god.
>
> (*Ba.* 68–71)

In *Acharnians* (240–65) Aristophanes offers a comic version of the procession as it might have been practised at a rural Dionysia, with celebrants carrying a basket of offerings and a phallos on their way to the sacrifice. As noted in Chapter 1, the sacrificial offerings for the City Dionysia were on a massive scale, and the meat was cooked and distributed in a giant state-sponsored feast. These two events – the *pompê* and the sacrifice at the altar of the temple of Dionysus – were the *sine qua non* of the City Dionysia, for without these elements there was no cult worship and no basis for the contests and other festivities.

Before the competitions took place, officials purified the theatre with the blood of a slit piglet they carried around the orchestra. Athenians undertook similar purification rites for meetings of the Assembly and Council, and for openings of temples, public buildings, and shipyards. Other pre-performance practices set the dramatic competitions squarely in the context of fifth-century civic and political life. The annual tribute paid to Athens by her allies in the Delian League fell due just before the City Dionysia, and the wealth was displayed in the theatre orchestra.[11] During the second half of the fifth century, part of the tribute went to pay for Pericles' great building programme on the Acropolis, indirectly linking the display in the orchestra to the glorification of Athens. Similarly, when Athenians fell in battle, their male offspring were raised at state expense and given full hoplite armour when they reached manhood. Before the first performances, the orphans who had come of age paraded through the orchestra in their new armour and took complimentary front-row seats for the performances. A herald also announced honours that the city had conferred on citizens and foreigners during the year and read out the names of recently freed slaves. The last activity helped protect the newly liberated by involving the theatre audience as potential witnesses to their manumission.[12]

The performances themselves shared a public and political function. In the dithyrambic competitions (ten choruses of boys and ten of men), each chorus consisted of fifty members drawn from the same tribe. In 508–07 the Athenian leader Cleisthenes organized the population of Attica into ten 'tribes', a democratic and egalitarian move intended to undermine the influence of old familial clans and local power bases. The dithyrambic competitions reflected these reforms, their tribal organization helping to solidify new civic loyalties.[13] On the next three days came the tragic contests, each day reserved for a tetralogy (three tragedies and a satyr play) by one of the three competing tragedians. We will deal with the specifics of tragic production in the next chapter. To fit all the events into four days, one of the five comedies (each written by a different playwright) probably followed the tragic tetralogy each day. The festival's final day would have featured the performance of the final two comedies, preceded by the twenty dithyrambic competitions. At some point during the Peloponnesian War (431–404), the festival reduced the number of comic productions to three in order to save money.[14] After the close of the festival, the archon in charge held a meeting of the Assembly in the theatre to evaluate the proceedings and to review the conduct of festival officials.

As with the City Dionysia, Athens tied other occasions to see tragedy to the god Dionysus. The Lenaia – a festival much older than the City Dionysia, held annually in late January – included a procession (without phallic elements) and sacrifice to the god. The city introduced theatrical performances at the Lenaia in 440. Three to five comic poets (the evidence is unclear) competed with a single comedy, and a prize was awarded to the best comedy and best comic actor. Tragic performances may have begun at the same time, with two playwrights (later three) entering two tragedies each, with no satyr play, and a prize for tragic acting introduced in 432. The Lenaia may have served as proving ground for younger talent, although Sophocles competed here occasionally (with a total of over 120 plays to his credit, this hardly surprises). It seems that a producer (*chorêgos*) at the Lenaia also could revive a tragedy first presented at the City Dionysia. The dramatic contests probably took place in the theatre of Dionysus, although some scholars believe another theatre existed in the (still undiscovered) sanctuary known as the Lenaion that lay just outside the city walls. Resident aliens of Athens could serve as the producers of comedies and tragedies, and they also could perform in the choruses, aspects of production we will discuss in the next chapter.

Athenians also attended tragedies at the various rural or 'agrarian' Dionysia that took place at the local deme level. As the popularity of the city festivals grew, so did Athenian hunger for theatre, and performances spread across Attica. We know little about these smaller festivals, save that they took place (presumably on different days) in the month of Poseideon, roughly our December. Some communities held processions on the model of the City Dionysia, such as the one parodied in Aristophanes' *Acharnians*, discussed above. Of 139 demes in Attica, we know of nineteen (generally the more populous ones) that held some sort of dramatic festival, as did the (non-deme) Attic communities of Brauron to the east and Salamis to the west. Plato (*Republic* 475d) describes Athenian theatrephiles going from deme to deme during the various agrarian Dionysia to catch different productions, and it seems likely that acting troupes toured with a repertory of plays. The local crowd could see revivals of successful tragedies, and we can assume that productions in Piraeus (the port of Athens) and Eleusis (the home of the Mysteries) were important affairs. We hear of Socrates walking to Piraeus to see a performance of Euripides' tragedies, and Sophocles and Aristophanes directed revivals of their plays at Eleusis towards the end of the fifth century.[15]

This brief look at the festival context should make us wary of viewing dramatic performances primarily as religious worship. Robert Parker reminds us that 'the poets saw their primary task as one of exploring human experience, not of honouring the gods'.[16] Nor should we approach tragedy as a form of 'high art' divorced from the social and political life of its audience. Although elevated in style, and frequently in character and setting, Greek tragedy remained grounded in festival contexts integral to the life of the city. No one who has struggled with a Greek text would deny that tragedies have a complex verbal dimension, but the complexities serve ends that have characterized all great popular theatre – the exploration of the concerns, tensions, and aspirations of the society from which they grew.

Notes

1 A full bibliography would run longer than this book. For a range of different-ent theories, see A. Pickard-Cambridge, *Dithyramb, Tragedy, and Comedy*, rev. T.B.L. Webster, Oxford, Clarendon Press, 1962, pp. 60–131; G.F. Else, *The Origin and Early Form of Greek Tragedy*, Cambridge, MA, Harvard University Press, 1965; W. Burkert, 'Greek Tragedy and Sacrificial Ritual', *Greek, Roman, and Byzantine Studies* 7, 1966, pp. 87–121; R.P. Winnington-Ingram, 'The Origins of Tragedy', in *The Cambridge History of Classical Literature*, eds P.E. Easterling and B.M.W. Knox, Cambridge, Cambridge University Press, 1985, pp. 258–63; R. Seaford, *Reciprocity and Ritual: Homer and Tragedy in the Developing City State*, Oxford, Clarendon Press, 1994, pp. 238–327; E. Csapo and W.J. Slater, *The Context of Ancient Drama*, Ann Arbor, MI, University of Michigan Press, 1995, pp. 89–101; and S. Scullion, '"Nothing to Do with Dionysus": Tragedy Misconceived as Ritual', *Classical Quarterly* 52, 2002, pp. 102–37.

2 A. Henrichs, 'Changing Dionysiac Identities', in *Jewish and Christian Self-Definition*, vol. 3, eds B. Meyer and E. Sanders, Philadelphia, Fortress Press, 1982, p. 158; also 'Loss of Self, Suffering Violence: The Modern View of Dionysus from Nietzsche to Girard', *Harvard Studies in Classical Philology* 88, 1984, pp. 205–40. C.P Segal, *Dionysiac Poetics and Euripides' Bacchae*, Princeton, NJ, Princeton University Press, 1997, offers a far-ranging interpretation of Dionysiac dualities. See also P.E. Easterling's masterful 'A Show for Dionysus', in *The Cambridge Companion to Greek Tragedy*, ed. P.E. Easterling, Cambridge, Cambridge University Press 1997, pp. 36–53.

3 My account owes much to Henrichs, op. cit. 1982, pp. 143–47. For a more imaginative treatment, see E.R. Dodds' appendix 'Maenadism' in *The Greeks and the Irrational*, Berkeley, University of California Press, 1951, pp. 270–82.

4 On cross-dressing, see R.J. Hoffman, 'Ritual License and the Cult of Dionysus', *Athenaeum* 67, 1989, pp. 91–115; and P. Vidal-Naquet, 'The Black Hunter and the Origins of the Athenian Ephebia', in *Myth, Religion and Society*, ed. R.L. Gordon, Cambridge, Cambridge University Press, 1981, pp. 147–85. For the Oschophoria, see Parke, op. cit. 1977 (Chapter 1, n. 9), pp. 77–80.

5 See Parke, op. cit., pp. 107–20; L. Deubner, *Attische Feste*, Berlin, Akademie–Verlag, 1932, pp. 92–123.

6 Archilochus, fr. 77. For the role of dithyramb in the development of tragedy, see Aristotle, *Poetics* 1449a1; R. Seaford, 'Dionysiac Drama and the Dionysiac Mysteries,' *Classical Quarterly* 31, 1981, pp. 252–75; Pickard-Cambridge, op. cit. 1962 (above n.1), pp. 1–38, 89–131; and G.F. Else, *Aristotle's Poetics: The Argument*, Cambridge, MA, Harvard University Press, 1957, pp. 149–63. Cf. Scullion, op. cit. (above n. 1), who rejects Aristotle and argues forcefully against the influence of Dionysiac ritual on the rise of tragedy.

7 The *aulos* had a single or 'beating' reed, and the *diaulos* had a double reed, comparable to our clarinet and oboe respectively, and not to a flute. See K. Schlesinger, *The Greek Aulos*, London, Methuen, 1939, pp. 45–81, and M.L. West, *Ancient Greek Music*, Oxford, Clarendon Press, 1992, pp. 81–107.

8 W.R. Connor, 'City Dionysia and Athenian Democracy', *Classica et Mediaevalia* 40, 1989, pp. 7–32, offers a convincing reappraisal of the institution of tragic performances in Athens, whose argument I follow; also M.L. West, 'The Early Chronology of Attic Tragedy', *Classical Quarterly* 39, 1989, pp. 251–54.

9 See Csapo and Slater, op. cit. (above n. 1), p. 107; A. Pickard-Cambridge, *Dramatic Festivals of Athens*, rev. J. Gould and D.M. Lewis, 2nd edn, Oxford, Clarendon Press, 1988, pp. 59–70; W.S. Ferguson, 'Demetrius Poliorcetes and the Hellenic League', *Hesperia* 17, 1948, pp. 133–35 n. 46; J.T. Allen, *On*

the Program of the City Dionysia during the Peloponnesian War, Berkeley, University of California Press, 1938.

10 A German scholar in 1796 first put forth the idea that women could not attend the theatre in Athens, invoking eighteenth-century moral concerns about public licentiousness. Much of the current polemic on the subject reflects the belief that a male-dominated fifth-century Athens would not allow women in the audience. For correctives, see A.J. Podlecki, 'Could Women Attend the Theater in Ancient Athens?' *Ancient World* 21, 1990, pp. 27–43; Csapo and Slater, op. cit. (above n. 1), pp. 286–87; C. Sourvinou-Inwood, *Tragedy and Athenian Religion*, Lanham, MD, Rowman & Littlefield, 2003, pp. 177–96; N. Spineto, *Dionysos a teatro: Il contesto festivo del drama Greco*, Roma, "L'Erma" di Bretschneider, 2005, pp. 292–315; and Chapter 1, n. 1 above.

11 Established after the defeat of the Persians at Salamis (480) and Plataea (479), the Delian League gave Athens pride of place for driving off the invaders. The League eventually became an extension of the Athenian empire, evidenced by the transfer of its treasury from Delos to Athens in 454. Allies initially provided a set number of ships annually for common defence, but monetary tribute gradually replaced material contributions.

12 On the pre-performance practices, see Pickard-Cambridge op. cit. 1988 (above n. 9), pp. 58–59; Parke, op. cit. 1977 (Chapter 1, n. 9), pp. 133–34; and S. Goldhill, 'The Great Dionysia and Civic Ideology', *Journal of Hellenic Studies* 107, 1987, pp. 59–64.

13 We might contrast the great Palio in Sienna, where the neighbourhoods within the city compete in a wild annual horserace. Unlike the dithyrambs at the City Dionysia, the Palio reinforces traditional ties of family and locale going back centuries, an antidote to the rootlessness of modern urban life.

14 See Pickard-Cambridge, op. cit. 1988 (above n. 9), pp. 63–67.

15 N.F. Jones, *Rural Athens Under the Democracy*, Philadelphia, University of Pennsylvania Press, 2004, pp. 124–58, notes that one of the demes lay within Athens' city walls, making the traditional term 'rural Dionysia' misleading. 'Agrarian Dionysia' better approximates the ancient *Dionysia kat'agrous* ('Dionysia in the fields'). See also Pickard-Cambridge, op. cit. 1988, pp. 42–56, and D. Whitehead, *The Demes of Attica*, Princeton, NJ, Princeton University Press, 1986, pp. 212–22. On the re-performance of tragedies at Attic deme festivals and beyond, see E. Csapo, *Actors and Icons of the Ancient Theater*, Chichester, Wiley-Blackwell, 2010, pp. 83–116; M. Revermann, *Comic Business*, Oxford University Press, 2006, 66–95: and C. Dearden, 'Plays for Export', *Phoenix* 53, 1999, pp. 222–48. See also E. Csapo, H.R. Goette, J.R. Green, P. Wilson, eds, *Greek Theatre in the Fourth Century B.C.*, Berlin, De Gruyter, 2014.

16 R. Parker, *Polytheism and Society in Athens* (esp. Chapter 7, 'Religion in the Theatre'), Oxford, Oxford University Press, 2005, p. 152.

3   Production as participation

As with all theatre production, mounting Greek tragedies at the City Dionysia in Athens involved the participation of many different parties who contributed their time, talent, energy, and money. The process differs greatly from what we are accustomed to in the modern theatre, and it bears closer examination. Given the city's integral involvement with dramatic festivals, let us begin with the administrative side of things before moving into the financial, creative, and performance aspects of tragic production.

The archon *eponymous*, one of nine annually selected Athenian leaders, oversaw the City Dionysia – the procession, the opening and closing ceremonies, and the dithyrambic and dramatic competitions. Associated with secular matters, the archon *eponymous* served as one of three senior magistrates, along with the *polemarch* (military commander) and the archon *basileus* (overseer of religious festivals such as the Eleusinian Mysteries, Anthesteria, and Lenaia, discussed in Chapter 2). As many of these offices were filled by lot, scores of different Athenians exercised control over the great theatrical performances at the City Dionysia during the fifth century, a festival viewed from an administrative standpoint as a secular, and not a religious, affair.

Shortly after taking his position in July, the archon *eponymous* nominated wealthy citizens to serve as financial producers, called *chorêgoi*, for the festival. A total of eight were required for the dramatic performances, one for or each tragedian (responsible for three tragedies and a satyr play) and one for each of the five comic playwrights (who entered a single comedy each). The *chorêgoi* for the dithyrambs were selected at the tribal level, presumably one or two from each of the ten tribes, to cover the costs of the boys' and men's choruses. Because expenses were tied largely to personnel and not to sets and scenery, the cost of producing a dithyramb with fifty performers was much greater than a tragic tetralogy with a chorus of twelve to fifteen, plus three actors, or a single comedy with a chorus of twenty-four singer-dancers and three or four actors.[1]

The selection of *chorêgoi* was part of the Athenian institution of 'liturgies', a form of service based on *noblesse oblige* by which the city selected wealthy individuals to support specific public activities.[2] Following the festival calendar, civilian liturgies occurred on a regular basis, and could involve paying for a chorus (the liturgist as *chorêgos*) or underwriting the cost of festival games (a *gymnasiarchos*). There were also military liturgies that called for donations to build a warship, or trireme (the donor as a *trierarchos*). Only the well off were compelled to contribute, and never more than once every two years. In actuality, citizens frequently volunteered, because liturgies provided the means of gaining social status and launching a political career. Alcibiades, the mercurial leader who played such a chequered role in the Peloponnesian War, boasted of his liturgies. At the end of the fifth century, a client of the speechwriter Lysias served as *chorêgos* eight times in nine years. We have other law court speeches where defendants point to their frequent liturgical sponsorship as evidence of their importance to the city, and of their innocence in the face of charges from less generous plaintiffs.[3]

In a case where a citizen felt put-upon at being selected as liturgist, he could find a voluntary replacement or ask another citizen to answer the call. If that person refused, the original draftee could bring a legal charge called *antidosis*, whereby he offered to exchange property with his counterpart and then undertake the liturgy![4] At the Lenaia, non-citizens who were resident aliens called 'metics' could serve as *chorêgoi*, an important opening into the life of the city and one that reflected this group's growing economic importance. Lowering the number of comedies performed at the City Dionysia and Lenaia during the Peloponnesian War freed members of the elite to provide needed military liturgies, and for a single year near the end of the war (406–05) the city instituted a *synchorêgoi* at the City Dionysia whereby two citizens combined to fund a single set of tragedies or a comedy. To get some idea of the expenses involved, a tragic *chorêgos* in 411–10 spent 3,000 drachmas on his tetralogy, and a comic *chorêgos* in 403–02 spent 1,600 drachmas on his comedy, at a time when a sculptor-mason working on the Erechtheum temple on the Acropolis was paid a drachma a day.[5]

The lengths to which some liturgists might go to secure victory reveal the competitive nature of dramatic performances in Athens. In the mid-fourth century, Demosthenes delivered a speech in court against a certain Meidias, who purportedly interfered with a dithyrambic chorus under Demosthenes' choregic sponsorship:

> The sacred apparel – for all apparel provided for use at a festival I regard as sacred until after it has been used – and the golden crowns, which I ordered for the decoration of the chorus, he plotted to destroy ... by a nocturnal raid on the premises of my goldsmith. ... But not content with this, he actually corrupted the trainer of my chorus; and if Telephanes, the *aulos*-player, had not proved the staunchest of friends, if he had not seen through the fellow's game and sent him about his business, if he had not felt it his duty to train the chorus and weld them into shape himself, we could not have taken part in the competition

... the chorus would have come in untrained and we should have been covered with ignominy. Nor did his [Meidias'] insolence stop there. It was so unrestrained that he bribed the crowned archon himself; he banded the chorus members against me; he bawled and threatened, standing beside the judges when they took the oath; he blocked off the side entrances.[6]

Evidently Demosthenes had a rough day in the theatre! Allowing for rhetorical exaggeration characteristic of the genre, the passage gives a sense of the efforts (financial and otherwise) that a liturgist might make to ensure success.

What of the deeper civic and political interests that dramatic liturgies could inspire? Consider a set of fascinating correspondences that scholars have pieced together about the early days of tragic performances at the City Dionysia. Phrynichus, an older contemporary of Aeschylus, wrote *The Capture of Miletus* (now lost), one of the few tragedies inspired directly by a contemporary historical event. Based on the Persian sack in 494 BC of a Greek city in Asia Minor, the play so distressed the Athenians (who had done little to help their distant countrymen) that they fined Phrynichus a thousand drachmas. Although the date is uncertain, *The Capture of Miletus* may have been produced in 492 when Themistocles was the archon *eponymous* and oversaw the play selection for the City Dionysia. It seems that Themistocles had supported the Ionian revolt in Asia Minor, setting himself in opposition to reactionary forces in Athens, just as he later persuaded the Athenian Assembly to build ships as the 'wooden walls' that would save the city against the Persians. As it turns out, Themistocles also served as *chorêgos* for Phrynichus' *second* tragedy on a contemporary theme, *Phoenician Women*, produced in 476. The body of the play has not survived, but we know that it included a messenger speech relating the defeat of the Persians at Salamis, a victory for which Themistocles deserved much credit. Celebrating a triumph rather than Athenian shame, *Phoenician Women* met with the response denied *The Capture of Miletus*. Phrynichus and Themistocles won first prize as playwright–director and *chorêgos* respectively.

Here the plot thickens. Themistocles was ostracized in 472 for alleged collusion with the Persians, a charge probably trumped up by rival Athenian politicians opposed to other aspects of his policy. Earlier that spring at the City Dionysia, Aeschylus achieved his first victory with the *third* tragedy on a contemporary theme, *Persians*. As with Phrynichus' *Phoenician Women*, Aeschylus tells of the defeat of the Persian navy at Salamis. By emphasizing Themistocles' contribution to that great victory, *Persians* offered tacit support to the beleaguered leader. The successful *chorêgos* of Aeschylus' play was the young Pericles, who at the outset of his political career positioned himself as Themistocles' successor. The subject is fascinating, and ancient historians have worked out many variations.[7] It suffices for our purposes to appreciate the close interconnection that could obtain in the production process among archon, *chorêgos*, playwright, and the tragedies themselves.

The *sine qua non* for dramatic productions was, of course, the playwright. We have little secure information about these men, but it does not seem likely that a fifth-century playwright made his living solely in the theatre. The purportedly self-authored epitaph of Aeschylus (525–456) highlights his role in battling the Persians at Marathon and fails to mention that he wrote tragedies. We know that Sophocles (496–06) played an important part in the political life of Athens, serving as state treasurer, as one of the elected generals (*stratêgoi*), and possibly as priest in the cult of the healer Asclepius. Generally speaking, however, the ancient biographical tradition is unreliable, converting details drawn from individual tragedies and comedies into facts about the poet's life: Euripides (480–06) was ripped apart by dogs (like Pentheus torn asunder by maenads in *Bacchae*); Aeschylus was chased from the stage for revealing the Mysteries (probably drawn from a joke in a lost comedy); Sophocles' election as one of the ten generals of Athens in 441–40 (attested by a reliable source) resulted from his victory with *Antigone* (which must then date to 442–41, a conclusion based on virtually no evidence). Even the generally accepted idea that Euripides spent his last years in self-exile at the court of Archelaus in Macedonia may have been conjured from a few references in *Bacchae* to those regions in the north.[8]

We do know with confidence that each of the tragedians began a theatrical tradition in his own family. Two sons of Aeschylus wrote tragedies, and one of them, Euphorion, won first prize in 431 BC against Sophocles and Euripides (whose *Medea* was one of his group of plays that was placed third in the competition). Euphorion's triumphant tetralogy may have included the revival of one or more of his father's plays. Revivals of earlier masterpieces are attested for the City Dionysia in the fourth century, but the intimate knowledge of Aeschylus' plays in the later fifth century strongly suggests that revivals of Aeschylus were instituted earlier, if not at the City Dionysia, then at local deme festivals. In addition to his sons, Aeschylus' nephew Philocles, purported author of over 100 plays, defeated Sophocles in the year that he produced *Oedipus Tyrannus*. Philocles himself had a son who wrote tragedies and is the butt of several Aristophanic jokes. Sophocles' son Iophon won several victories, even competing against his father (given Sophocles' longevity, this makes sense), and he may have fathered an illegitimate son who also wrote tragedies. After Sophocles' death in 406/5, his grandson and namesake produced his *Oedipus at Colonus* posthumously at the City Dionysia of 402/1. In 405, either a son or a nephew of Euripides directed the posthumous tetralogy that included *Bacchae* and *Iphigenia in Aulis*, and the same relative may have written tragedies himself. So, too, in comedy, Araros directed some of the later plays of his father, Aristophanes, supporting the view that playwrights worked in only one genre, tragedy or comedy, but not in both.[9]

We have fairly reliable information that Aeschylus wrote eighty-two plays (seven extant, with the names of sixty-eight others), Sophocles 123 (seven surviving and the titles of [all?] 116 others), and Euripides ninety-two (nineteen surviving and sixty-one other titles). Although the least successful of the three great tragedians in terms of prizes (winning only five victories, one of them posthumously), Euripides seems to have been granted a chorus every year that he proposed a tetralogy to the archon. It is both a testimony to his later popularity and a happy accident of history that so many of his plays survived. Ten of his tragedies were selected *c.* 200 AD for use in schools, and copies of their texts continued to circulate. In addition, a Byzantine manuscript has come down to us with these same plays (only *Trojan Women* is missing), along with nine *other* plays in a quasi-alphabetical grouping (Greek letters E, H, I, K). Without this manuscript, we would have lost such Euripidean masterpieces as *Heracles, Helen, Suppliant Women* [*Iketides*], *Iphigenia in Aulis, Ion*, and the only fully extant satyr play, *Cyclops* [*Kyklops*].

These three tragedians dominated the fifth-century theatre. In Aristophanes' *Frogs*, they are the only playwrights deemed worthy to compete for the right of returning from Hades to save the city, and later ancient literary historians refer to them collectively as the 'Three Tragic Poets'. But the names of other tragedians and the titles of some of their lost plays have survived. In addition to the aforementioned Phrynichus and the half-legendary Thespis, Choerilus and Pratinas lived in the half-generation before Aeschylus and both may have produced tragedies at 'agrarian' Dionysia before the inauguration of the City festival, where they competed as well. Among contemporaries of Sophocles and Euripides, the playwrights Ion, Achaeus, and Agathon stand out, but the names of dozens of others have come down to us. Foreign names among the victory-lists for directors (who usually also were the playwrights) indicate that non-Athenians and metics could enter plays in the competitions at dramatic festivals. We have the text of only three per cent of the tragedies produced in the fifth century, and perhaps 10 per cent of the titles, reminding us of how much we have lost, and also of how active the theatre was in classical Athens.[10] Just as we understand Shakespeare's plays as part of the vital Elizabethan and Jacobean theatrical scene in England, so the mastery of tradition and innovative brilliance of Aeschylus, Sophocles, and Euripides reflect the lively theatrical culture of fifth-century Athens.

We know little about the selection process for plays at the City Dionysia, save that a playwright would apply for a chorus by reading/reciting a part of his work before the archon *eponymou*s. As a tragedian's reputation grew, it became easier for his work to be selected, and the author of the winning productions any given year was entitled to a chorus the following year. Once the archon assigned the three successful tragedians their respective *chorêgoi* and the playwrights chose their *aulos*-player (probably drawing lots for first pick), the production process was under way.

The first meetings surely involved the playwright and *chorêgos* working out the parameters of the production based on budgetary concerns. They would determine not only material outlay – costumes, properties, exceptional stage equipment, and special effects – but also the rehearsal period. The *chorêgos* was responsible for paying a salary of some sort to the chorus members and the *aulos*-player, and also for providing a banquet after the production closed. We can imagine the meeting between Aeschylus and Pericles in the summer of 473, where the playwright outlined his *desiderata* for *Persians*: a full chariot entrance for the queen, regal garments for her and rich robes for the chorus to set off the rags of the defeated Xerxes, the effects (if any) required for raising the ghost of Darius, and so on. We only can guess at the many compromises that must have been made between a poet's original conception and the actual performance. Similarly, we have no way of knowing what ideas may have found their way into a production (and even into the text) thanks to a *chorêgos* who was drawn into the project and eager for its success.

The playwright himself usually served as stage director, or *didaskalos* ('teacher'); the Greek phrase for directing a play was *didaskein choron*, 'to teach a chorus'. The victors' list (*didaskaliai*) indicates that the prizes were awarded for directing, not for writing, meaning that a play was judged more in terms of its production than as an authorial creation in its own right. At the Lenaia of 425, for example, *Acharnians* won for best comedy, but the prize went to Kallistratos who directed the play, not the 23-year-old Aristophanes who wrote it.

The playwright–director also served as choreographer, and he composed the music that was sung by the chorus and occasionally by one or more of the actors. In the years before the institution of the actor's prize in 449 BC, the playwright seems to have been his own leading actor as well. As far as we can tell, the tragedian also designed the costumes, and possibly the masks, always working with the *chorêgos* who had to cover the expenses. We must wait for Shakespeare and Molière before we meet again such consummate men of the theatre, playwright–directors who had all artistic aspects of production under their control, and whose task was to mould those elements into a performance that would do justice to the dramatic texts they had written.

The term for directing, 'to teach a chorus', underlines the importance of choral training. Here lay the major expense and the most time-consuming rehearsals, working with a group to bring together music, movement, and a highly poetic text. A good deal of learning took place via oral repetition (Athenian education – such as it was – operated in similar fashion), and we cannot assume that the performers could read.[11] The choral melodies were taught by ear, and we have ancient testimonia of Euripides singing one of his odes to his chorus at a rehearsal. So, too, the *didaskalos* and *diaulos* player must have worked out the dance movements with the chorus members 'on their feet', much as choreography is developed today.

The same twelve performers (the number grew to fifteen at some point in the fifth century) played the chorus in all four plays – three tragedies and a satyr play – composed by a given tragedian.[12] To get a sense of what this meant in practice, consider Aeschylus' production of the *Oresteia* in 458 BC. The same chorus members appeared as Argive elders in *Agamemnon*, captured slave-women in *Choephori*, the terrifying Furies in *Eumenides*, and a band of randy satyrs in the lost satyr play *Proteus*. Not only were masks, costumes, and personae different, but the style of movement, the music, the level and quality of emotion, and countless other factors shifted from play to play. With only a single performance at the City Dionysia, the chorus had to master a wide range of material without the benefit of preview audiences, although we must assume that the final rehearsals (at least) were held in the theatre.

Given a long and involved rehearsal period, the notion that the text and lyric metres that have survived were ever purely those of Aeschylus or Sophocles or Euripides seems extremely unlikely. Much of what was performed in the orchestra resulted from the give and take between the tragedian (juggling his input as playwright, lyricist, composer, choreographer, and director) and his chorus, with the *diaulos* accompanist making major contributions as well. As with every new script, new ideas surely came up during rehearsal, demanding flexibility on the part of playwright and performers alike. It is probable that the dramatist viewed his original script as a starting point, and then spent the early rehearsals adjusting the play to the performers. Although the fifth-century playwright possessed extraordinary artistic autonomy, his work on the production was necessarily collaborative.

About the selection of the chorus members we know nothing. Presumably there was some audition for interested parties, with the specifics of the playwright's project and the remuneration offered by the *chorêgos* as incentives to participate. At the City Dionysia the chorus consisted of male citizens, not professional actors, although it is possible that remuneration was sufficient to constitute a second income. A group of choral semi-pros might find themselves called upon for a deme revival of a play they had performed at the City Dionysia, or they might balance their schedule between the Lenaia one year and the Dionysia the next.

A theory that has generated much scholarly interest links the teaching of the chorus to the military training of ephebes, male youths on the point of maturity.[13] Proponents adduce ancient evidence that tragic choruses were divided into ranks and files, suggesting strict rectilinear patterns of movement based on the military analogy with marching and drill. However, the sources are late, mainly a professor in Athens named Pollux who dedicated his work to the emperor Commodus (161–92 AD). Pollux's conclusions reflect the theatre and the theatrical conventions of his day, over 600 years after Aeschylus, and we should be wary of assuming that his views on staging, theatre space, and choral movement reflect the situation in fifth-century Athens. How many choral sections in the *Oresteia*, for example, can we imagine danced in ordered rank and file like a march or military drill? The great *kommos* between the chorus of women, Orestes, and Electra? The binding song of the Furies around Orestes, or their final benedictions over the city of Athens? The visionary lyrics of Cassandra that eventually draw the chorus into the dance? The evocation of the sacrifice of Iphigenia, or the choral lament over the slain Agamemnon? We could multiply examples, but the point is clear. The thesis that tragic choruses provided ersatz military training fails where it matters most, in performance. Better to conclude that participation in a Greek tragic chorus was open to male citizens generally (and to male metics at the Lenaia), and was not restricted to boys on the verge of a beard.

In the earliest tragic performances, the playwright himself acted the most important roles and procured the services of fellow-actors to fill out his cast. Given that the performers were masked (a convention discussed in Chapter 4), an actor could play several parts in any given tragedy. *Persians*, our earliest surviving tragedy, requires only two actors. Perhaps Aeschylus chose not to play the Messenger (much the biggest part) and the ghost of Darius, performing instead the roles most problematic for the Athenian audience, the Persian queen and her son Xerxes, whose destruction of Athens had taken place only seven years earlier. At some point in the fifth century a third actor became available, and we know that Aeschylus took advantage of the addition in his *Oresteia* of 458.

In 450/49, the city assumed responsibility for procuring and paying actors, initiating a prize for best tragic actor at the City Dionysia, followed by a similar contest at the Lenaia (around 432). As with comic and tragic playwrights, actors performed in one genre only, and prizes for comic per-formers also were awarded at the Lenaia in the fifth century and after 329 at the City Dionysia. Although we have no direct evidence for the reasons behind this development, the state sponsorship of actors speeded up a pro-cess that had been in train for some time, namely the division of labour between playwriting and acting. Ancient testimonia tells us that Sophocles stopped performing because of the weakness of his voice, dubious in its spe-cifics but credible as a sign of a general trend. We have no indication that Euripides ever acted; he first competed at the City Dionysia in 455 BC, only five years before it became impossible for playwrights to perform leading roles in their own plays. And it is difficult to imagine Aeschylus at age 67 undertaking the role of Clytemnestra in the *Oresteia*, produced three years before Euripides' debut.

Whatever the reason for the change to city-sponsored acting, it led to a more even-handed distribution of the best actors. No longer could a finan-cially committed *chorêgos* simply buy up the most accomplished performers in any given year. With the institution of the prize for acting, the three tragic playwrights would draw lots to pick one of the three actors chosen for the festival, who in turn would provide the other actors needed to perform the tetralogy. Each group invariably included two additional men capable of playing a variety of speaking roles, and also might involve a fourth mute actor who took on such parts as the silent Pylades in Euripides' *Electra*, as well as other supernumeraries.[14] The situation gave rise to diminutive acting companies, a master-actor and his (small) band of apprentices, competing for public support each year and ready to serve the playwright who was allotted them.

Only the leading actor of each of the competing tetralogies was eligible for the acting prize, although we cannot be sure whether it honoured the best set of performances over the course of a given tetralogy, as seems likely, or whether it rewarded the best performance in any single play. In either case, the character(s) played by the lead actor (called the protagonist or 'primary competitor') would have been scrutinized with special interest and, for that reason, could establish a privileged relationship with the audience. Although it seems likely that the theatre public would recognize the leading actors even in masks, one of the purposes of the earlier *proagôn* may have been to announce the roles played by each of the three protagonists. After the annual competitions, the winning actor's name was inscribed on the official list of victors, alongside that of the victorious *didaskalos* (director) and the *chorêgos* (producer), and he was preselected for the competition in the following year. That the public record of contributions to the *polis* included the names of actors is remarkable, given the low social status associated with actors throughout most of the history of theatre.

The celebration of acting and actors had its negative side as well, reaching its nadir in the late fourth/early third century, when the tragedies of Aeschylus, Sophocles, and Euripides were revived more as star-vehicles than as integrated productions. As Aristotle observed, 'the actors are [now] more important than the poets'.[15] Widespread interpolations by actors further contaminated the texts, until the Athenian leader Lycurgus (*c.* 330) passed a law establishing an official copy of the plays of the three great tragedians and requiring that all city-sponsored revivals follow those scripts.

The selection of the three leading actors must have been based on their previous public performances (both in major and in minor festivals), supplemented when necessary by auditions before the archon *eponymous*. Although the random selection process seems to have prohibited playwrights from writing with specific actors in mind, we have counter-evidence to suggest that tragedies were tailored to a certain actor, or at least a certain kind of actor. Ancient testimonia link Aeschylus to two actors, Cleander and Mynniscus; Sophocles is singled out for having written parts for specific actors, where the names Cleidemides and Tlepolemus come up; and Euripides' later plays often demand singing skills from actors that may not have been generally available. Three of his extant plays – *Andromache*, *Ion*, and *Trojan Women* – require that *two* actors sing, and the monodies of Andromache and Peleus, Ion and Creusa, and Hecuba and Cassandra are central to their respective plays.[16] Unless performers were available who could handle these difficult lyric sections, Euripides would not have included them.

On the model of the great Elizabethan playwright–actor teams of Marlowe and Alleyn, of Shakespeare, Kempe, and Burbage, some form of ongoing collaboration between playwright and actor must have characterized fifth-century Athenian theatre. We know that the prize for acting did not have to go to the protagonist in the tetralogy that won best play for the *didaskalos* and *chorêgos*. Because both the victorious playwright–director and actor were guaranteed a place in the following year's competition, one or the other may have been allowed first pick, enabling the tragedians to write parts for specific actors. Whatever the circumstances of selection and rehearsal, state sponsorship and public recognition make it clear that the actors played a central role in Athenian tragic drama.

In total, some 1,250 artists and performers participated annually at the City Dionysia. The dithyrambic competitions required ten to twenty poets and as many *chorêgoi*, 500 men and 500 boys who made up the twenty choruses, and twenty *aulos*-players. For the tragic contests, there were three poets, three *chorêgoi*, three aulos-players, thirty-six to forty-five chorus members, and nine actors (plus supernumeraries and supplemental choruses when necessary); for the comedies, five playwrights, five *chorêgoi*, five *aulos*-players, 120 chorus members and fifteen or more comic actors for the five comedies. To this number we should add the various trainers, builders, costumers, rehearsal assistants, and others who worked behind the scenes.

As impressive a figure as this is, it remains small when compared to the most essential participants in the theatre of Dionysus, the crowds who gathered in the audience. We will discuss the physical nature of the theatre in the next chapter, but a fair estimate of the crowd at the performances in fifth-century Athens is roughly 6,000 to 8,000 on each of the four days of the City Dionysia. It seems likely that Athenian men, women, and children, resident aliens, slaves, and foreigners alike came to watch the plays, in keeping with the inclusionary nature of the festival and of most Dionysiac cult. We are unsure when admission began to be charged and what the price was, but it seems that during at least part of the fifth century the audience paid two obols (one-third of a drachma) per seat. At some point the city established a *theoric* fund to subsidize tickets for the poor, a practice that probably began in the fourth century.[17]

To provide judges for the contests, each of the ten tribes had a jar filled with names of male citizens in attendance, and one was drawn from each jar just before the performances began. The random drawing of judges was aimed at avoiding bribery and partisanship, a process similar to that for choosing jurors and filling political offices by lot. At the conclusion of each set of performances, the judges marked their ballots anonymously and placed them in the voting urn; they were drawn out one by one, until a majority (or plurality) for a given contest was achieved.[18]

Judging the plays and the actors offered only the most formal way in which an Athenian spectator participated at the City Dionysia. The lively accounts in comedy indicate that the audience laughed, applauded, and hissed; they raised a din by kicking the wooden benches with their feet; when the plays bored them they ate the food they brought, and if things got deadly, they threw it as well.[19] Surely the tragedies elicited a more decorous response than satyr plays and comedies, but we must not imagine the hushed crowds that follow the dimming of the lights in a modern indoor theatre, or the programmed response of a 'live' audience in a television studio. After all, the city had gathered to see itself represented in, and challenged by, the dramatic competitions. Production as participation meant that the audience, no less than the playwrights, producers, and performers, were central to what was happening, part and parcel of the energy of the theatre.

Notes

1 On the expense of dithyrambs compared to dramatic performances, see P. Wilson, 'Costing the Dionysia', in *Performance, Iconography, Reception: Studies in Honour of Oliver Taplin*, eds M. Revermann and P. Wilson, Oxford, Oxford University Press, 2008, pp. 112–14. Recall (Chapter 2, above) that Attic 'tribes' do not imply racial or ethnic links, but reflect the Cleisthenic reforms aimed at transferring loyalties to the city and away from traditional economic and social hierarchies.

2 P. Wilson, *The Athenian Institution of the* Khoregia: *The Chorus, The City, and the Stage*, Cambridge, Cambridge University Press, 2000.

3 See P.J. Rhodes, 'Political Activity in Classical Athens', *Journal of Hellenic Studies* 106, 1986, pp. 132–44.

4 V. Gabrielson, 'The Antidosis Procedure in Classical Athens', *Classica et Mediaevalia* 38, 1987, pp. 36–45.

5 Wilson, op. cit. 2008 (above n. 1), pp. 88–127, concludes that for the City Dionysia of 415, the *polis* spent roughly 79,000 drachmas, and private expenditure totalled an additional 94,000 drachmas. The combined outlay would fund a dozen naval triremes for a year, about 5 per cent of the annual public expenditure on military activity at the height of the Athenian empire.

6 Demosthenes, *Against Meidias*, 16–17, in *Orations*, Vol. III (J.H. Vince, trans.), Cambridge, MA, Harvard University Press, 1935, pp. 16–19 (with minor changes).

7 A.J. Podlecki, *The Political Background of Aeschylean Tragedy*, Ann Arbor, University of Michigan Press, 1966, pp. 8–26, 125–29, and his introduction to *Aeschylus' 'Persians'*, Englewood Cliffs, Prentice-Hall, 1970, pp. 4–11. See also W.G. Forrest, 'Themistokles and Argos', *Classical Quarterly* 10, 1960, pp. 221–41.

8 M. Lefkowitz, *The Lives of the Greek Poets*, 2nd edn, Baltimore, MD, Johns Hopkins University Press, 2012, pp. 1–5 and 70–103, exposes ancient biography for what it usually is – post-Classical legend and invention, with details pulled from tragedies and comic parodies.

9 D.F. Sutton, 'The Theatrical Families of Athens', *American Journal of Philology* 108, 1987, pp. 9–26. Compare the great old families of the circus, where different acts worked under the same tent, but a family of high-wire artists did not produce lion-tamers, and vice versa.

10 Although more than a century old, A.E. Haigh, *The Tragic Drama of the Greeks*, Oxford, Clarendon Press, 1896, pp. 395–415, 463–81, remains useful for playwrights and titles. On lost and fragmentary plays, see T.B.L. Webster, *The Tragedies of Euripides*, London, Methuen, 1967; D.F. Sutton, *The Lost*

Sophocles, Lanham, MD, University Press of America, 1984; O. Taplin, *The Stagecraft of Aeschylus*, Oxford, Clarendon Press, 1977 (index under 'Aeschylus / fragmentary plays'); the Loeb editions listed in the Preface; *Sophocles: Selected Fragmentary Plays*, Volume I, eds A.H. Sommerstein, D. Fitzpatrick and T. Talboy, Oxford, Oxbow Books, 2006; *Sophocles: Selected Fragmentary Plays*, Volume II, eds A. H. Sommerstein and T. Talboy, Oxford, Oxbow Books, 2011; *Euripides: Selected Fragmentary Plays*, Volume I, eds C. Collard, M.J. Cropp and K.H. Lee (Warminster: Aris & Phillips, 1995); and *Euripides: Selected Fragmentary Plays*, Volume II, eds C. Collard, M.J. Cropp and J. Gilbert, Oxford, Oxbow Books, 2004.

11 Ancient writing usually prompted human speech rather than silent reading. Most fifth-century Athenians could not read; when necessary, they were read to. See Plutarch *On Listening to Lectures* 46b; Herodotus 1.48.1; Thucydides 1.21.1 and 1.22.4; Polybus 36.1.7 and 38.4.8; also Csapo and Slater, op. cit. (Chapter 2, n. 1) pp. 10 (#13) and 360 (#305); R. Thomas, *Literacy and Orality in Ancient Greece*, Cambridge, Cambridge University Press, 1992, pp. 61–73, 101–27; and S. Flory, 'Who read Herodotus' *Histories?*' *American Journal of Philology* 101, 1980, pp. 12–28.

12 The anonymous *Life of Sophocles* claims that Sophocles expanded the tragic chorus, which means that at some point the chorus grew to fifteen, and the biographer credited his man. The change may have reflected the desire to include a larger number of citizens in tragic productions.

13 J.J. Winkler, 'The Ephebes' Song: *Tragôidia* and *Polis*', in *Nothing to do with Dionysos?* eds J.J. Winkler and F.I. Zeitlin, Princeton, NJ, Princeton University Press, 1990, pp. 20–62. However, the institution of ephebic training is not attested in the fifth century, and we should not read the practice back into the early days of Athenian democracy. See L. Kozak, 'Greek Government and Education: Re-examining the *ephêbeia*', in *A Companion to Ancient Greek Government*, ed. H. Beck, Chichester, John Wiley & Sons, 2013, pp. 302–16.

14 In some cases, the 'three-actor rule' allows us to figure out which actor played which role(s), and how role-doubling worked. For ancient actors and acting generally, see *Greek and Roman Actors: Aspects of an Ancient Profession*, eds P. Easterling and E. Hall, Cambridge, Cambridge University Press, 2002.

15 Aristotle, *Rhetoric* 3.1403b31.

16 The title character in Euripides' *Alcestis* sings a monody, as does her son, Eumelos. It seems unlikely that the child's part (otherwise silent) was played by one of the three actors; more likely a talented boy was pulled from the dithyrambic competitions. In Euripides' *Phoenician Women*, Antigone and Jocasta each sing a monody, but these parts were played by the same actor. See further discussion in Chapter 5.

17 E. Csapo, 'The Men Who Built the Theatres', in *The Greek Theatre and Festivals*, ed. P. Wilson, Oxford, Oxford University Press, 2007, esp. pp. 96–103. See also Chapter 4, n. 6.

18 C. Marshall and S. van Willigenburg, 'Judging Athenian dramatic competitions', *Journal of Hellenic Studies* 124, 2004, pp. 90–127, present the various possibilities.

19 R.W. Wallace, 'Poet, Public, and "Theatrocracy": Audience Performance in Classical Athens', in *Poet, Public, and Performance in Ancient Greece*, eds. L. Edmunds and R.W. Wallace, Baltimore, MD, Johns Hopkins University Press, 1997, pp. 97–111.

4   The theatre of Dionysus

At some point early in the fifth century an area on the south slope of the Acropolis became home to the performances of the City Dionysia. Located just above the temple of Dionysus Eleuthereus, in the precinct dedicated to the god, the hillside gradually assumed the recognizable form of a Greek theatre. However, we must remember that the remains visible today – primarily the greatly altered theatre of the Roman emperor Nero (first century AD) and a certain Phaedrus (third or fourth century AD) – bear a problematic relationship to the performance area of the fifth century BC. The nature of the evolution in the shape and function of the theatre from that early period has generated much speculation, and not a little controversy. It will help us make our way through the maze if we first consider the situation of tragic productions *before* there was a theatre of Dionysus at all.

The original city performances of dithyrambs and tragedies probably took place in the central open space of the agora (civic centre/market) called the *orchêstra* ('dancing area').[1] Sloping gently down from the foot of the Acropolis that lies to the southeast, the agora developed into the hub of the city, the site of political, judicial, commercial, and religious activities (see Plate 1). Here were located the meeting places for the Council, the law courts, civic stoas, other public edifices, cult shrines and altars, private shops, commercial buildings, and food stalls (see Plate 2). The broad Panathenaic Way ran diagonally through the agora, and there the grand procession of Athens' greatest festival wended its way, immortalized on the Parthenon frieze. Starting by the cemetery and potters' quarter just outside the city gates, the procession ran alongside the *orchêstra* area before rising up to the entrance of the Acropolis itself. In the other direction, the Panathenaic Way joined the Sacred Way, heading down to the sea and the city of Eleusis, the route taken by the initiates to the Eleusinian Mysteries. The market area also housed the famous Altar of the Twelve Gods, the spot from which all distances from Athens were calculated, where suppliants came for asylum, and also where the *pompê* of the City Dionysia stopped to perform a choral dance (discussed in Chapter 2). In both a real and a metaphorical sense, the agora was the centre of the *polis*, and the possibility that early tragedies were performed there speaks to their importance in Athens.[2]

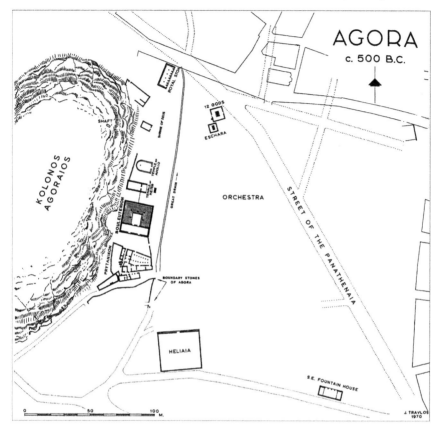

Plate 2 Map of the Athenian agora *ca.* 500 BC.

The term *orchêstra* indicates that the area was set aside for dancing, and that accommodating a chorus was its defining criterion. We infer from the sparse literary evidence and from the absence of archaeological remains that no permanent theatrical edifice existed in the agora, that audience members sat on temporary tiered wooden benches (*ikria*). Rather than a built-up theatre, the *orchêstra* was a space where people gathered to watch a performance in an area large enough for a chorus to dance. It was out of doors, open to the elements and the light of day, with no preconceived shape or ideal configuration.[3]

The move to a location linked specifically to Dionysus on the opposite (south) slope of the Acropolis may have coincided with the formal institution of the City Dionysia and organization of competitive performances. Or perhaps the increasing popularity of the theatrical performances necessitated the shift to a larger and less encumbered space. In any event, the hillside rising up from the temple and precinct of Dionysus formed a natural *theatron* (literally, 'place to see'), shielding the proceedings from the north wind that blew in early spring and offering more spectators a better vantage than was possible in the agora (see Plate 3). Gradually the south slope of the Acropolis was built up, with a covered hall (Odeion) added in the mid-fifth century for music concerts, epic recitations, and the *proagôn* of the City Dionysia, and a new temple to Dionysus erected in the fourth century.[4]

The physical parameters of this early theatre are of great importance for understanding the dramatic instincts of the Greeks and the way in which their tragedies worked in performance. However, the complicated archaeological record frustrates our efforts at reconstruction, because the performance space shifted several times over the 900 years in which the area served as a theatre. The current remains date from the first to the third centuries AD, some 500–700 years after Aeschylus' *Oresteia*. We must think away the stone seats in the cavea, the paved semi-circular orchestra, and the stone stage (*proskênê*, or proscenium) in front of the back façade (*skênê*, literally 'tent'). Scattered among the extant ruins are bits of the cement that made the orchestra watertight for mock naval battles in the Roman period, traces of the Christian basilica in the eastern *eisodos*, and remnants of the Byzantine fortification wall that ran across the *skênê* (henceforth, simply 'skene'). Remains dating from the original fifth-century theatre are scant and adulterated, leaving room for endless – and often reckless – hypothesizing.

What can we say with a modicum of confidence about the earliest theatre of Dionysus? Starting with the orchestra, there is no substantive evidence that its original shape was circular. Recent examination of the archaeological record, including comparison with other theatres of the fifth century, indicates that there are no theatrical remains from the early period that indicate the original 'dancing area' was circular.[5] As we might expect from the highly practical Greeks, the shape of the orchestra did not differ from the space defined by the seating area in the front, and the terrace wall supporting the orchestra in the back, a retaining wall that kept the packed earth of the dancing floor from eroding down the slope. As a result, the early orchestras tended to be a slightly irregular rectangle.

The important point is that the fifth-century Greeks acknowledged *no pre-established template* governing the shape of the theatre cavea or orchestra, but instead developed and adapted their theatres according to local topography. They had no visual, theatrical, or ritual commitment to a circle per se. No firm evidence substantiates the claim that the circular threshing floor (often adduced in handbooks on Greek theatre) influenced the development or shape of the early theatre orchestra. Perhaps theatre history owes this last idea to the wistfulness of moderns who have lost the feel of the wheat and the chaff; it owes little to recent archaeology, which has unearthed no early circular orchestras. The form of the Greek theatre, including the orchestra, did not become standardized until relatively late, probably under the influence of the theatre at Epidauros (with the first bona fide circular dancing place) built in the late fourth/early third century.

Plate 3 Photograph of the theatre of Dionysus in Athens (early twentieth century).

Although some stone seating blocks dating from the fifth century have been found in the theatre of Dionysus, they seem to have provided only the first row of seats (*prohedria*), reserved for the priest of Dionysus and other dignitaries. We know from Aristophanes that most of the audience sat on wooden benches, and we can assume that others sat or stood on the ground above these temporary bleachers.[6] To put this in architectural terms, the early theatre was conceived more as a space than as a building. It lacked the inherent controls of programmatic construction and architectural order that defined, for example, the temple and the stoa, the most formally fixed of Greek buildings.

Another misconception about the theatre of Dionysus involves the presence of a permanent backdrop rising behind the orchestra, a back wall that could support an elevated stage for the actors. As far as we can tell, the earliest permanent (stone) foundations in the theatre of Dionysus date from the fourth century, radically simplifying our picture of the theatre of Aeschylus, Sophocles, and Euripides. We can dismiss the many reconstructions that feature an elaborate stone façade, or projecting areas at the two ends (*paraskênê*), or an inner entrance area (*prothyros*) receding from a long wooden colonnade, and so on. Furthermore, without the secure anchor of a permanent (stone) building for wooden additions, we cannot assume that the fifth-century theatre possessed a playing area defined by an elaborate backdrop. Most surviving tragedies do call for a back façade with central entrance, an innovation that may date from the production of the *Oresteia* in 458 BC.[7] That need was met by a wooden skene building, the back wall and door of which served as the theatrical facade.

Today we associate Athens with remarkable stone and marble buildings, but the construction of these permanent structures required massive wooden scaffolding and great quantities of wood for roofing, especially the temples.[8] The theatre's temporary bleachers and skene-building were well within the Athenians' capacity. Their eventual replacement in stone over the fourth century followed the pattern of other Greek buildings, the so-called 'petrification' of the earlier form.

We are left, then, with a trapezoidal orchestra area, backed by a wooden façade with a central door, fronted by a row (*prohedria*) of stone seats and then wooden bleachers, with two side entrances into the orchestra between the seating area and the façade (see Plate 4). All extant tragedies can be staged in such an area and with these basic elements. Some scholars insist that certain comedies of Aristophanes call for more than one door, but their arguments tend to reflect modern concerns for spatial difference and specificity not required in Greek drama.[9] It makes practical sense to assume that productions of tragedy and comedy shared the same wooden façade during the City Dionysia. If two or three doors were available for comedy, then we would expect an experimentalist like Euripides to use them. However, none of his extant plays call for more than one façade entrance, and his *Suppliant Women* and *Andromeda* (lost) require *no* such central door. Greek tragedy exhibits what one critic has called an 'aesthetic of abstinence',[10] and in such a theatre the single door in the skene and the side entrances of the *eisodoi* are necessary and sufficient.

The backdrop – which could represent a palace, temple, house, tent, even a cave – coincided with the longer outside wall of the wooden skene-building. There the actors changed costumes and masks without being seen, and made their entrances through the central door onto the playing area. Some theatre historians have used an interpolated passage in Aristotle's *Poetics* (about Sophocles' introducing scene-painting) to reconstruct elaborate scenographic systems for the façade, but it appears that scene-painting played

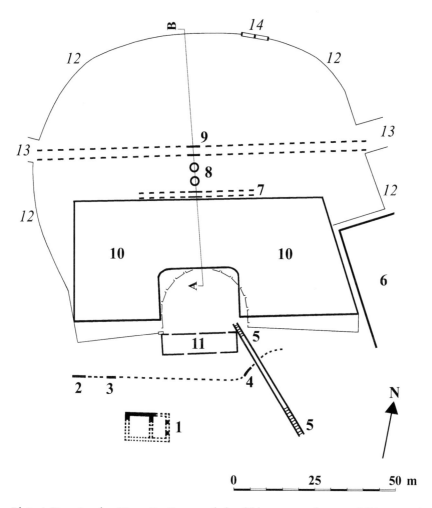

Plate 4 Drawing by Hans R. Goette of the fifth-century theatre of Dionysus in Athens. 1: Temple of Dionysus. 2, 3, 4: retaining wall. 5: drainage channel. 6: Odeion of Pericles. 10: seating banks. 11: skene building.

a minimal role (if any at all) in fifth-century productions.[11] The skene structure was strong enough to support actors on its roof, an area that came to
be known as the *theologeion* ('place where the gods speak') because stage
divinities often appeared there. Access to the roof for human characters
came by means of a ladder from within the skene-building through the ceiling, or from behind the structure. The gods and 'elevated' mortals usually
arrived from above, via the *mêchanê* ('machine'), giving us the Latin phrase
deus ex machina, 'god from the machine'. A lever-and-fulcrum apparatus
located behind the skene would raise the actor(s) high above the façade to
suggest their movement through the air, and then lower them onto the roof
of the skene-building.[12]

Another vexed question about the ancient theatre of Dionysus is whether
a wooden stage raised above orchestra level stood in front of this temporary backdrop. No extant tragedy requires a raised playing area (except
for the *theologeion*), and we are better off assuming there was no such
stage.[13] Those who claim that the plays demand distinct performing areas
for the actors and for the chorus betray a basic misunderstanding of the way
tragedy works. Fifth-century plays require free (and frequent) interaction
between chorus and actors, as we shall see in the exemplary plays in Part II.
In the second century AD, Pollux wrote that 'the skene belongs to the actors
and the orchestra to the chorus', but he was describing the Neronian theatre
in Athens. Then a raised stage served the demands of a different kind of
drama, in which the chorus existed independent of, and frequently tangen-
tial to, the action.[14]

The idea that a low raised stage gave an actor visual and acoustic prominence vis-à-vis the chorus fails to grasp the physical relationships and scale
involved in the ancient theatre. In a space the size and shape of the theatre
of Dionysus, most of the spectators look down on the action, some from a
fairly steep angle, as we can see from Plate 3, and from the reconstructed
model of the wooden seating banks (one of several possibilities) on Plate 5.
A three-foot raised stage against the back façade – the furthest distance from
the audience – hardly constitutes a gift to the actor, for one gains visual and
oral power in such a space by proximity to the audience. Unlike the carefully planned theatre built at Epidauros some two centuries later, the hillside
theatre in Athens had anything but perfect acoustics. In the fifth century,
the theatre's back wall was not a large stone façade (which would act as
an effective sounding board), but a relatively small wooden construction.
Recall the basic principle of acoustics, that sound intensity varies inversely
with the square of the distance, which means that if an actor standing ten
feet from the audience moves back to a distance of thirty feet, the intensity
of his voice drops to one-ninth of what it was at the first position.[15]

With the audience sitting in bleachers and others spread above them on
the hillside, the midpoint of the orchestra (however it was shaped) provided
the strongest acting area, and we find evidence in the tragedies themselves
that the playwrights recognized the fact.[16] In play after play the dramatists

Plate 5 Model of a possible reconstruction of the seating banks in the fifth-century theatre of Dionysus.

literally 'orchestrate' key speeches and scenes, setting them up in the Greek equivalent of downstage centre. Here, for instance, were located the prop altars required for supplication or asylum in Aeschylus' *Suppliant Women*, Sophocles' *Oedipus Tyrannus*, and Euripides' *Andromache*. The tomb of Darius in Aeschylus' *Persians*, that of Agamemnon in *Choephori*, and that of Proteus in Euripides' *Helen* also were placed orchestra centre.[17] That the tragedians fully exploited the best acting area is hardly surprising. They worked in the theatre, not in the library, and they used the performance space available to them to best advantage.

The essential question about any performance space is how it engages the audience. Irrepressibly three-dimensional, large, and out of doors, the theatre of Dionysus differed fundamentally from the indoor venues that house modern audiences. Epitomized by the frame of the proscenium-arch, the modern theatre reflects the central assumption of theatrical realism, namely that the spectator is a hidden observer looking in on a specified location through an invisible fourth wall. The Greek theatre aims at precisely the opposite effect, a sense that the audience has gathered in a public place to be addressed, and confronted, by the play. The empty space of the Greek theatre encourages us to imagine the scene for ourselves, guided by the words and gestures of the performers.

Take, for example, the action of *Choephori* that moves from the tomb of Agamemnon to the palace of Clytemnestra and Aegisthus, and once there 'shifts' from outside to inside to outside of the palace, all accomplished without altering the setting or backdrop. In *Eumenides*, the action begins outside the temple of Apollo at Delphi, then goes inside the temple, then moves to the temple of Athena in Athens, and finally ends up in the court of the Areopagos, again with no fundamental alteration in set pieces or background. In his lost *Women of Aetna*, the only tragedy we know written specifically for production outside of Athens (Syracuse in Sicily), Aeschylus changed the location *five times* in the course of the drama. Plays such as Sophocles' *Troilus* (lost) and Euripides' *Children of Heracles* exhibit what we might call 'flexible geography', where the action begins at one place and gradually slides (if we stop to think about it realistically) some geographical distance. Collapsible dramatic time is a concomitant of a flexible notion of space, and also poses problems only for the literal-minded. To ask, for example, how the Herald and Agamemnon can arrive from Troy so soon after the beacon fire brings the news of victory in *Agamemnon* is to take up the temporal equivalent of 'how many children had Lady Macbeth'.

The playwright/director used the *ekkyklêma* or 'roll-out machine' to expose interior scenes: Eurydice lying dead on the household altar in *Antigone*, Ajax in his tent surrounded by the butchered animals in *Ajax*, the hero bound to the pillar of the house he has destroyed in *Heracles*. Here, too, the playing area remains flexible, for in these instances (among others) the exposed area gradually shifts from inside the house/palace back to the open air.[18] Unlike realistic drama that demands the strict logic of spatial identity (and with it the convention that a new 'look' is needed to signal a new location), the Greek theatre exploited the possibilities of flexible setting and a transitive notion of indoor and outdoor space. The audience accomplished the necessary adjustments with the strongest of theatrical forces, their own imaginations, sparked by the words and actions of the actors and chorus.

All modes of access to the playing area channelled the performers into the orchestra and out towards the audience. The central door of the façade opened directly onto the orchestra, immediately confronting the actor with the audience. Coming in from either side of the back façade, the two *eisodoi* or 'entrance roads' – also called *parodoi* or 'side roads' – were angled slightly downstage into the orchestra, not upstage towards the backdrop. Because these entrances were aimed in their direction, some of the audience could see actors and chorus approaching from a distance, and often in some display. For example, the *eisodoi* accommodated the arrival and departure of horse- or mule-drawn carriages in Aeschylus' *Persians* and *Agamemnon*, in Sophocles' (lost) *Triptolemus*, and in Euripides' *Electra*, *Trojan Women*, and *Iphigenia in Aulis*.[19] Contrast a proscenium stage where entrances from the wings – through side doors of a box-set, or out of 'nowhere' in the ballet – allow the performers to direct their focus across the playing area or even upstage, towards their fellow players and not out to the house. So, too, the vomitoria of a thrust stage enable actors to enter with their backs to much of the audience, directing their movements and energies upstage rather than towards the spectators.

Addressing a speech towards the back façade would have been extremely rare in the theatre of Dionysus, due to its size, poor acoustics, and the lack of a stone wall to reflect the sound. The vaunted genius of Greek theatrical design did not emerge fully formed at the start, and problems of audibility directly affected the relationship between audience and performer. The fifth-century theatre in Athens was not an intimate space, and acting there was of necessity forceful and outwardly directed.

The arrangement of entrances, the confrontation with the audience, and the size of the theatre reinforced the public nature of Greek tragedy. Neither the plays nor the space in which they were performed sustain the idea that individual psychology and character-revelation are the stuff of ancient drama. Most modern and contemporary plays rely on a process of inner burrowing, progressively narrowing the focus until it delivers the psychological equivalent of a close-up. Greek tragedy works in a different way, presenting a dynamic exploration of life writ large, where tragic issues and conflicts are aggressively public. Bred as most of us are on a drama of interiors, with the world collapsing to the size of a living room, a television screen, a computer monitor, or a hand-held device, we easily forget that Greek theatre took place in the open air. In Athens, the panorama of southern Attica provided the wider theatrical backdrop – sky, sea, the sun, the distant hills and rocky terrain, the river Ilissos, the city walls, the Acropolis looming behind, the very earth on which some of the audience sat – the ever-present, natural correlatives to the characters' and chorus' words and actions.

The outdoor setting means that the theatre of Dionysus lacked the illusion-making capacities of the modern stage, enclosed by walls and a roof, where performers are confined to a relatively small area and electric lights illuminate the action. Guided by the actors' speech and gestures, the Greek audience created the pre-dawn atmosphere at the opening of *Agamemnon* and *Iphigenia in Aulis* and the pitch-black darkness of *Rhesus*, even as they sat under the bright Mediterranean sun.[20] Drawn together in that common light, the audience saw not only actors and chorus but also each other, made aware of their collective roles in creating the performance. Compare the kinds of responses fostered in such an environment with those arising from the darkened room of a modern theatre, where each spectator is involved (more or less) in a private, even intimate relationship with the performance. In the theatre of Dionysus, the emotional reactions were 'scaled up' by the simple fact that the 'lights' shone on performers and audience alike.

The open, public nature of the ancient theatre helps to explain its most basic convention, the masking of actors and chorus. In a theatre the size of the one in Athens, the primary acting tool was the voice, not the face, which would all but disappear. Far from hindering the actor, the tragic mask projected the persona of his character outward to the audience. Because mask-wearing in the Athenian context seems inextricably linked to the idea of outdoor performance, let us consider the place and function of masks here, rather than postpone discussion to the following chapter that examines other conventions of tragic production.

By focusing on the practical function of masks, I do not mean to underestimate their deep psychological and even metaphysical significance, or to skirt the issues of identity and disguise that are relevant to tragic character. Drawing on such considerations, scholars have proposed a number of theories to account for masks in ancient performance. They allow the actor to lose himself in alternative identities, fitting for a servant of Dionysus, the god of ecstasy (*ekstasis*), literally 'standing outside' oneself. Masks confront the audience with ambiguities of appearance and change, instantiating the conflicting urge to schematize and to personify. They enable the playwright to present characters in terms of social role and type, rather than as the sum of personal characteristics. Alternatively, masks blur the lines between a group (grasped by recognizing similarities) and separate individuals (identified by isolating differences). Via sympathetic magic and symbolic incarnation, they empower the wearer to override divisions of gender (man/woman), species (human/animal), and ontological category (mortal/god).[21] Much of the anthropological study of mask-wearing focuses on ritual and religious contexts, areas that have significant overlap with Greek tragedy. We discussed in Chapter 2 the place of masks in various Dionysiac cults, and there may be a link between such ritual masking and dramatic performances.

On the other hand, we should emphasize that *all* 'impersonating' performers in the Greek theatre – every actor and chorus member in every tragedy, comedy, and satyr-play, in every Attic festival that included theatrical performance – wore masks. If tragedy developed from the dithyramb, then the link with ritual mask-wearing is much weaker than scholars admit, for the dithyrambic chorus members did not wear masks. The ancient testimonia on early tragedy suggest that masks were adopted *after* the first tragic performances. The legendary Thespis is said to have smeared his actors' faces with wine lees or white lead (the cosmetic of the day), later introducing masks made of linen. A predictable (if not particularly reliable) evolution emerges from the tradition: the tragic playwright Choerilus improves the mask, Phrynichus introduces women's masks (and, so, female characters), Aeschylus uses terrifying and highly coloured masks, and so on.

Whatever the truth about the first tragic masks, the fact that all dramatic performers in the fifth century wore them means that an Athenian would have been as surprised to see an unmasked tragic actor interpreting a role as we would be to see masked performers in *Annie Get Your Gun*. As a scholar observed a century ago, 'to wear a mask was to act a part, and the idea that it was ever possible to act a part or to perform a play without wearing a mask was one which never occurred'.[22] Regardless of the psychological, cultural, ritual, and metaphysical significance for the Greeks, masks were above all an accepted theatrical convention. Mask-wearing was not a self-conscious attempt to alienate the audience or to invoke a magical or ritual past, or to contrast the flux of reality with the false notion of fixed character, as it seems to be for modern theorists and the contemporary avant-garde. Modern directors of tragedy looking for meaningful equivalents between our conventions and those of the Greeks would do well to keep this in mind.

The ancient Greek language identified a human being metonymically with his or her head or eyes, using such expressions as 'dear head' (meaning 'loved one') and the phrase 'eye of [something]', where we might use the term 'heart' or 'inner fire' of a thing. The Greeks employed the same word, *prosôpon*, for 'face', 'countenance', 'mask', and 'dramatic character'. Sophocles exploits these meanings in *Oedipus Tyrannus*, when the hero returns wearing a mask that shows his gouged eye-sockets, his face now reflecting his true character, a man who was blind to, and is now blinded by, his own identity. In *Bacchae*, Euripides delves even deeper into the connection between mask and character. Possessed by the god Dionysus, Agave holds what she thinks is the head of a lion she has killed, but which in fact is the head of her son, represented by the actor's mask. The ironies go further, for the actor playing Agave previously played Pentheus; she holds up the symbol of that earlier role, which has been dismembered by her own Dionysian frenzy. Combining the image of a tragic character with a self-conscious reference to the theatre, Euripides links dramatic illusion to the destructive power of Dionysus.

In Greek tragedy, both characters and spectators must face what they would rather not, a paradox epitomized by the unflinching stare of the actor's mask. It is hard to imagine a character looking into the terror and instability of tragedy *without* the shield of a mask, for in real life we instinctively would close our eyes. The mask confronts the audience as well, far more powerfully than the naked eye in that large outdoor theatre. The wide-eyed gaze of the tragic mask does not scatter or divide, but focuses and encompasses, compelling the attention of the entire theatre.[23] Paradoxically, by forcing its gaze out, the tragic mask draws the audience in, for each spectator projects his or her reactions onto its surface.

Observe how the fixed image of a human face seems to reflect the emotions of the situation around it, appearing to alter with description and circumstance. A self-portrait of Van Gogh, for example, possesses its own intrinsic qualities, but when the narrator tells us it was the last he painted before his suicide and the camera zooms in, we begin to see hopelessness, anguish, despair. And yet the same portrait reveals a hard earned, if tenuous, peace when we hear one of Van Gogh's happier letters read in the background.[24] In similar fashion, a theatre audience revises and re-construes a mask's physiognomy when the character's circumstances, attitudes, and emotions change. The convention of masked acting brings the audience' imagination vitally into play, tapping the ancient theatre's greatest resource.

Tragic masks and costumes also gave an immediate sense of character-type, gender, age, social status, and economic class, conveying the central tragic conflicts between old and young, men and women, gods and mortals. Comic masks fulfilled the same generalizing and informational ends, but added the possibility of satire. In Aristophanes' *Knights*, for example, the two servants of Demos ('The People') seem to have worn masks resembling the well-known Athenian generals Demosthenes and Nicias. We hear that the mask-makers thought better of fashioning a comparable portrait-mask linking the Paphlagonian servant to the warmongering politician Cleon (*Knights*, 230–33). The joke plays on the fact that Cleon's face is to frightening to imitate.[25]

For all their dramatic power and mystery, masks allowed a single actor to play multiple roles (including different ages and genders) in the same play. Once established as a convention, masks obviated many of the demands that concern us as heirs to theatrical realism. We are bothered if the mother in Ibsen's *Ghosts* looks younger than her son, or if the family members in Pinter's *The Homecoming* sound as if they came from anywhere other than north London. Because the characters and chorus in Attic tragedy all belonged to the tribe of mask-wearers, questions about the appropriateness of the actor's age, look, and gender did not arise, freeing the audience to concentrate on other matters.

Chief among these other concerns was language. The large, open mouth of the tragic mask emphasized the words that came from it, as if they provided the essence of dramatic character and the key to the action.[26] Rhetoric and oral exchange dominated the performance culture of fifth-century Athens, and the ancient actor appeared above all as a speaker. The enlarged orifice of his mask epitomized the tragic situation, where words and suffering seem co-extensive, the mouth always capable of speech, even in the face of the unspeakable. Like a ballet without limbs to dance it, Greek tragedy would cease if the mouth were to close.

Here, the theatre of Dionysus conspired with the tragic mask. A space where most of the audience sat above ground level demanded that performers literally kept their heads up, always projecting forward and out in order to be seen and heard. It is remarkable how frequently tragic texts indicate head movements, especially with the arrival of a new character, as if to ensure that the actor catches the audience in his full, broad sights. Even mute characters wear the possibility of their verbal intervention, silent but never silenced. Consider Pylades in Aeschylus' *Choephori* who says nothing the entire play, only to break his silence for three brief lines, advising Orestes to perform the unthinkable and kill his own mother. In Euripides' *Electra*, produced some forty years later, we expect the mute Pylades to speak at a key moment like his Aeschylean predecessor. But this Pylades *never* speaks, a twist on the tradition that suggests the absence of the gods in the sordid world of Euripides' play.

For all the physical distance between actor and audience in the theatre of Dionysus, both parties found themselves drawn together by natural surroundings in a natural light. Stage conventions that seem exotic to us provided practical and effective means to make that common world sustain dramatic life, producing a compelling experience for the audience. To understand more fully how tragic art and artifice combined, we will consider other dramatic conventions in the next chapter. But we should never lose sight of the fact that the Greek theatrical drive was towards reality, a grounding of issues in a public forum where the human world was set in meaningful relationship to nature, a theatre where the world was included rather than shut out.

Notes

1 There are no archaeological remains. The original *orchêstra* probably lay to the north of the later Odeion of Agrippa (a roofed concert hall erected in the first century BC), which took advantage of the natural slope of the agora, with seats at the higher, southern end looking down on the stage to the north. See J.M. Camp, *The Athenian Agora*, London, Thames & Hudson, 1986, pp. 46, 89, 183–84; and J. Travlos, *Pictorial Dictionary of Ancient Athens*, New York, Praeger, 1971, p. 8 fig. 5, p. 21 fig. 29.
2 In the Attic demes of Rhamnous, Aixone, and Ikaria, the theatre was located in the agora and also served as the meeting place for the local assembly. By the late third century, the theatre of Dionysus had superseded the Pnyx as the meeting place for the Athenian Assembly as well.
3 See R.E. Wycherley, *The Athenian Agora*, vol. 3: *Literary and Epigraphical Testimonia*, Princeton, NJ, American School of Classical Studies, 1957,

48   *The social and theatrical background*

pp. 162–63, 220–21; also Csapo and Slater, op. cit. (Chapter 2, n. 1), pp. 133 (#65, #66).

4 See Travlos, op. cit. (above n. 1), pp. 387–92, 537–52.
5 Csapo, op. cit. 2007 (Chapter 3, n. 17), pp. 105–06, and H.R. Goette, 'An Archaeological Appendix', pp. 116–21; R. Rehm, *The Play of Space: Spatial Transformation in Greek Tragedy*, Princeton, NJ, Princeton University Press, 2002, pp. 37–41; H.R. Goette, 'Griechische Theaterbauten der Klassik- Forschungsstand und Fragestellungen', in E. Pöhlmann, ed., *Studien zur Bühnendichtung und zum Theaterbau der Antike*, 1995, Frankfurt am Main, Studien zur klassischen Philologie 93, pp. 9–48; and *The Architecture of the Ancient Greek Theatre*, eds R. Frederiksen, E.R. Gebhard, and A. Sokolicek, Aarhus, Danish Institute at Athens, vol. 17, 2015.
6 Aristophanes, *Thesmophoriazusae* 395. Entrepreneurs leased the right to erect and disassemble these bleachers for each City Dionysia, receiving some part (per- haps all) of the entrance fees (2 obols) charged for each day's performance, the equivalent of a day's wage for an unskilled labourer before the Peloponnesian War, and perhaps one-third of that value by the end of the fifth century (with wartime inflation). See Csapo, op. cit. 2007, pp. 88–115, and D.W. Roselli, *Theater of the People: Spectators and Society in Ancient Athens*, Austin, TX, University of Texas Press, 2011, pp. 63–86.
7 Taplin, op. cit. 1977 (Chapter 3, n. 10), pp. 452–59, argues that Aeschylus introduced the façade in 458 with his production of the *Oresteia*. It seems more likely that the backdrop appeared in earlier tragic productions. See R. Seaford, *Cosmology and the Polis: The Social Construction of Space and Time in the Tragedies of Aeschylus*, Cambridge, Cambridge University Press, 2012, pp. 337–39, and R. Hamilton, 'Cries Within and the Tragic Skene', *American Journal of Philology* 108, 1987, pp. 585–99, esp. 595–99.
8 J.J. Coulton, *Ancient Greek Architects at Work: Problems of Structure and Design*, Ithaca, NY, Cornell University Press, 1977.
9 A.M. Dale, 'Aristophanes, *Vesp.* 136–210', in *Collected Papers*, Cambridge, Cambridge University Press, 1969 (org. 1957), pp. 103–18, demonstrates that a single door is all that is needed (along with a window or two in *The Women of the Assembly* and *Wasps*); also C.W. Dearden, *The Stage of Aristophanes*, London, Athlone Press, 1975, pp. 50–74; and Taplin, op. cit. (above n. 7), pp. 438–40. K.J. Dover, op. cit. (Chapter 1, n. 8), pp. 21–24, 83–84, 106–08, 197–98, and 'The Skene in Aristophanes', *Proceedings of the Cambridge Philological Society* 192, 1966, pp. 2–17, makes the strongest case for two doors.
10 George Steiner, *Antigones*, New Haven, CT and London, Yale University Press, 1984, p. 227. J. Davidson, 'Theatrical Production', in *A Companion to Greek Tragedy*, ed. J. Gregory, Oxford, Blackwell, 2005, pp. 194–211, provides an excellent summary of fifth-century production practices.
11 A.L. Brown, 'Three and Scene-Painting Sophocles', *Proceedings of the Cambridge Philological Society* 210, 1984, pp. 1–17.
12 Attempts to clarify how this device worked have not met with general approval. See D.J. Mastronarde, 'Actors on High: The Skene Roof, the Crane, and the Gods in Attic Drama', *Classical Antiquity* 9, 1990, pp. 247–94. I use the term *theologeion* for the platform on the roof, and refer to an appearance of a divinity on high as a *deus ex machina*, whether the god 'flies in' or mounts the platform.
13 An Attic red-figure *chous* (a small jug for pouring wine) dated *ca.* 420 BC depicts a single comic actor on a trestle stage, with two spectators seated in chairs. This seems an impromptu affair with no connection to the theatre of Dionysus. Although a raised stage could lift an actor above the chorus, it would need sufficient depth to accommodate the *ekkyklêma* (Chapter 3), impinging signifi- cantly on the orchestra playing area, and, depending on its length along the

skene building, could restrict entrances along the *eisodoi*, as one can tell from Plates 4 and 5.

14 Pollux, 4.123. See R. Rehm, 'The Staging of Suppliant Plays', *Greek, Roman and Byzantine Studies* 29 (3), 1988, pp. 276–83; also F.E. Winter, '*Greek Theatre Production*: A Review Article', *Phoenix* 19, 1965, pp. 106–10. C.P. Gardiner, '*Anabainein* and *Katabainein* as Theatrical Terms', *Transactions of the American Philological Association* 108, 1978, pp. 75–79, shows that the terms 'go up' and 'go down' do not imply a raised stage, but suggest that the Greeks shared our convention of upstage and downstage for directing actors' movement away from or towards the audience.

15 B. Hunningher, *Acoustics and Acting in the Theatre of Dionysus Eleuthereus*, Amsterdam, Noord-Hollandsche Uitg., 1956. Of course, the percentage change in sound intensity decreases the further an audience sits from the action.

16 The skene-roof and machine offered stronger areas, but appearances on high were reserved for special occasions.

17 See Rehm op. cit. 1988 (above n. 14), pp. 263–307.

18 N.C. Hourmouziades, *Production and Imagination in Euripides*, Athens, Greek Society for Humanistic Studies, 1965, pp. 9–13, 83–108, argues that Euripides maintains a clear distinction between 'interior' and 'exterior'. His discussion of the *ekkyklêma* proves the opposite – an exposed interior gradually loses its specificity and merges with the outside, blurring places and spatial boundaries.

19 For chariots, see G. Ley, *The Theatricality of Greek Tragedy: Playing Space and Chorus*, Chicago, IL, University of Chicago Press 2007, pp. 69–83. The idea that an exit out the stage-right or stage-left *eisodoi* signalled, respectively, departure to the country or to the city is of late date and implies a geographical specificity foreign to tragedy.

20 The claim that performances began at dawn – 6,000 to 8,000 people finding their way in the dark? – arises from the mistaken notion that a typical tragedy takes two and a half hours to perform. If so, and assuming pre-performance ceremonies, a tragic tetralogy, and a single comedy, the performance day would last some 14 hours (allowing time for costume changes between plays), requiring a sunrise start in order to end before dark. However, played at speed, even the longest tragedies (*Agamemnon* and *Oedipus at Colonus* at about 1,700 lines) take roughly 110 minutes to perform, while shorter plays (*Choephori* ca. 1,100 lines) under an hour and a quarter. Satyr-plays were shorter still – *Cyclops* has some 700 lines, although *Alcestis* (performed in the fourth spot usually reserved for a satyr-play) has 1,160 lines. See P. Walcot, *Greek Drama in Its Theatrical and Social Context*, Cardiff, University of Wales Press, 1976, pp. 11–21.

21 See D. Wiles, *Mask and Performance in Greek Tragedy*, Cambridge, Cambridge University Press, 2007; F. Frontisi-Ducroux, 'In the Mirror of the Mask', in D. Lyons (transl.), *A City of Images*, Princeton, NJ, Princeton University Press, 1989, pp. 150–65; T. Harrison, 'Facing Up to the Muses', *Proceedings of the Classical Association* 85, 1988, pp. 7–29; A.D. Napier, *Masks, Transformation, Paradox*, Berkeley, University of California Press, 1986; and A. Lesky, *Greek Tragedy*, H.A. Frankfort (transl.), 3rd edn, New York, Barnes & Noble, 1979, pp. 27–46.

22 F.B. Jevons, 'Masks and the Origin of Greek Drama', *Folk-lore* 27, 1916, pp. 173–74.

23 See P. Meinick, 'The Neuroscience of the Tragic Mask', *Arion* 19, 2011, pp. 113–58; and (more generally) 'The Embodied Space: Performance and Visual Cognition at the Fifth Century Athenian Theatre', *New England Classical Journal* 39.1, 2012, pp. 3–46.

24 I take the idea from John Berger's classic *Ways of Seeing*, New York, Penguin, 1972, pp. 27–28; he uses Van Gogh's painting of a wheat field with crows to make the point.

25 The mask-makers' fear also may refer to Cleon's unsuccessful prosecution of Aristophanes (or his *chorêgos*) two years earlier, charging that his *Babylonians* harmed the city. The fate of this lost comedy and of Phrynichus' *Capture of Miletus* (discussed in Chapter 3) is all that we know of theatrical censorship in fifth-century Athens.

26 Illustrations on vases indicate that the fifth-century mask had a relatively small mouth, with wide-open mouths dating from *c.* 300. What we may have here is evidence of changing conventions of visual representation and not necessarily changing masks. The late testimony of Pollux that various colours of masks represented different temperaments (cf. the medieval notion of humours) probably reflects Hellenistic innovation.

5   Conventions of production

I daresay that audiences in most cultures and historical periods have felt that the dramatic characters in their theatre represented (or were intended to represent) intelligible human beings – whether the form was the American musical, Jacobean tragedy, German *Sturm und Drang*, the Peking opera, Brecht's *Lehrstücke*, medieval Mystery plays, Noh drama, or a Broadway production of *Death of a Salesman*. To appreciate the fact that audiences of different cultures and periods viewed their theatre as realistic is to acknowledge the conventional nature of all theatrical representation. A fifth-century Athenian (*mutatis mutandis*) transported to London to see a revival of David Storey's *The Changing Room* would think the production riddled with artifice and convention, presenting a picture far less compelling than, say, Aeschylus' *Seven Against Thebes*. Such an audient might consider the images and language of the locker room too specific to reveal much of value about 'real people', preferring the story of the struggle between two mythical brothers at Thebes for the very reason that it seems closer to the reality of a human situation. Similarly, what strikes *us* as conventional and 'artificial' in a performance of Greek tragedy (or Japanese Kabuki, or Indian Kathakali) would seem to a Greek audience (or their Eastern counterpart) normal and appropriate.

The conventionality of all theatrical performance is worth belabouring, for we cannot hope to understand a given dramatic style or period without grasping the nature of its accepted artifice. To call Greek theatre stylized, conventional, or artificial illuminates little, because the same attributes describe every other drama, even that which strikes a modern audience as perfectly lifelike.[1] Although linguistic metaphors frequently obscure more than they clarify, understanding a given set of theatrical conventions is not unlike learning a foreign language. We realize that our native tongue (with its rules, grammar, syntax, and idioms) is no more or less 'natural' than another, but that any language allows us to represent and operate on the real (non-linguistic) world. As our facility with new languages increases, we come to understand that each tongue has its own strengths and weaknesses, enabling it to work at some tasks better than others, to describe the physical world or to sustain abstractions, with more or less concision, fluidity, power, subtlety, complexity, and specificity.

In similar fashion, to understand and take advantage of the communicative opportunities of a foreign theatrical mode, we must become familiar with the relevant conventions that inform its operations. We then can translate as necessary, using the appropriate conventions from our own theatre. Shakespeare provides an illustrative example. The diction and verse in his plays strike us as highly artificial compared to everyday English, and yet the actor playing Hamlet will fail if he sounds like a poetic metronome. On the other hand, if the actor delivers the 'To be, or not to be' soliloquy like a crisis-centre operator, then he ignores the structure, thought, and mode of expression implicit in the metre and the language. We fault the former for failing to make the convention his own, the latter for ignoring the integral connection between theatrical form and content. We fault both for failing to engage the material, because the play demands a living character whose mental processes, emotions, and style of speech are mutually informing.

In this chapter we will examine the major conventions that provide the form and expressive mode of Greek tragic theatre. The term 'convention' is used in a loose sense, a tacit agreement among the various participants in a performance, both on-stage and in the audience, that allows the drama to unfold in a meaningful way. I will concentrate on those conventional aspects of tragic texts and performance that might strike us as odd, recalling that a fifth-century audience would consider them part of the dramatic furniture. Naturally, the Greek tragedians could and did use these dramatic givens in innovative and shocking ways, but the conventions per se would seem no stranger to a Greek audience than an invisible fourth wall in a proscenium stage seems to us.

We have already discussed the constraints and possibilities implicit in a large outdoor theatre where the performers wore masks. Before looking at other conventions, let us begin with the question of dramatic illusion in tragedy, which forces us in turn to consider approaches to characterization and acting style. We then will examine the functions and modes of the chorus (including a brief look at different metrical forms), followed by a discussion of the conventions of dramatic rhetoric, including stichomythia (alternating dialogue), messenger speeches, and formal debates or *agôns*. Prophecies and curses often play a decisive role in the stories, and they deserve our attention as elements in tragedy that seem foreign to our way of thinking. We next examine costumes, props, and the function of corpses in the plays. To understand how tragedies begin and end, we will look at the prologue and the *deus ex machina*, followed by a brief account of the satyr play, an essential part of the tragic competitions at the City Dionysia. A conclusion will summarize these conventions in terms of the relationship they establish with the audience, the most important factor to keep in mind when considering appropriate modern equivalents.

In and out of the scene: dramatic illusion, character, and tragic acting

Some critics believe that the actors in Greek tragedy never acknowledged the audience as such, and the audience in turn were never encouraged to view the play as a play, but were caught in a kind of spell where the fiction implicit in the performance went unquestioned. According to this view, the audience watching a tragedy operated in one basic mode, that of belief – or, as is more commonly put, 'a willing suspension of disbelief' – and, as a result, the dramatic illusion of the performance was complete.

This form of presentation might appear to characterize much of the drama on stage, television, and screen today. We understand that the actors represent real people whose lives unfold before us, and we are expected to focus our attention on them and *not* on the manner by which their story gets told. Applied to narrative cinema, for example, we remain unconscious of camera angles, changes in perspective, variations in narrative technique (flashbacks, monologues, voice-overs), references to other films, lighting and special effects, all the interventions of the medium itself. We may note in passing the signs of artifice behind a commercial film, but we are meant to subordinate them to the illusion of a 'real' event.

Brief reflection suggests that this is not how we actually watch a film or a play, for we are (intermittently) made aware of the means, as well as the matter, of production. Greek tragedy operates similarly. The genre was highly conscious of the Homeric tradition that preceded it, alert to the ways in which other playwrights and poets had treated the same stories, alive to the political situation facing the city, and so on. Above all, the tragic playwrights explored the dynamic relationship between the characters on stage and the audience, manipulating with artistry (and an admirable will-ingness to experiment) the spectators' perspective on, and commitment to, the action. They constructed their tragedies to implicate the audience emo-tionally and intellectually, consciously and unconsciously, not only in the story but also in the process of its performance.

Dramatic 'illusionists' also position themselves against the trendy view that theatre is always self-referential, endlessly fabricating and unravelling a skein of signifiers that only the naïve would consider to be of any 'real' substance. Although Greek theatre neither maintained nor depended on seamless dramatic illusion, the argument that it did so is an understandable reaction against the once popular belief that any drama with such strange conventions as masks and chorus could not represent intelligible people in recognizable situations, or present characters whom an audience could loathe, reject, learn from, laugh at, and sympathize with.

Once we entertain questions about dramatic illusion and the tragic thea-tre's relationship to reality, a wide range of issues emerge as problematic, including what we mean by such fundamental concepts as personal identity and agency. In what sense can we think of Sophocles' Oedipus as real, or as a person? Is he a dramatic figure with human capacities, or a fictional construct where we locate our own acts of consciousness? When we introduce the actor, the complexities multiply. What does it – or did it – mean for or an actor to 'play' Oedipus? Does he act a part, perform a role, or is there any sense in which he 'becomes' the character? In classical Athens, how did the audience react as they watched this process? Were they conscious of seeing a human being, or a mythical figure, or an actor?

The case of Oedipus is difficult enough, but consider what the fifth-century audience thought when a god took the stage. Did their response alter fundamentally in such plays as *Eumenides* and *Ion*, where one of the deities was Athena, the patron goddess of the city where the plays were performed? On those occasions did the audience give themselves over to the fiction of the performance? Or did they react as if in a game of make-believe, with the character Athena serving as a prompt to their imagination? Did they watch in a detached, critical mode, attending to the rhetoric of her speech and enjoying the innovations of the scene? Or, did they hear the goddess's pronouncements as relevant to the city itself, above and beyond their connection to the play?

Simply posing these questions helps us to realize that a lively interplay between belief and incredulity, between emotional proximity and distance, must have operated in the Greek theatre as it does at some level in even the most 'realistic' of dramatic presentations now. After all, unquestioning belief on the audiences' part would convert spectators into agents, ready to intervene in the action. On the other hand, nothing but distance would turn us into objective observers, emotionally unaffected by the highly charged situations facing the characters. We might react like a hardened paramedic who takes the pulse and blood pressure of every walk-in, or worse, like some avant-garde composer interested in sampling strange arhythmias for their musical quality, rather than for the possibility of a heart attack.

If an aestheticized and distanced response were all that was intended in Greek tragedy, then we would expect a different kind of writing and a different mode of presentation. As Aristotle points out, the great advance that tragedy made over epic was the appearance of characters 'as living and moving before us' (*Poetics*, 1448a.24–25), that is, characters as embodied. The physical presence of the actor defined the earliest drama, and the actor remains the irremovable obstacle in the path of those who view Greek tragedy (or the theatre in general) as a sophisticated playground for mental and artistic games, as opposed to a place of live, and lived, human experience. With all due respect for the life of the mind, there is something inhuman about not responding to the humanity of dramatic characters who come to life before us in performance.

The audience of Greek tragedy witnessed recognizable events happening to intelligible human characters (and, occasionally, highly anthropomorphic gods) as they made choices and discovered the consequences. The responsibilities of the audience included participating with the performers in investing the characters and their dramatic situation with significance and credibility. Yet the form of the plays and the context of their performance also compelled the audience on occasion – and in a manner guided by the playwright and production – to view these same characters and circumstances as elements in a consciously constructed drama that pointed to a world beyond the theatre.

Take, for example, the highly poetic, image-charged language of Greek tragedy. Given its full weight and complexity, the language takes on a life of its own, appropriate not only to the immediate situation, but also to the overall dramatic project. We recognize how fitting it is in *Agamemnon* that the king who threw a net on Troy is netted in the bath, just as Orestes (who traps Clytemnestra in *Choephori*) is snared metaphorically by the Furies in *Eumenides*. But we also realize that the concatenation of images works through the trilogy independently of character and plot, part of the larger case that Aeschylus wishes to make. Through the power of its language, the *Oresteia* expands in scope and texture, alerting us to the wider setting as it deepens the significance of specific moments. The process is one in which the audience shifts from the immediate dramatic situation to the larger world of the play, and then moves beyond it, formulating responses appropriate to each level, inspired by their initial commitment to the dramatic illusion.

A more obvious sign of the tragedians' interest in keeping the audience alive to the fact of performance involves dramatic irony and humour. Although not a formal convention, the practice of employing ironically charged words and disruptive language alters the audience's response to the action. Take, for example, the ubiquitous word-play in Sophocles' *Oedipus Tyrannus* on the name of the hero, *oidipous*, literally 'swollen foot' but also containing the Greek word *oida*, 'I have seen' = 'I know'. At times the repetition of the name draws us into a horrified sympathy with the protagonist; at other times it distances us from his individual plight, encouraging us to view the play as an exemplary tale about human ignorance and blindness.

In Euripides the difference between the characters' knowledge and that of the audience can become so involved that we delight in the play of irony for its own sake. In *Helen*, for example, Euripides alters the standard story of the heroine's abduction, presenting a version in which a phantom goes to Troy while the real Helen spends the war years in Egypt. When the Greek Teucer lands there on his way home, ignorant that the Greeks and Trojans have fought for a phantom, he meets the real but unrecognized Helen and wishes her the best, then curses Helen of Troy and prays for her death. The ironies are rife, and the audience cannot help but enjoy the play of illusion – that is, until Euripides returns us to the stark reality of the war as Helen laments the suffering inflicted in her name on innocent Trojan women.

Although not normally associated with tragedy, humorous moments scattered through the plays pull the audience out of the immediate circumstance with a laugh, only to drop them back with a vengeance. In Euripides' *Heracles*, for example, the goddesses Lyssa ('Madness') and Iris arrive unexpectedly in the middle of the play, sent by Hera to drive Heracles mad. Lyssa argues that Heracles has done nothing to warrant such punishment, prompting Iris to respond: 'The wife of Zeus did not send you here to exercise your sanity' (857). Madness appears as the voice of reason and is chided for it, the kind of pointed Euripidean humour that momentarily takes the audience out of the dramatic situation. However, the playwright then conveys Heracles' madness so vividly that irony and humour vanish, as the play moves from quibbling divinities to human slaughter.

Tragedy also calls attention to itself by referring to (and even parodying) scenes from earlier tragedies, introducing a more complex sense of representation and illusion. Again Euripides is the master, and his parody in *Electra* of the recognition scene between Electra and Orestes in *Choephori* splits the focus of the audience. Part of our interest lies in the earlier treatment by Aeschylus, the other part in the Euripidean version played out before us. Distrust of such quirky dramatic practices once led scholars to delete the passage as spurious, but recent critics have recognized that Euripides systematically involves the audience in this kind of dialectical relationship, alternating between their belief in the illusion of the play and their awareness that they are part of the process by which that illusion occurs. The ambiguity that results in *Electra* ultimately serves dramatic ends, for the Old Man insists on the validity of the traditional signs of Orestes' identity against the sophistic arguments of Electra. He proves to be right, confounding Electra's view that Orestes is too heroic and manly to return home incognito.

Euripides is not alone in exploiting the theatrical conventions available in Greek tragic production. As we shall see in Chapters 6 and 7, Aeschylus and Sophocles also use these basic elements – the prologue, stichomythic exchanges, the messenger speech, curses and prophecies, the chorus, the *deus ex machina* – not only to serve a narrative based on dramatic illusion, but also to explore the processes by which the audience is caught up in that illusion. In so doing, the tragedians force the audience to confront the material of the play, asking them to consider new perspectives and perhaps even reorder their priorities when they leave the theatre.

What do these observations regarding dramatic illusion and its violation tell us about the style of acting in Greek tragedy? No handbook on ancient acting has come down to us, and even if it had done, we would be suspicious of how representative it was, given what we know of the many conflicting approaches to acting today. We know that acting style changed over the course of the fifth century, judging from the anecdote in Aristotle's *Poetics*. The old actor Mynniscus who had performed for Aeschylus, and lived long enough to win the actor's prize for a Euripidean trilogy in the 420s, criticizes a young actor, Kallipides (who won his first acting prize in 418), for overly realistic mimesis, likening his efforts to those of a monkey who can imitate anything.[2]

In Plato's fourth-century dialogue *Ion*, a Homeric rhapsode answers Socrates' questions about the 'process' behind his performances. The rhapsode speaks as if he were possessed by the roles, that the characters were playing him, that he served as a conduit for the poet (or playwright, the difference here is immaterial) and succeeded best when he was least conscious he was acting. This is not the description of acting we would expect from a theatre so frequently characterized as 'stylized' or 'conventional'. According to the Roman Cicero in the first century BC, the tragic actor Aesopus performed in a manner that we would call 'emotional identification' with his character:

> What can be more fictitious than poetry, plays, the stage? However, in this genre I myself have often seen the eyes of the actor flashing from behind his mask as he spoke ... [quoted lines]. And then he would say, lowering his voice to a pitiable tone ... [quoted lines]. He seemed to be weeping and grieving as he spoke these lines.

We have ample evidence that such close identification between actor and character had a correspondingly strong emotional effect on ancient audiences.[3] Tragic productions struck the original performers and spectators as realistic, far more so than classicists who privilege spectacle, semiotic multiplicity, and meta-theatricality would have us believe.

This does not mean that tragic acting portrayed the idiosyncratic and the personal – the standard rule in contemporary psychological realism – over the generic and typical. As we recall from Chapter 4, masked acting in a large outdoor theatre imposed on Greek tragedy a generic account of human existence. Characters operated more on an ethical than on a psychological level, their status depending on qualities that were socially recognized and sanctioned, not on peculiarities of individual behaviour or consciousness. According to Aristotle, tragedy did not concentrate on presenting individual characters as much as on imitating an 'action' [*praxis*]. By action Aristotle meant something like a plot, a structuring of events that tells a story of some gravity and importance, and from which the audience derives appropriate pleasure.[4] Whatever the original audience's responses to tragedy, it seems unlikely that they arose dazzled by the detailed portraits of highly individualized characters. Rather, they were moved by a mythic narrative. one performed by actors who gave that story great emotional power.[5]

Tragic acting style took its cue from the outdoor theatre, the scale of the dramatic events, and the form the material was given. Acting was big-voiced, front-footed, and fully displayed, not low-key, withdrawn, and inner. Aristotle tells us that the main metre adopted for speeches and dialogue – iambic trimetre (three sets of double-iambic feet, each line scanned $^x {}^- {}^\smile {}^- / {}^\smile {}^- {}^\smile {}^- / {}^\smile {}^- {}^\smile {}^x /$ where $^-$ is long, $^\smile$ is short, and ^{x} is either long or short) – was more conversational than epic dactylic hexametre.[6] This fact should warn us against adopting the false analogy between tragedy and musical theatre or opera. Tragic dialogue was neither sung nor accompanied by music, but was deemed to follow the rhythms of common speech, although controlled more formally and expressively than day-to-day conversation.[7] The actor did most of his work through his voice, and the primary attributes of a would-be performer were the quality and range of his vocal powers.

Ancient actors usually played more than one role, but the task may have been slightly easier than it first appears. With very few exceptions, there is little indication in the tragic texts (and none in other sources) that the diction of different characters – queen or nurse, king or servant, male or female, Greek or foreigner, god or mortal – was marked in any individualized way. We may contrast, for example, the Professor's speech with that of Waffles in *Uncle Vanya*, or the prose of Roderigo with the verse of the Moor in *Othello*. Like Bottom in *A Midsummer Night's Dream* who would 'aggravate' his voice to play Thisbe, tragic actors may have changed their pitch and delivery when performing different characters. But even if they did – if there were, for example, a characteristic 'vocal quality' for an old woman or a herald – the audience would have recognized the distinctive voice of each actor behind the mask.

The fact of vocal recognition means that doubling roles folded the issues of dramatic character back into the larger patterns of the play, an opportunity that the playwrights fully exploited. For instance, the same actor likely played both Agamemnon and his rival Aegisthus in *Agamemnon*; both Electra and Clytemnestra, the estranged mother and daughter of *Choephori*; Heracles and Deianeira, the husband and wife who never meet in the course of *Women of Trachis*; Antigone and Haimon, who finally join off-stage in a 'marriage to death' in *Antigone*; Orestes and Clytemnestra, avenging son and murdered mother in Sophocles' *Electra*; Agave and Pentheus, both the mother and the son she kills in *Bacchae*. In Sophocles' *Ajax*, the division of parts probably broke down along the lines of loyalty or antipathy for the title character. The protagonist played Ajax and his half-brother Teucer; the second actor, the 'deuteragonist', portrayed Odysseus (sympathetic to Ajax) and Tecmessa (Ajax's wife); and the third actor, 'tritagonist', performed the roles of Athena, Menelaus, and Agamemnon (Ajax's enemies in the play).[8]

Actors performing tragedy in contemporary productions are usually free of the demands of role doubling, and from the prodigious vocal projection required in the theatre of Dionysus. Nonetheless, attention to the words and to the flow of speech and dialogue provides the surest guide for any actor or director who wishes to take advantage of Greek tragic form. To be avoided is the temptation to convert Greek tragic figures into modern characters by adopting a mode of delivery best suited for domestic/living-room drama – mumbling, using exaggerated breathing as an emotional marker, making inarticulate acknowledgements and prompts, taking long pauses to convey moments of gravity, and employing other irregular patterns of speech and silence. Tragedy demands a different, but no less expressive, discipline, one that subordinates psychological marking via speech/non-speech habits to the 'acoustic mask-wearing' appropriate to its subject and scale.[9] In Greek tragic theatre, the development of character through the forward movement of speech and dialogue serves the action of the drama; it is not an end in itself.

Ancient discussions of gesture (*cheironomia*) indicate that physical expression played an important part in tragic acting. Judging from the extant plays, the most important gestures involved ritual actions associated with mourning the dead, and we can tell from vase paintings and from the texts themselves something of how they looked. The same is true of gestures connected with pouring libations (liquid offerings), swearing oaths, and making supplication. The last example holds particular importance, because supplication (placing oneself at the mercy, and protection, of another) provides the organizing principle of several tragedies, giving rise to the sub-genre of the suppliant play: Aeschylus' and Euripides' *Suppliant Women*, Sophocles' *Oedipus at Colonus*, Euripides' *Children of Heracles*, and several others.[10]

By incorporating patterns of movement and gesture drawn from contemporary ritual and religious practice, the tragedians incorporated important elements of fifth-century life into the world of the heroic figures that inhabited their stage. Here and elsewhere, a thoroughgoing anachronism operated in Greek tragedy, making powerful and immediate contact with the experience of the original audience.[11] The actors presented the spectators with a mythic vision of the contemporary world writ large, and not (as in most modern productions) a version of the heroic world writ small.

The Greek chorus

The chorus represent the least understood aspect of Greek tragedy and the one most rarely honoured, both in productions and in critical writing on the ancient theatre. This situation is unfortunate, because what distinguishes the earliest drama from its later offspring is the presence of the chorus, or more specifically, the coexistence of two contrasting modes of presentation: the rhetoric, or speech of the actor (usually in iambic trimetre, noted above), and the *mousikê* of the chorus, a combination of dance, music, and verse in a variety of metres, traditionally referred to as 'lyric' (although we must remember that tragic choral 'lyric' was accompanied by the *diaulos*, not the lyre).

The difference between rhetoric and lyric, between actor and chorus, has been expressed in a variety of ways. The opposition between individuated character and the undifferentiated chorus influenced Nietzsche's vision of the wellsprings of theatre in *The Birth of Tragedy*. In more pragmatic terms, the actor/chorus dialectic did much to energize theatrical group-work and the revival of alternative theatre in the 1960s and 70s. The distinction between language as lyric (chanted and sung, accompanied by the *diaulos*, filled with imagistic and temporal leaps) and language as rhetoric (used for narrative, argumentative, and persuasive purposes) informed the old critical polarities of connotation and denotation, and has found a new critical life in terms of poetic versus public discourse. Considering the non-verbal aspects of choral performance, we may contrast the power of dance and the emotional valence of music with the rational, logic-bound order of speech, drawing on the traditional dichotomy of reason and passion, or of left- and right-brain activity. We also can view these modal differences in terms of McCluhan's 'hot' medium of language (requiring greater audience participation to complete the experience) and the 'cool' medium of the chorus's lyric and dance (which offers much greater sensory input and so 'does more of the work' for the audience).[12]

However one construes the differences between the rhetoric of the actor and the lyric of the chorus, the interplay between the two expressive modes sets Greek tragedy apart from later drama. Compare the popular Broadway and West-End fare that consists of people in a room talking, or the contemporary avant-garde 'theatre of images' that provides one stage picture after another with minimal narrative or storyline. At best, each offers but half of the possibilities inherent in Greek tragic form. Some critics argue that opera or musical theatre offers a helpful analogy to Greek tragedy, but the apparent similarities strike me as superficial and misleading. The power of speech is absent or extremely attenuated in opera, with simple libretti that lack forceful argument, persuasive rhetoric, cut-and-thrust dialogue, and meaningful public debate. Similarly, the opera's use of dance – usually balletic interludes or atmospheric folkdance – bears little resemblance to the combination of poetry, song, and movement that constitutes the Greek chorus.

As for the comparison of tragic lyric to popular music theatre, a central tenet of the integrated musical asks that a song (or song and dance) reveal character, or signal a major development in the plot, or (in less well-crafted pieces) offer a 'vehicle' for the star. Think how often in a musical number a character establishes his or her situation, a couple falls in or out of love, an important decision is reached, a discovery made, a deal struck, and so on. As we shall see, the choral lyric of tragedy rarely serves so explicit a function. By providing a different mode from the rhetoric of the actors, the chorus engages the play in an ongoing dialogue with itself. Through the different 'voices' of that dialogue – sometimes complementary, sometimes additive, sometimes opposed one to the other – the tragedy takes shape and comes to dramatic life.

Choral practicalities

We can get a better handle on how the lyric differs from the surrounding action by looking at the practicalities of choral performance. The initial arrival of the chorus into the theatre usually took place through one or both of the side entrances called *eisodoi* ('roads in') or *parodoi* ('side roads'), giving the name *parodos* to the first chorus. Frequently the metre for the choral entrance is anapaests – a combination of ˇ ˇ ¯ and occasionally ¯ ˇ ˇ in a repeating pattern – often referred to as 'marching anapaests', although tragedies in which the chorus could be said to move in military fashion are hard to find. There are formal processions, as in the opening of Aeschylus' *Choephori* where the slave women enter the theatre with libations for the tomb of Agamemnon, and in Euripides' lost *Phaethon*, where the chorus enter singing a wedding hymn. In some tragedies the choral entrance is drawn out purposely, as in Aeschylus' *Persians*; in others the chorus arrive with a sense of urgency and dispatch, as in Euripides' *Alcestis* and *Medea*, or with a festive excitement, as in *Ion* and *Electra*. On rare occasions the chorus are discovered in the orchestra when the play begins, moving into place in a 'cancelled entry' that the audience understands to have occurred before the drama begins. Aeschylus in *Eumenides* and Euripides in *Suppliant Women* pre-set their choruses in this fashion, discussed in Chapters 6 and 8.

Once established in the orchestra, the chorus sing and dance a series of odes over the course of the play, usually designated by the general term *stasimon* or 'standing song'. The name does not imply immobility but simply indicates that the chorus are already present before the audience. When a choral song is preceded immediately by an actor's exit and is followed by an actor's entrance, the term 'act-dividing song' seems a more appropriate term than the generic *stasimon*, signalling the importance of choral placement in structuring the drama.[13]

Although there are odes with no metrical response (called astrophic), most choral songs consist of paired stanzas, a *strophê* (meaning 'turn', henceforth strophe) and *antistrophê* ('counter-turn'). In this strophic structure the metrical pattern in one stanza repeats precisely in the next, then a different metrical pattern is introduced in a new strophe, which is followed precisely in its antistrophe, and so on: a—a' /b—b' /c—c'/. Sometimes an independent passage called a mesode ('middle song') is inserted between the two parts of a strophic pair, marking a rhythmical break before the pattern of the strophe repeats in the antistrophe: a—mesode 1—a' /b—mesode 2—b'/ and so on. To bring a choral lyric to a close, the playwright occasionally employs an epode ('after-song') that does not correspond precisely to any of the preceding strophic pairs. The tragic playwrights work complex elaborations on the basic schemes, and a breakdown of the metrical patterns can prove helpful in grasping the movement of the lyric. Although we should not mistake the pattern on the page for the experience of an audience, a director of Greek tragedy would do well to remain alert to the interlocking musical patterns, observing the way the lyric brings together different subjects and motifs by virtue of repeated rhythms and movement, or emphasizes tonal shifts by introducing a break in the pattern.

The precise nature of the dance of the chorus has been lost, but we gain some insight from the content and substance of the songs, from the representation of dancers on Attic vases and in sculpture, and from the lyric metres themselves. Given the verbal complexity of the chorus, we can assume that tableaux and gesture played an important part in tragic choreography. When the lyric included threnodic elements and other aspects of mourning rites, or dealt with sacrifice, weddings, athletic contests, or military actions, the dance drew on recognizable gestures and movements from those contexts. When the chorus sang of the natural and animal world, we may assume that their dance reflected the power and beauty of nature, as (for example) the closing lines of the parodos of *Bacchae* suggest: '... to the mountains, to the mountains. Happy / like a colt with its grazing mother / the bacchant leaps and gambols on its young, strong legs' (*Ba.* 164–69).

The chorus generally moved and sang in unison, although individual dancers could move independently while the group maintained the basic rhythm, and solo voices could emerge when dramatically effective (as in the parodos of Euripides' *Ion*, discussed in Chapter 9). At times the chorus divided into two half-choruses, allowing one group to move with less restraint while the other carried the song, and vice versa. In modern terms, Greek choral dancing seems closer to synchronized modern dance than to ballet, more in the mould of expressive movement than kinaesthetic abstraction.

Although we assume close co-ordination between the dance figures and the carefully constructed lyric rhythms, we should avoid associating specific metres with a particular set of movements or a single emotional effect. A rough scale of physicality from constrained to wild would put the steady and somewhat repetitive anapaests at one end and dochmiacs at the other. A syncopated rhythm, the dochmiac suggests tension, anxiety, and even abandonment, with the metrical foot ˘ ‒ ‒ ˘ ‒ in repeated patterns, capable of great variation, including the resolution of all the long syllables into shorts (˘ ˘˘ ˘˘ ˘ repeated) as at line 1330 of *Oedipus Tyrannus*, where all but one syllable is short. In between anapaests and dochmiacs lie a variety of metrical systems, open to a wide range of emotional and choreographic possibilities.[14]

English translations rarely aim to capture the lyric variation of the original, a wise course given the limitations of English syntax. As a fully inflected language, ancient Greek uses the endings of words and not their order to signal grammatical function in a sentence. By offering maximum flexibility in terms of word placement, the Greek language allows for remarkably complex metres to be repeated precisely without sacrificing intelligible meaning. To identify these lyrical patterns, a commentary on the Greek text can prove an essential guide, for the editor usually provides a breakdown of all the choral metres. Of course, strict allegiance to the original metrical scheme is neither possible nor desirable in a modern translation or choreographed production. But sensitivity to this aspect of choral lyric can help anyone working on Greek tragedy to appreciate more fully the essential dramatic role of the chorus, suggesting places for modern theatrical equivalents to metrical responsion.

At the end of most Greek tragedies, the chorus leave the orchestra through an *eisodos*. Frequently their exit constitutes the culminating action, as in Aeschylus' *Persians* where the elders accompany Xerxes in a dirge back to their homes, or in *Eumenides*, where a secondary chorus leads the Furies out of the theatre towards their new home in a cave below the Areopagos.

At the end of Sophocles' *Women of Trachis*, the chorus form part of the funeral cortège for Heracles, and they perform a similar function in *Ajax*. An effective variation on conventional choral exits occurs in Aeschylus' *Agamemnon*, where the chorus members do not leave together, but depart in small groups after taunting the tyrant Aegisthus. Their exit underlines the unsettled political situation in Argos, the *polis* fragmented following Aegisthus' and Clytemnestra's coup. In a more formal acknowledgement of closure, several plays of Euripides end with choral 'tags', short truisms about the unpredictability of events, after which the chorus presumably exit in silence. Although we cannot be certain, a few tragedies may have ended with no choral exit, substituting a final tableau followed by the audience's applause and whatever passed for the ancient curtain call.

In five extant tragedies – Aeschylus' *Eumenides*, Sophocles' *Ajax*, Euripides' *Alcestis* and *Helen*, and *Rhesus* (once attributed to Euripides, but now considered a fourth-century drama) – the chorus leave the theatre *during* the play, allowing for a second *parodos* when they re-enter the orchestra. In *Eumenides*, the departure of the chorus of Furies in pursuit of Orestes facilitates the shift in scene from Delphi to Athens. Orestes re-enters the empty orchestra (which now represents Athena's sanctuary on the Acropolis), followed shortly by the Furies in their second *parodos*. A similar change in scene occurs in Sophocles' *Ajax*. Tecmessa and the chorus leave the theatre to find Ajax, allowing the tortured hero to enter an empty stage, which now represents a desolate part of the Trojan beach, and there he commits suicide. In *Alcestis*, the chorus join Admetus in bearing the corpse of Alcestis out of the theatre, a procession modelled on a fifth-century funeral. After a scene between Heracles and a household servant (played in the absence of the chorus), the funeral party returns to an empty stage. Admetus contrasts their desolate homecoming to his joyful arrival with Alcestis years before on their wedding night. By voiding the playing area, Euripides conveys not only the collective sense of loss brought on by Alcestis' death, but also the transformation that takes place in Admetus.

Choral identity

But what *is* a tragic chorus, and what relationship does it have to the mythic figures whose story the play dramatizes? The tragedians always present their choruses as a defined group with a credible reason for its presence on the scene – the elders in Aeschylus' *Persians* await news of Xerxes' expedition, the Furies in *Eumenides* pursue Orestes, the women of Corinth answer the cries within the house in *Medea*, the crew of Greek sailors accompany Odysseus and Neoptolemus on their mission to Lemnos in *Philoctetes*. At some point in every tragedy, however, the chorus undermine normal assumptions about character consistency. For example, is raising a ghost the kind of thing Persian elders do? Why should the immortal Furies bind Orestes in the manner of a fifth-century Athenian cursing his enemy to render him ineffective at a trial? Do local women worry about the violation of the ideals of a rival city, as they do in the 'ode to Athens' in *Medea*? These questions may seem absurd, but they follow directly from the way some critics and productions have insisted on the continuity and consistency of character in the Greek chorus.

We would do better to approach a tragic chorus with a flexible notion of identity.[15] Consider, for example, the chorus of Asian slave-women in Aeschylus' *Choephori*. Literally 'bearers of pourings [for the dead]', they enter bringing offerings to Agamemnon's grave at the command of their mistress Clytemnestra. These women urge Electra to convert the offerings designed to placate Agamemnon's spirit into pourings that will rouse his anger and hasten Orestes' return. Later they provide a list of (Greek) mythological monsters against which to view Clytemnestra's murder of her husband. They act as key players in the plot, persuading the Nurse to change her message and lure Aegisthus to his doom. As the murder of Clytemnestra approaches, the chorus alter their point of view, distancing themselves from the matricide so as not to be implicated. They conclude the play by assuming the voice of the house of Atreus, recounting the bloodshed of the past and hoping for a brighter future.

Clearly, these libation-bearers do more than their name and background can account for. Capable of partisan agency in the drama, they prove equally capable of stepping away from the action, providing changing perspectives and commentary, bringing dramatic pressure to bear where and how the playwright chooses. We see similar flexibility in the choruses of Sophocles and Euripides. The arrival of the group always makes 'realistic' sense, coming as attendants to the main character, sympathetic friends, elders of the city, visitors, suppliants seeking help or asylum, and so forth. This 'initial condition', however, does not limit the chorus' dramatic function, and their 'identity' can be tested, contradicted, and put aside as the needs of the play demand.

The theatrical gains from the flexible chorus are enormous. To take one example, the chorus of women in Euripides' *Helen* sing the following passage in their long-delayed first *stasimon*:

> Fools! who look for glory in war,
> in the shock of spear against shield,
> you senselessly try to stop
> once and for all the labour of mortal life.
> Must contests of blood decide
> these things? Then strife will
> never leave the cities of men.
> You see what these men won – wedding chambers
> in the Trojan earth, and they could have
> settled it with words, their strife over you.
> Ah Helen!

(*Hel.* 1151–60)

This group of captured Spartan women entered the play 900 lines earlier, having left their washing to dry on the banks of the river Nile. Now, in their long delayed first *stasimon*, they sing a diatribe against war. Euripides has not constructed a set of circumstances, or presented a psychological profile, that would account for this change in choral sensibility. Nor would the original audience have expected such an undertaking, or found it necessary. The chorus's outburst conforms to a message that the play develops in several ways, but none of them dependent on the realistic conversion of the chorus from washerwomen to anti-war protesters.

Although looking for character consistency in the chorus seems something of a red herring, maintaining the gender of the group is not. Of the thirty-one extant tragedies from the fifth century, twenty-one have female choruses, and they frequently stand in solidarity with a female protagonist. Their stories compelled both the males on stage and in the audience to consider situations and emotions foreign to their own. A similar imaginative sympathy would have operated towards choruses of slaves, captives, suppliants, barbarians (non-Greeks), the old, and the weak. It is important that the chorus of Aeschylus' *Seven Against Thebes* and Euripides' *Bacchae* are female, standing in opposition to the male protagonist. It makes dramatic sense that Medea has an initially sympathetic group of women at hand, and the same can be said for Deianeira in *Women of Trachis*, Creusa in *Ion*, Andromache in her tragedy, and many others. Similarly, the fact that the choruses of *Agamemnon* and *Antigone* are male highlights the gender conflicts and transformations essential to those plays.

A ritual chorus?

By approaching the chorus as a multifaceted but gender-specific entity, we cease to limit the group to a single function or point of view, resisting a scholarly tendency that goes back centuries.[16] The idea of a consistent choral character has recently taken a new twist, however. Some scholars now identify the tragic ensemble as a 'ritual chorus' existing outside of the dramatic fiction, like those that celebrated rites of passage, athletic victories, festivals dedicated to various gods, and so forth. According to Albert Henrichs, 'all instances when the chorus refers to its own dancing in extant tragedy may be interpreted in terms of its extra-dramatic identity as a performer in the ritual dance.' When a tragic chorus imagines performing at a different time and place, their 'choral projection' further distances them from the onstage action, reminding the audience that they are, in fact, a 'ritual chorus' that could perform elsewhere. Extending this view, one scholar asserts that 'choral projection is not an exceptional state for the chorus to be in but what tragic ritual is really about'.[17]

I believe that this approach to the chorus makes a nonsense of the plays, and I shall try to explain why. It is true that tragic choruses often refer to singing and dancing in ritual contexts, including hymns praising Delphi and Apollo, songs honouring Dionysus, wedding hymns and epithalamia, funeral laments and threnodies, girls' choruses, victory odes, and so on. However, choral performances in tragedy represent a *mixing* of these genres, designed for dramatic effect. As Herington reminds us, the innovation in tragic lyric did not lie in discovering new metres, but in 'its fusion of the known metrical genres within the compass of a single work'.[18] This means that tragic choruses disregard the essential element that defines choral ritual: strict adherence to the purity and rigour of the form. So, for example, in Euripides' *Helen* the title character sings a lament that she labels a 'paean' for the dead (*Hel.* 167–78), a ritually perverse association of a hymn of praise to a god with human mortality. Similarly, in Sophocles' *Antigone* (806–82) and Euripides' *Suppliant Women* (990–1030), wedding hymns become funeral dirges, a conflation of two rituals that highlights the horrific emotional reversals experienced by the characters and chorus on stage.

In Euripides' *Electra*, the chorus join Electra in welcoming Orestes and Pylades after the murder of Aegisthus. The women sing an epinician-like ode (*El.* 860–79) while they crown the young men, invoking the ritual commemoration of athletic prowess for the 'beautiful and noble' victor. But Euripides portrays Orestes as far from heroic, having stabbed Aegisthus in the back at a ritual sacrifice at which he was an invited guest. When Orestes presents his sister with the corpse of Aegisthus to abuse, the audience understands that the elevated victory hymn heightens the contrast between a false heroic image and the brutal realities of the play, hardly the 'choral projection' to a distant ritual context that scholars imagine.

Comparing Heracles' madness to a Bacchic celebration run amok, the chorus in Euripides' *Heracles* call into question the nature of the lyric they are performing, referring to the *aulos* that accompanies a crazed dance (*HF* 877–79). The chorus themselves are dancing to an *aulos* in the orchestra, so their performance comes to signify the inverted Dionysiac ritual they describe. By transforming the choral dance in the theatre into its own 'negative image', Euripides asks the audience to consider the fabric of song that once praised Heracles as victor and now unravels into disorder and madness. In their final lyric, after the hero has blindly killed his family, the chorus doubt what song they should perform next: 'What groans, / or dirge, or song of death, what dance / of Hades should I take up?' (1025–27). The chorus answer the question by never singing and dancing again, over the last 350 lines of the play. Through their collective stillness and silence, Euripides suggests that the tragic lyric adequate to the experiences of *Heracles* has yet to be written.

The most famous example of a chorus calling its own activities into question occurs in the second stasimon of *Oedipus Tyrannus*. At this point, Apollo's oracles seem unfulfilled, and the shifting eddies of fortune appear so random that they threaten any sense of human purpose. If such is the state of the cosmos, the chorus wonder 'Why is it necessary for us to dance?' (*OT* 895–96). Although their question is deeply self-referential, it remains closely bound to the action of the play. Why *should* choruses dance? If events occur only at random, what allegiances are there to the city, the gods, and the notion of a 'cosmos' (the Greek for 'order'), the very things that a tragic chorus gather to explore and celebrate at the festival of Dionysus? By virtue of the chorus's own self-examination, Sophocles raises a fundamental question about the purpose of theatre. To assume the fifth-century audience would have seen the chorus as performing a ritual lyric independent of the dramatic context makes no sense of the play they were watching.

Nonetheless, scholars with little or no theatrical experience insist that the Athenians 'failed to distinguish dramatic from other, non-dramatic choroi', and claim that we misread Greek tragedy if we refuse to see that it functions *as* ritual.[19] Let us meet this claim head on. The strongest case for seeing tragedy as a form of choral ritual has been made for Euripides' *Bacchae*. The chorus represent followers of Dionysus, the god of the theatre festival in which the play took place, and meta-theatrical elements abound, as discussed in Chapter 4. In terms of choral performance, the *parodos* resembles a dithyramb in style, diction, and theme, recalling Dionysiac ritual processions in other contexts.[20] The god's epiphany leads to exultation among his chorus of Asian followers, and he has converted the entire Theban population into worshippers of his cult. One 'ritualist' scholar concludes: 'The whole point of the experience seems to lie in becoming part of the shared choral ritual.'[21]

Bacchae also presents the horrific murder and dismemberment of a son by his mother, struck mad by the god whose ritual the audience (the claim goes) has come to share. The chorus of Asian bacchantes, played by masked Athenian citizens, sing in triumph: 'A beautiful endeavor it is to drench / your hands in the blood of your child' (*Ba.* 1163–64). If this is the 'shared choral ritual' of Dionysiac worship championed by recent scholars, then Euripides goes out of his way to expose its terrible, destructive nature. A ritual that turns on itself in this way is so far removed from what we associate with the term that we must conclude, for the ancient audiences as for us: tragedy was *not* coextensive with ritual. We would be doing Greek tragic theatre a great disservice if we were to adopt the current fashion of viewing the tragic chorus as an independent ritual entity whose perspective is only tangentially connected to, or shaped by, the play that calls that chorus into being.

Chorus–actor interchange

In addition to singing and dancing on their own, the chorus can share the lyric with a dramatic character in a *kommos*, literally 'beating' the breasts, a gesture of mourning. As the term suggests, *kommoi* frequently arise in moments of extreme grief: the return of the defeated Xerxes at the end of *Persians*; following the suicide of Jocasta and the blinding of Oedipus in *Oedipus Tyrannus*; during the final appearance of the heroine in *Antigone*, when her wedding hopes end in a funeral procession. On other occasions, characters and chorus can interact in a lyric dialogue, where they maintain their respective modes of rhetoric and lyric. As we will see in Chapter 6, Cassandra and the chorus in *Agamemnon* share such an exchange, but with the roles reversed – Cassandra sings and the chorus speak, until the prophetess draws the group into her dance and together they share a *kommos*.

Actors sometimes use lyric metres on their own, singing a monody ('solo song').[22] The title characters in both Euripides' *Ion* and *Electra* enter an empty orchestra performing a monody, much like a chorus arriving in the *parodos*. After an opening section of anapaests (again, modelled on a choral entry), Ion sings a work song as he sweeps the temple precinct with his broom. The fact that his lyric is divided into a strophe and antistrophe suggests that dance movements accompanied his song. In *Electra* the protagonist returns with a water-jug filled from the well, singing and dancing a lament for her miserable fate. The formal structure emphasizes Electra's distress, for she separates each strophe and antistrophe with a short mesode that interrupts the metrical correspondence, underlining her wretched situation as a married virgin without status, a royal princess dying on the vine.

To convey utter isolation at a moment of great dramatic intensity, Euripides sometimes gives his character a monody. Evadne suddenly appears in *Suppliant Women* ready to leap onto her husband's funeral pyre; after years of silence, Creusa confesses her rape by Apollo in a moving solo song in *Ion*. After singing, the character often presents the material again in regular dialogue metre. For example, Alcestis 'dies' first in a beautiful song, and then she plays out the death scene in rhetoric. Cassandra in *Trojan Women* sings a perverse wedding hymn in honour of her union with Agamemnon, and then she explains to her mother why the occasion deserves celebrating. The process of 'going through things twice' is highly conventional, for we find no examples where a speech on the same general topic *precedes* an actor's monody or shared *kommos*. In other words, the 'repetition' does not imply inauthentic behaviour or rhetorical posturing, but quite the opposite. The character has undergone an experience of sufficient power and importance to warrant presenting it in two different modes, forcing the audience to grapple with the different perspectives and emotional responses that each elicits.

Just as actors can adopt the medium of the chorus in a *kommos* or a monody, so the chorus occasionally speak. Editors usually assign their dialogue lines to a single *coryphaeus*, or chorus-leader, who takes on the role of group representative, as in the Furies' dialogue in the trial scene of *Eumenides*. At other times, we may hear various voices from the chorus, as in the exchange after the death of the king in *Agamemnon*, when each member speaks his view on the best course of action (*Ag.* 1348–71). Lines also may have been divided among different speakers in the more conventional utterances of the chorus, such as identifying new arrivals, bidding farewell to departing characters (covering their exit), and offering a short break between long speeches. As for this last function, recall that in a large theatre with masked actors the source of any given utterance might be unclear to the audience. Tragedy adopts the convention that the chorus can offer a brief comment on what they've just heard, or call for moderation between the contending parties, before the next character begins speaking.

Although tragic choruses usually do not 'make speeches', we find an exception in Euripides' *Heracles*, where the *coryphaeus* delivers a twenty-three-line speech (longer than Aegisthus' entire part in *Choephori*, or Eurydice's in *Antigone*). The chorus leader focuses on the chorus's impotence to resist the tyrant Lycus, and he concludes by wishing that he and his fellow elders could regain their youthful prowess. This unprecedented speech by a chorus member emphasizes the group's *weakness*, accentuating the gap left by Heracles' absence and the desperate need for his return.

Why a chorus?

Perhaps the most important function of the tragic chorus is to open up the drama to non-linear possibilities that a strict narrative can inhibit or deny. Time and again choral lyric introduces striking images of the natural world, in the manner of the extended epic similes discussed in Chapter 1. In *Agamemnon*, for example, the images of the vultures orphaned of their young, the eagle and the pregnant hare, the lion cub who turns from pet to killer, the nightingale singing of her loss, take on a life of their own. Through the choral lyric, human activities in the *Oresteia* are viewed against the vast backdrop of nature and prove to be both at one and at war with the natural world.

Intermingling past, present, and future, the chorus also free tragedy from a strict temporal sequence. By introducing examples from myth, they encourage the audience to view specific dramatic actions within the (relatively) timeless context of mythic paradigms. Space and location also become transmuted in the performance of lyric. The chorus of *Heracles* evoke various points at the edge of the known world; the Danaids in Aeschylus' *Suppliant Women* (776–83) and the chorus in *Bacchae* (402–16) sing an 'escape' ode, conjuring a location far from their immediate problems.

We read that the chorus represent the ideal spectator, the city, the common man or woman, the fifth-century world-view opposed to the archaic ethos of the heroic characters, the voice of the poet, and (as discussed above) a ritual ensemble that stands outside the drama. We do better to understand the chorus as theatrical raw material that the playwright shapes as the mood and plot demand. They share information, ask questions, make comments, interpret events, offer parallels from myth, evoke and conflate rituals, and expand the play across time and space. Freed from strict determinants of identity, character, and ritual function, the tragic chorus influences the audience as much as the action. Through their lyric and dance, they cast disturbing shadows back on the scene we have just watched, or throw an interpretive filter over what will transpire. They ask the audience to consider elements not directly related to advancing the plot, and yet essential to the workings of the play.

Modes of talking: messenger speeches, stichomythia, prophecies, and formal agôns

Messenger speeches

We have discussed how tragic lyric can extend over time and space, bringing the past and future, the distant and remote, to bear on events in the play. An important convention of tragic rhetoric, the messenger speech also brings an off-stage world into the theatre, but in a more focused and emotionally immediate manner. The theatrical opposite of a chorus engaged in music, song, and movement, the Messenger stands alone, a performer stripped of everything but his capacity to hold the stage with the narrative he delivers.

Rarely given a name, the tragic Messenger subordinates character to dramatic function. Here, if anywhere in Greek tragedy, the text speaks through the actor. Modern productions fail to grasp the theatrical power of these remarkable speeches, substituting for hard-edged narration a personally felt, angst-ridden account. Imbued with a sense of 'I was there', such performances are at odds with the form, in which the 'I' defers almost completely to the 'there'. The audience should focus on the narrated events of the message, *not* on the Messenger – the blinding of Oedipus, the suicides of Antigone and Haimon, the madness of Heracles, the dismemberment of Pentheus. A messenger speech makes its strongest impact when the actor serves as the medium through which the audience create the off-stage events in their own imaginations.

As with their tragic choruses, the playwrights always provide a reason for the Messenger's presence: Alcestis' handmaid describes her mistress's farewell to the house; a servant of Medea brings the news of Glauke's immolation; a member of Creon's entourage reports the fatal events in the cave in *Antigone*; and so on. This explanation establishes that a credible eyewitness will relate accurately what was said and done, and in almost every case we trust the message to be the truth.[23] The Messenger frequently sets up the narration as if he or she were part of an audience, either privileged to be there or forced to observe what no one would want to see. In *Heracles*, for example, the Messenger reports how all the household – family and servants – participated in the sacrifice to celebrate Heracles' return and purify the house after the murder of Lycus. But confusion reigns among the servants at the strange behaviour of Heracles. One of them asks, 'Is our master playing, or has he gone insane?' (*Her.* 952). This comment by a concerned onlooker points toward the truth, for Hera has struck Heracles mad, driving him to hunt down his wife and children.

As this example demonstrates, a convention within messenger speeches involves quoting someone else on the scene. In Euripides' *Bacchae*, the second Messenger reports the words of both mother and son, Agave who is possessed by Bacchic frenzy and Pentheus who is spying on their mysteries. Agave calls on her fellow Bacchantes to uproot the tree where her son sits, and the Messenger follows with Pentheus' desperate appeal: 'Mother, it is I, your son / Pentheus, whom you bore to Echion. / Mother, please, have mercy. I have done wrong, / but I am your son. Don't kill me' (*Ba.* 1118–21). Through their own words, crazed Agave and doomed Pentheus come to life in a moment of tragic clarity, before we hear the grisly details of dismemberment: 'They raised the cry of sacrifice. One woman bore an arm, / another a foot still in its boot, then they stripped his ribs, / ripping off the skin, every hand blood red / as they played ball with Pentheus' flesh' (1133–36).

Although there are few passages in drama more gruesome than this, the convention of the Messenger does not mean that *all* violence in Greek tragedy takes place off-stage. Physical pain, brutality, and even bloodshed do occur within sight of the audience: the hero commits suicide on stage in Sophocles' *Ajax*, the suppurating wound of the title character in *Philoctetes* remains constantly before us, the tormented Heracles exposes his pain-wracked body in *Women of Trachis*, a battered son dies in the arms of his father in Euripides' *Hippolytus*. Rather than simply a way to avoid on-stage violence, the Messenger exploits the audience's capacity to visualize and re-animate that violence in their minds' eye. We might compare the messenger's report to a radio play or podcast that depends on the imaginative participation of the audience for its success. Those who have worked in radio drama stress the medium's incomparable visual richness,[24] and the same quality infuses messenger speeches in tragedy. Here, language and imagination do the work that modern theatre and film have surrendered to technical wizardry, graphic visuals, and special effects.

Stichomythia

Cut-and-thrust dialogue called stichomythia ('story by lines') represents another important convention of tragic rhetoric. It can take several forms, normally alternating single lines of dialogue between two characters, but also two lines per speaker (distichs) or only half a line each (hemistichs), not unlike a pentametre line in Shakespeare split between two actors. Employed in a variety of circumstances, stichomythia usually signals a quickening of tempo and focusing of dramatic energy, often leading to a decision. In its neutral function, it can mark the transition from the end of one speech to the beginning of the next. For example, the stichomythic exchange initiated by the chorus-leader in *Agamemnon* manoeuvres the Herald to describe the disastrous storm that destroyed the Greek fleet (*Ag.* 538–50). Playwrights also use stichomythia to introduce and welcome a new arrival on-stage, important in a large outdoor theatre (as noted above), where the actors are masked and character identity may not be self-evident.

As part of his experimentation with tragic form, Euripides used stichomythia in bold new ways. In *Ion*, for example, Creusa's first meeting with her (unrecognized) son generates over *one hundred* lines of stichomythia, by far the longest stretch of such dialogue in tragedy. Here, the rapid exchange of questions, answers, and reactions replaces the series of speeches we would expect to establish the dramatic situation. By using stichomythia to provide important background information, Euripides ironically emphasizes the fact that mother and son, intimately connected by blood and symbolically drawn together in dialogue, remain separated thanks to the self-serving secrecy of the god Apollo.

In Euripides' *Electra*, the old Tutor and Orestes share a stichomythic exchange to map out the murder of Aegisthus. After thirty-five lines alternating between the two, Electra suddenly enters the dialogue, replacing the troubled Orestes as interlocutor and introducing her own diabolical plan to kill her mother. The catechistic form of stichomythia also can help a character understand the larger context of which he or she has been unaware. In *Heracles*, for example, Amphitryon's dialogue with his son guides Heracles to realize that he has killed his family in a fit of god-sent madness. In *Bacchae* the stichomythic exchange between Cadmus and his daughter draws Agave out of her Bacchic frenzy, and she sees that the lion's trophy she holds in her arms is actually the head of her son Pentheus.

Frequently a character employs stichomythia to convince another to change his mind. Clytemnestra's dialogue with her husband in *Agamemnon* persuades him to walk on the tapestries against his own better judgement. In *Philoctetes*, Neoptolemus has a series of stichomythic exchanges with Philoctetes and with Odysseus that highlight the difficult choices facing him. Time and again the young man repeats the question *ti drasô*, 'What shall [should] I do?', reminding us of the strong ethical dimension in Greek tragedy.[25] By means of stichomythia, characters focus on the issues of choice, decision, and action through engagement and dialogue with others, and not through abstract speculation.

The rapid exchange of alternative points of view also reflects the process of cross-examination by which Athenian juries reached their verdicts. The law courts intermixed long prepared speeches with these short exchanges, a pattern we observe in court-influenced tragedies such as Sophocles' *Ajax*, where Menelaus, Teucer, and Agamemnon present competing arguments for and against the burial of Ajax. Let us turn to this more elaborate convention of tragic rhetoric, the formal debate between two characters, called an *agôn* or 'contest'.

The theatrical agôn

Political debates in the Assembly and legal cases in the law courts provided the inspiration for many scenes on the Greek stage. We find a formal trial scene in Aeschylus' *Eumenides*, a fitting culmination to a trilogy imbued with legal terminology and metaphor, as we shall see in Chapter 6. Scenes of political debate on the relative merits of democracy figure prominently in both Aeschylus' and Euripides' *Suppliant Women*, and in Sophocles' *Oedipus at Colonus*. References to specific Athenian political and legal practices occur throughout the plays, reminding us of the thoroughness with which the mythic and heroic characters articulate fifth-century concerns.

In a tragic debate or *agôn* ('contest'), a character makes his or her case as if speaking before a body of jurors or voters; then the second party responds, often point by point like a defence lawyer or political opponent. The formal verbal contest encourages the audience to grapple with the arguments, apply them to the issues of the play, and reach their own judgement. At times the playwrights expose the manipulation of these rhetorical structures to serve the ends of power; at other times they question the efficacy and appropriateness of public debate itself.[26]

The second half of *Ajax* consists primarily of arguments between Teucer and the brothers Menelaus and Agamemnon over the burial of Ajax. These *agôns* challenge and ultimately affirm an ethical principle central to Greek society – the right of even the enemy dead to receive burial. At a crucial juncture, Ajax's erstwhile enemy Odysseus adds his voice to that of Teucer, helping to ensure that funeral rites take place. In *Medea*, the first encounter between Medea and her estranged husband takes the agonistic form of prosecution and defence. In presenting his case, Jason inverts almost everything the audience knows to be true, flouting the very aspects of Greek culture with which he claims to have blessed Medea. He resembles those fifth-century Athenian politicians (and their modern epigones) who clothe personal advantage in terms of justice, making a mockery of the values and institutions they ostensibly support.

Euripides scrutinizes various argumentative strategies in other plays. In *Alcestis*, Pheres arrives during the funeral procession for Alcestis (who has sacrificed herself for her husband), precipitating a bitter debate with his son Admetus. The two men escalate their mutual recriminations until the funeral situation is virtually forgotten. In this *agôn*, neither party wins, and the debate itself – played out before Alcestis' corpse – seems grossly out of place. In *Trojan Women*, Hecuba confidently assumes that she can demonstrate the bankruptcy of Helen's sophistry and persuade Menelaus that his unfaithful wife deserves to die. Hecuba's faith in the efficacy of words proves as ill-founded as it is poignant, for the scene exposes the futility of rational discourse when events have reached this stage. No matter what anyone says, Menelaus will welcome the beautiful Helen back to his marriage bed and Hecuba's suffering will continue.

An even more problematic *agôn* involves the tyrant Lycus and Amphitryon in *Heracles*. Intent on killing Heracles' family (who have sought protection at the altar of Zeus), Lycus unleashes a verbal assault on the absent Heracles for using a bow, fighting from a distance like a coward, rather than in man-to-man combat like a hoplite warrior. In response, Heracles' father Amphitryon mounts a point-by-point defence of his son's choice of weapon, failing to confront Lycus' with his own blatant cowardice in violating the rights of suppliants. Some scholars point out the topicality of the debate for fifth-century military strategy; others argue that the bow represents a problematic image of Heracles' courage. But neither of these explanations accounts for the presence of such an extended debate – especially given the dramatic situation – that changes nothing.

Perhaps Euripides lingers over these speeches to force the audience to consider what lies *behind* the convention itself. Full of contemporary sophistry and 'legalese', the bow debate dramatizes a 'miss', an *agôn* of ineffectiveness, a failure to engage the important matters of the play. The fifth-century audience may have recognized an indirect reference to the mis-directed speeches that made up a good portion of public debate during the Peloponnesian War, in full swing at the time of the play's production. If so, then Euripides uses the convention of the formal *agôn* to expose how public rhetoric can skirt or even *displace* crucial issues, rather than confront them directly.[27]

Prophecies, dreams, oaths, and curses

In a world that lacked the explanatory and predictive powers of modern science, ritual divination played a significant role, and tragedy reflects these practices by featuring an array of prophets and prophecies. Theseus pro-claims in Euripides' *Suppliant Women*, 'Unclear matters, about which we have no secure knowledge, / seers help us understand, by examining the flames in fire, / the folds of entrails, and the flight of birds' (*Supp*. 211–13). In Greek tragedy, prophets and oracles inevitably speak the truth, and char-acters who reject their (usually) dire predictions suffer them nonetheless. Onstage seers such as Teiresias (*Oedipus Tyrannus*, *Antigone*, *Phoenician Women*, *Bacchae*), Cassandra (*Agamemnon*, *Trojan Women*), and Theanoe (*Helen*), and off-stage prophets such as Calchas (*Agamemnon*, *Iphigenia in Aulis*) and Helenus (*Philoctetes*) reveal errors or crimes of the past and disclose what lies ahead. Polymnestor, Eurystheus, and Medea (who attain prophetic powers near the end of *Hecuba*, *Children of Heracles*, and *Medea* respectively) alter the trajectory of their plays as they come to a close. Gods from the machine (discussed above) and within the dramas (Prometheus in *Prometheus Bound*, Athena in *Eumenides*, the ghost of Darius in *Persians*) fulfil prophetic functions by extending our understanding of events into the future.

Prophetic missions to Apollo's oracle at Delphi or Zeus' at Dodona occur time and again. Both Deianeira and Heracles recount the oracle that came from Dodona in *Women of Trachis* (169–72, 1164–74). In *Andromache*, Orestes travels to Dodona, but after he rescues Hermione in Thessaly, he changes course for the sanctuary at Delphi. Theseus (*Hippolytus*), Aegeus (*Medea*), and Orestes (*Choephori*, and both Sophocles' and Euripides' *Electra*) arrive onstage after consulting the Delphic oracle. Sent from Tyre on a choral mission to Delphi, the chorus of *Phoenician Women* must remain in Thebes because of the Argive invasion. In *Oedipus Tyrannus*, we hear of *five* separate pilgrimages to Apollo's oracle, each of signal importance to the play (discussed in Chapter 7). Both Xuthus and Creusa in *Ion* have come to inquire at Apollo's shrine, and the god's sanctuary provides the setting for the play, discussed in Chapter 9.

Dreams also hold a special place in tragedy, often requiring a prophet or otherworldly figure to interpret. A nightmare impels Atossa to appear before the chorus in *Persians*, and they urge her to call on the gods and her dead husband Darius for help. A dream motivates Clytemnestra to make offerings at Agamemnon's tomb in *Choephori* and in Sophocles' *Electra*. In *Eumenides* the murdered queen appears as a ghost in the Furies' dream. Hecuba wants assistance from the Trojan prophet Helenus or Cassandra to interpret her nightmare, which seems to augur danger for her son Polydorus and daughter Polyxena (*Hec.* 67–97). Read properly, dreams in tragedy – like prophecies and oracles – tell an inevitable truth.

In their efforts to affect the future, tragic characters swear oaths and utter curses, invoking the gods as witnesses and guarantors.[28] After supplicating Aegeus, Medea compels him to swear that he will provide her sanctuary in Athens (*Med.* 731–58). The prominence of this oath encourages us to contrast Aegeus' vow with the false oaths sworn earlier by Jason (20–3, 160–5) and denounced by the chorus: 'The grace of oaths has departed; no longer does respect / for oaths remain anywhere in Greece' (439–40). As we shall see in Chapter 8, Athena insists that Theseus exact an elaborate oath from the Argive Adrastus (*Supp.* 1183–1212), an issue of great relevance to the Athenians who were negotiating an alliance with Argos in the year of the play's performance at the City Dionysia.

Old curses return at the end of *Agamemnon*, when Aegisthus boasts over the corpse of Agamemnon, recounting his father Thyestes' curse on the house of Atreus (*Ag.* 1577–1611). Oedipus curses the murderer of Laius, who proves to be Oedipus himself (*OT* 246–51), and he curses his own son Polyneices, adding to the tragedy of his future (*OC* 1370–96). Hyllus curses his mother Deianeira (*Trach.* 807–12), who later kills herself. Ajax prays that the Furies curse the Atreidae and the Greek army (*Aj.* 839-44), and Teucros does the same (1175–79, 1389–92).

We see the tragic results of curses and oaths most powerfully in *Hippolytus*. By keeping his vow not to speak of Phaedra's illicit passion (*Hipp.* 611–12, 657–60), the chaste young man pays with his life. Convinced of his son's guilt, Theseus uses a curse granted him by Poseidon to bring about Hippolytus' death (885–90). His son swears an oath to Zeus that he did nothing to Phaedra (1025–31, 1191–93), but Theseus rejects this out of hand. Reunited at the end of the play, Theseus wishes he could undo what he prayed for, and the dying Hippolytus wishes he could turn Poseideon's gift back on the giver: 'Would that the race of men could curse the gods!' (1411–15).

Costumes, props, and corpses

Rather than reflecting historicist notions of Bronze Age, archaic, or heroic attire, the costumes worn by tragic performers resembled contemporary fifth-century clothing, what we would call 'modern dress' for the Greeks, This aesthetic applied not only to the characters' domestic and public clothing, but also to military apparel, armour, and hand props (swords, bows, and the like). The contemporary look of the actors, coupled with anachronisms from the civic, political, and military spheres, suggests that the tragedies set during the mythic wars at Troy or Thebes and produced in the last third of the fifth century would have brought the Peloponnesian War (431–04) immediately to mind.

This is not to imply that an Athenian spectator saw his next-door neighbour onstage, or mistook tragic action for a slice of life. Nonetheless, the actor playing Agamemnon in *Iphigenia in Aulis* dressed more or less like a contemporary and spoke a poetic, but recognizable, version of Athenian speech, far more so than did the rhapsode performing Homer. Agamemnon's concerns about how to prosecute the war, and what sacrifices it was worth, spoke directly to those gathered in the theatre of Dionysus. Modern productions could do worse than aim for a similar combination of distance and proximity vis-à-vis their intended audience.

Bridging the gap between the heroic characters and the fifth century, tragic costumes and props often mirrored specific aspects of Athenian ritual life. Evadne appears in her wedding dress in Euripides' *Suppliant Women*, in marked contrast to the chorus who wear the black robes of mourning. So, too, Cassandra in *Trojan Women* perversely celebrates her upcoming wedding with Agamemnon, to the point of carrying her own nuptial torches, normally borne by the mothers of the bride and groom. In *Alcestis*, Admetus dresses in black with his hair cut in mourning when he leads Alcestis' funeral procession. At the end of the play, Heracles miraculously hands back the resurrected Alcestis, who is dressed and veiled like a bride, and Admetus accepts the 'stranger' much as a husband would have taken his new wife at an Athenian wedding.

As well as contemporizing ritual activities, prop and costume elements indicate the status and age of the characters: staffs for old men such as the chorus of *Heracles*, and for blind prophets such as Teiresias in *Antigone*; swords for Aegisthus' guards in *Agamemnon*; special robes to indicate service to a god for Cassandra in *Agamemnon*, the Pythia in *Eumenides*, and the priestess Theonoe in *Helen*; wands wound with cotton to identify supplicants in the various suppliant plays; and so on. Costumes could take on a realistic flavour, as in some of Euripides' plays, parodied mercilessly by Aristophanes in his comedies. The shipwrecked Menelaus arrives in tatters in *Helen*, and his change of costume near the end of the play signals a return to his old warrior self. In *Electra* the embittered protagonist bemoans her rags, and makes much of the water-jug she hauls back from the spring.

However, she rejects her husband's help in carrying the water, and she refuses the chorus's offer of festive clothing, oppressed as much by her wilful self-martyrdom as she is by her poverty.

For all his notoriety, Euripides was not the first to employ costumes and props to suggest suffering and deprivation. Aeschylus builds the climax of *Persians* around the return of the defeated Xerxes, who arrives in rags. The Greek word for his apparel, *stolos*, Aeschylus also uses for Persia's naval fleet destroyed at the battle of Salamis. Arrayed in tattered garments and bearing an empty quiver, the young king symbolically wears the defeat of his empire. Sophocles, too, uses distressed costumes to suggest the abject suffering of his hero, from the suppurating wound and wild appearance of the title figure in *Philoctetes* to the robe-poisoned Heracles in *Women of Trachis*, borne on a litter and crying out in anguish.

More common than the representation of physical agony in tragedy is the appearance of corpses or the remains of the dead, often requiring a corps of mute actors to bear them on- and off-stage. A formal procession escorts the body of Alcestis out for burial, and a similar cortège brings the corpse of Neoptolemus into the theatre in *Andromache*. The bodies of the recovered seven against Thebes are paraded in the orchestra in *Suppliant Women*, and (after their off-stage cremation) the secondary chorus of their orphaned sons return bearing the urns with their ashes. In *Antigone* burial provides the catalyst for the tragic action: Antigone chooses to bury Polyneices in spite of Creon's decree outlawing such rites. Although Antigone dies for her deed, it is Creon who must bury the corpses of his loved ones at the end of the play. He returns carrying the body of his son, Haimon, only to learn of his wife's suicide. Revealed on the *ekkyklêma* draped over the household altar, she provides a chilling image of the death of Creon's home. These and other spectacles of the dead recall the importance of death ritual for the Greeks (discussed above), where the family prepared the corpse and performed the funeral rites.

Corpses, costumes, and props often come together at significant dramatic moments. Sophocles has the tortured heroine in his *Electra* hear the (false) news of her brother's death, and she mourns over his ashes in what she thinks is his funeral urn. Miraculously, the empty container leads Electra to the living Orestes, who reverses the trick at the end of the play. He uses the purported corpse of Orestes to lure Aegisthus on-stage, only to reveal the body of his mother Clytemnestra, whom he has murdered. In Euripides' *Trojan Women*, the Greeks hurl Astyanax, the young son of Hector and Andromache, from the (off-stage) walls of Troy. His broken body is carried onstage, cradled in the great shield of his father, a chilling symbol of the death of the city's hopes, and the cruelty of its conquerors.

Perhaps the most daring conjunction of costumes, corpse, and dramatic action occurs in Euripides' *Bacchae*. In the famous 'drag scene', Dionysus dresses Pentheus in women's clothing so that he can spy on the Bacchic mysteries. We laugh at his cross-dressing ('Is my head cover sitting right?'

'How is the line of my dress?' *Ba.* 930–31, 935–36), but the fact that he has fallen under the god's spell gives the laughter a vicious twist. The woman's garment that Pentheus wears reaches down to his feet, not normal for Athenian dress but standard for burial raiment. Dionysus readies Pentheus not only for the Mysteries, but also for his funeral.[29] At the end of the play, Cadmus returns with the dismembered bits of Pentheus' body torn apart by the Theban women, an appropriate image for the fragmentation that Dionysian union can unleash.

In some tragedies, stage props provide the locus for choice, symbolizing the dilemma facing the tragic hero. In Sophocles' *Ajax*, the sword that Ajax received as a gift from Hector comes to represent his outmoded heroism, and it serves as the means of his suicide. In *Philoctetes*, Helenus' prophesies that the hero's bow must be brought to Troy if the Greeks are to take the city. For the marooned Philoctetes, the weapon is his sole means of survival; for Odysseus, it guarantees the victory that he must obtain at all costs; for Neoptolemus, the bow represents the ethical dilemma he faces, which he resolves by returning the weapon to the wretched hero who entrusted it to him. In the final scene of Euripides' *Heracles*, the protagonist also confronts his bow – the attribute of his heroic labours, but also the instrument of his family's murder. By taking up the weapon, Heracles metaphorically shoulders his tragic past and acknowledges a hostile future, transformed into a new kind of hero when he leaves for Athens.

Less violent props include the letter that Phaedra leaves after her suicide in *Hippolytus*, although its false accusations lead Theseus to curse his son. The letter in *Iphigenia among the Taurians* works in a restorative fashion – when the heroine reads it aloud, its contents spark the recognition of her and her brother Orestes. In *Ion* the tokens that Creusa exposed with her baby operate similarly, establishing Ion's true identity. Last-minute recognition via tokens from the past recurs in other plays of Euripides, and it proved the mainstay of recognition scenes in the New Comedy of Menander, which became the most popular theatrical genre in the latter part of the fourth century.[30]

Starting and stopping the play: prologue, *deus ex machina*, and the gods' view

Like most plays, Greek tragedies come 'out of nowhere' and adopt some form of closure at the end. In various ways, the opening section maps out the dramatic terrain, provides the horizon line against which we are to see the key events, and clarifies the theatrical impulse that generates the subsequent action. Similarly, the manner in which a tragedy ends can confirm or frustrate our sense of resolution, turning us back to the issues of the play in a thoughtful, chastened, or deeply puzzled way.

Aeschylus' *Persians*, our earliest surviving tragedy, opens with the entrance of the chorus, appropriate for a play concerned with a people rather than an individual protagonist. The gathering of elders at the home front represents the counterpart to the expedition in Greece that they evoke in their song. At the close, their *kommos* with Xerxes marks a fitting ending, for the mournful procession out of the theatre reverses their hopeful arrival at the start of the play. Usually, however, Greek tragedy begins not with the chorus but with a dramatic character delivering a prologue before the chorus arrive. Sometimes the speaker is the protagonist (Eteocles in *Seven Against Thebes*, Deianeira in *Women of Trachis*, Helen in *Helen*); sometimes a less important character (Aethra in *Suppliant Women*, the ghost of Polydorus in *Hecuba*); and sometimes a character we never see or hear from again (the Watchman in *Agamemnon*, the god Hermes in *Ion*).

Often another character joins the opening speaker, giving a stronger impetus to the action, as audience-directed monologue shifts to actor-to-actor dialogue. In Euripides' *Medea*, for example, the Nurse welcomes the audience into the play, evoking the legendary journey of Jason and the Argonauts, only to displace the heroic world with one of domestic and marital turmoil. The arrival of the Tutor with Medea's and Jason's children confirms the gap between the epic past and the apparently mundane present. The scene between the Nurse and Tutor is unique in tragedy, consisting of two household servants, a scenario more at home in Greek comedy. Their dialogue establishes a familiar and contemporary tone, important in a play that exposes the destructive nature of the heroic code that leads Medea to slaughter her children.

The most dramatically charged prologues begin immediately with dialogue, such as the scene between Antigone and Ismene in Sophocles' *Antigone*. This opening conflict prefigures the greater oppositions that emerge over the course of the play. Sophocles goes further with his prologue in *Ajax*, exploiting *three* different perspectives.[31] Speaking from the *theologeion* (the roof of the skene-building), Athena urges Odysseus to enjoy the plight of his rival Ajax, whom the goddess has driven mad. From his position below, Odysseus refuses to mock a fellow-mortal, fearful that he could end in the same situation. The goddess summons Ajax from his tent, and he enters with the scourge he has used against the sheep's carcasses, thinking he has been torturing Odysseus. Caught between the beasts and the goddess, Ajax embodies his tragic condition, to which Odysseus finds himself drawn in pity, foreshadowing his role as champion of Ajax's burial at the end of the play.

Some opening scenes, such as that of Euripides' *Alcestis*, involve two gods. While Apollo delivers his monologue, Thanatos ('Death'), a kind of folkloric bogeyman, arrives to claim Alcestis. His onstage appearance establishes death (at least in this play) as a physical character, from whose clutches Heracles can wrestle away Alcestis later. A debate ensues between Apollo and Thanatos, arguing their respective plutocratic and egalitarian principles, a humorous note that resurfaces several times in the play. Performed as the fourth offering in Euripides' tetralogy of 438, *Alcestis* took the place of a satyr-play, even though it lacks a satyr chorus, as we will discuss in the next section.

Euripides returns to the two-god prologue in *Trojan Women*. Poseidon describes the disaster at Troy following the Greek conquest, pointing out to the audience the prostrate Hecuba, who took her position in the orchestra in a cancelled entry. The arrival of Athena transforms the opening from a monologue about the past to a dialogue about the future. Angry at the Greeks' desecration of her temple and rape of Cassandra, Athena persuades Poseidon to destroy their ships on the return home. Although the gods never reappear after the prologue, the opening exchange colours the audience's response to the escalation of Greek brutality during the play, for we know they will suffer in turn.

Euripides produced many variations on conventional openings, until his prologues developed into a kind of sub-genre like his messenger speeches, with repeated elements and modifications recurring in play after play. In his innovative version of the story of *Electra*, for example, Euripides gives us *two* prologues.[32] A down-to-earth Farmer emerges from his rustic cottage to deliver the opening monologue, explaining that he was given Electra in marriage, but he has respected her desires and not slept with her. His speech deftly establishes the innate difference between his honest and direct nature and the self-martyring tendencies of his wife, who joins him briefly on her way to fetch water. After the Farmer leaves for the fields and the stage empties, we expect the chorus to enter in the *parodos*. Instead Euripides gives us a second prologue. Orestes returns incognito from exile, staying far from the palace for fear of being recognized. In this double prologue, Euripides introduces radical variants in the received myth, matched (as we shall see) by the manner in which he brings the play to a close.

Turning to the end of tragedies, the most difficult convention to understand is also the most familiar, the so-called *deus ex machina*, Latin for 'god from the machine'. Tragedians used the machine (*mêchanê*), a kind of crane, to suggest the arrival of a god from afar. At other times gods and goddesses appeared on the roof of the skene-building, which came to be called the *theologeion* ('place where a god speaks'). Taking their cue from Aristotle's dissatisfaction with the *deus ex machina* ending of *Medea*, Renaissance critics viewed the appearance of a god as the mark of an inept plot requiring a last-minute resolution.[33] This description fits few, if any, Greek tragedies. When it does seem to apply, a closer look reveals a lively dramatic tension at work between the body of the play and its dénouement.

The appearance of a divinity near the end of a tragedy interrupts the action, surprising the dramatic characters and audience alike. Although the device became increasingly popular later in the fifth century, not every tragedy employs it, and one cannot predict on the basis of earlier action whether a god will appear at the end. The *deus*-figure usually provides an explanation for what has transpired, outlines what lies ahead, and offers the aetiology for a cult connected with the tragic events. The combination of summary and prophecy carries the material of the play into the fifth century, in that audiences usually had some knowledge of the cult described by the god. Even with this link to the 'present', the sense of closure provided by a *deus ex machina* varies enormously from play to play. Irony, iconoclasm, and subterfuge can operate no less than the sense of fulfilled expectations and ritual closure.

One mustn't confuse the utterances of a highly theatrical divinity with divinely sanctioned truths from Olympus, or conclude that the god provides the key to the play's meaning. Take, for example, the *ex machina* appearance of the Dioskouroi, Castor and Pollux, at the end of Euripides' *Electra*. The entrance of the twin gods (the brothers of Clytemnestra and Helen) is neither required by the plot nor expected by those onstage. Pollux remains silent, following the convention of a dramatic mute like Pylades earlier in the play. However, his brother – played by the same actor who performed the Farmer, the Old Tutor, and Clytemnestra earlier – has much to say. Castor insists that Apollo bears the responsibility for the murder of Clytemnestra, a proposition that receives little support from Electra and Orestes, who committed the matricide. Castor then reveals that the Trojan War was fought over a phantom, and not the real Helen, part of Zeus' plan to unleash strife among mortals. Turning to the future, the god arranges for Electra to marry Pylades, who will set up her former husband (the Farmer) in a profitable business. Orestes will be absolved of his crime by a trial in Athens, which will establish a cult of the Furies, and then Orestes will leave to found an eponymous city in Arcadia.

The *deus* speech in *Electra* gains little purchase on the play as experienced by the characters or the audience. Euripides has revealed the all-too-human motivations for murder, and the claim that it was Apollo's fault convinces only the gullible. The god's assurance that happiness awaits brother and sister has little effect on Orestes and Electra, who stand drenched in their mother's blood. After an initial question, they barely acknowledge the voice from on high. For all the excuses, revelations, and promises uttered *ex machina*, Castor cannot break through to the mortal sphere, where guilt and regret, finally acknowledged, are not easily dismissed. It is as if Castor were trying to rewrite the ending at the last minute, like a media spin-doctor, convincing the audience that something contrary to their experience has, in fact, taken place.

As we see in *Electra*, the *deus* convention allows the playwright to delve into the relationship between human characters and their gods. At the end of *Hippolytus*, Artemis abandons her dying disciple and leaves the *theologeion* – as an immortal, she wants nothing to do with death. Forsaken by the goddess he has served so loyally, Hippolytus forgives his father for his fatal curse and affirms the value of human, mortal connection.[34] At the opposite end of the spectrum, Euripides' *Bacchae* reveals a god that is too much *like* a human. Having struck Agave mad and caused her to kill her own son, Dionyus manifests himself in triumph on high. Confronted with the horror of Pentheus' death and dismemberment, Agave's father Cadmus cries up at the deity: 'Gods should not be like men in their anger' (1348).

On other occasions, the *deus* resolution seems so improbable that it forces the audience to focus on the situation that *almost* transpired, in the manner of Gay's *Beggar's Opera* and Brecht's *Threepenny Opera*. Euripides offers the clearest example in *Orestes*, where a triple-levelled dénouement accentuates the horror of the play even as it ostensibly vanishes. After killing Helen and setting fire to Menelaus' palace, Orestes stands on the *theologeion* representing what's left of the palace roof, holding a sword at the throat of Menelaus' daughter, Hermione. Menelaus himself looks on helplessly at the orchestra level, locked out of his burning home. Suddenly Apollo appears from the machine and halts the proceedings, announcing that Helen was spirited away before her death and now dwells as an immortal among the stars. Apollo then directs Orestes to put down the sword and take Hermione as his wife, a union that Menelaus accepts without protest. Not leaving anyone out, the god arranges for Electra to marry Pylades, and a tragedy of blood-crazed madness arrives at its 'happy ending'.

Over half of Euripides' extant tragedies conclude with a god or goddess appearing on high. But Sophocles, too, utilized this theatrical device, and we know that in his lost *Niobe* Apollo and Artemis appear on the roof in the middle of the play. While her immortal brother speaks, Artemis uses her bow to shoot down the daughters of Niobe, who stand in the palace courtyard behind the façade.[35] Sophocles ends *Philoctetes* with a *deus* figure, Heracles, who appears unexpectedly on the *theologeion*. Loathe to credit Sophocles with the theatrical daring of Euripides, some scholars argue that Heracles' command that Philoctetes go to Troy makes for a perfectly natural, rather than a deeply problematic, ending to the drama. Similar issues posed by the *deus ex machina* arise at the close of Euripides' *Suppliant Women* and *Ion*, discussed in Chapters 8 and 9.

In a variation on the *deus ex machina* convention, a mortal character can arrive in godlike fashion and effect a sudden change. As discussed above, the goddesses Lyssa and Iris appear out of the blue in Euripides' *Heracles* and strike the hero mad. The end of the play features the no less unexpected arrival of the Athenian hero Theseus, who redeems on a human level what the gods have destroyed from above. His efforts to convince Heracles to persevere and make his life in Athens raise questions about what constitutes real heroism, and what kind of gods are worth worshipping.

If the *deus*-like Theseus brings comfort and encouragement, the appearance from the machine of the protagonist in Euripides' *Medea* does the opposite. Jason rushes on-stage ready to break down the palace door and save his sons, and we expect the *ekkyklêma* to roll out revealing their dead bodies. Nothing prepares us for Medea's appearance on high in a chariot of the sun, her children's corpses draped over the railings. Invested with all the properties and functions of a stage divinity, Medea taunts her estranged husband, predicts his unheroic death, and proclaims the founding of a festival and holy rites in Corinth that will expiate guilt for the children's murders. In this *coup de théâtre*, Medea triumphs absolutely, and yet she no longer resembles the woman with whom we sympathized before. Euripides places her in the position of a stage goddess to emphasize the dehumanizing effect of what she has done, and what has been done to her. The fact that Medea will make her way to Athens, the city of the original performance, locates the challenges of the play very much in the world of the audience.

The satyr play

It may seem odd to call the fourth play of each tetralogy a 'convention', but the inclusion of a satyr play as part of the City Dionysia seems sufficiently strange to justify approaching it as the conventional way Athenians brought their tragic competitions to a close.[36] Although they feature a chorus of satyrs (male demigods with small erect penises, hairy legs and buttocks, and goat-like hoofs), these plays do not resemble the comedies that also were performed at the festival.[37] Aristophanic comedy features contemporary scenarios (invented plots rather than dramatized myths), freewheeling protagonists (with no heroic pedigrees), mounds of bodily-driven humour and innuendo (scatological and otherwise), and more sexual jokes and puns than Shakespeare. Satyr plays, on the other hand, are fully dependent on the world of tragedy, and the chorus find themselves incongruously caught in mythic or heroic situations, sometimes linked to one of the tragedies that came before, as we shall see in the next chapter. Given the satyrs' intimate association with Dionysus in myth and in numerous depictions on Attic vases, their appearance onstage inevitably brought the Athenian audience back to the god of wine and the theatre.

Given the scarcity of material, one can only speculate how these plays worked, and what fifth-century audiences took from them. Only a single satyr play survives intact, Euripides' *Cyclops*, but we have roughly half of Sophocles' *Ichneutae* (*Trackers*), the titles of some forty-two others by several playwrights (of which we have roughly 350 lines in total), and *Alcestis*, which took the place of the satyr play in Euripides' tetralogy of 438 (noted above). The preferred settings seem to be some wild place (the Cyclops' cave in Mt Aetna in Euripides' play, Mt Cyrene in Arcadia in Sophocles' *Trackers*, the island of Seriphos in Aeschylus' *Net-Haulers*). Trapped in these locations, the satyrs form a homosocial band freed from the constraints of political and family life, often under the 'leadership' of an older satyr, Papposilenus. Longing for escape, they indulge in libidinal fantasies of wine and women. The first they attain, the second they only dream about, and their childlike waywardness lend these cowardly semi-divine man–beasts a quality more endearing than threatening.

Reconstruction of the fragments suggests that romance does play a part, but only for the main characters – roughly half of the satyr plays of Aeschylus and Sophocles whose plots can be reconstructed involve a hero, human or divine, marrying a new bride, sometimes one rescued from the lascivious chorus.[38] The chorus's dedicated hedonism and juvenile fantasies, the non-public and non-domestic settings, and the apparently happy endings, suggest that satyr plays offered psychic release from the high stakes of tragedy. As discussed above, most extant tragedies have female choruses, and many have female protagonists. Their harsh predicament asks the audience (primarily male Athenian citizens) to step outside their own experience and circumstance. Satyr plays do just the opposite, offering a fantasy escape from the difficult ethical choices and wrenching emotional journey of the tragedies that went before.[39]

The *agôn* in the audience

Many tragic conventions appear self-evident, and we might expect something similar in any attempt to represent intelligible characters in a dramatic context. But even in such standard conventions as costume, speech, and gesture, Greek tragedy built a more immediate relationship with its audience than we often are led to believe. The costumes were contemporary, the specialized gestures reflected the world of familiar ritual activity, and the dialogue, although poetic, adopted a rhythmical form closer to everyday speech than its epic predecessor. Even the complex lyrics of the chorus contain elements from other genres well known in the fifth century, including cult hymns, epinician odes, wedding songs, funeral laments, and so on.

More elaborate conventions involving rhetoric and formal debate point to the world of the Athenian Assembly, the law courts, the agora, the day-to-day arguments and decision-making that played a key role in democratic life. Even the appearance of stage divinities reveals a tendency towards incorporating the local and familiar. Zeus, the father and *primus inter pares* of the Olympian gods, seems never to have appeared on the Attic stage, although characters often invoke and pray to him. On the other hand, Athena, the patron goddess of Athens – whose image adorned public buildings, freestanding sculpture, and the coins of the city – appears several times. In the initial setting or in the destination of the protagonist at the end, many tragedies forge an especially strong link with the city of Athens. The playwrights do not imply that their city offers a refuge from tragic conflict; on the contrary, the city where the audience have gathered represents the place where tragedy must be confronted.

The conventions of Greek tragic theatre return us to our starting point, the performance culture of Athens, where a participatory democracy played out its political and ethical concerns in an aggressively public fashion. The conventions of theatrical representation allowed for a variety of contemporary elements to enter, and indeed to inform, the dramatizations of ancient myth and legend. Empowered by such conventions, and the willingness to experiment with them, the tragic playwrights brought their stories home to the audience with such urgency and power that, paradoxically, they transcend their local origins and speak across the centuries.

Notes

1 To use a familiar example, Bertolt Brecht fostered his 'estrangement- (or alien-ation-) effect' to confront the audience with contradictions in the social and economic system that appeared on the bourgeois commercial stage as either natural or inevitable.

2 Aristotle *Poetics*, 1461b.26–1462a. 4. E. Csapo, 'Euripides on the floor-sweepings: the limits of realism in classical acting and performance styles', in Easterling and Hall, op. cit. (Chapter 3, n. 14), pp. 127–47, notes that the old actor faults Kallipides for inappropriately detailed character imitation, not for 'over-acting'.

3 Cicero, *De Oratore* 2.46.193. As Socrates says in Plato's *Republic* (10605c10–d5), 'When the best of us hear Homer or some other tragic poet imitating a hero in mourning … you know how we feel pleasure and give ourselves up to it, how we follow in sympathy …' See P. Walcot, op. cit. (Chapter 4, n. 20), pp. 51–53; O. Taplin, *Greek Tragedy in Action*, Berkeley, University of California Press, 1978, pp. 159–71; and, generally, W.B. Stanford, *Greek Tragedy and the Emotions*, London, Routledge & Kegan Paul, 1983.

4 Aristotle, *Poetics* 1449b25 on *praxis*; see 1453b12 on the pleasure appropriate to tragedy. The nature of this 'tragic pleasure' has been much debated – does it imply some intrinsic delight in watching those worse off than ourselves? Does it arise from the purging or cleansing of our emotions, principally pity and fear? Or does it align these emotions with intellectual perceptions about events that may seem unlikely, but in dramatic presentation achieve a probable shape and structure? Or does tragic pleasure come from an 'insight experience' that results from the clarification of highly charged dramatic events? See, for example, S. Halliwell, 'Aristotle's Poetics', in *Cambridge History of Literary Criticism*, vol. 1, *Classical Criticism*, ed. G.A. Kennedy, Cambridge, Cambridge University Press, 1989, pp. 158–75.

5 On the primacy of narrative in Greek tragedy, see P.E. Easterling, 'Narrative on the Greek Tragic Stage', in *Defining Greek Narrative*, eds. D. Cairns and R. Scodel, Edinburgh, Edinburgh University Press, 2014, pp. 226–40, and N.J. Lowe, *The Classical Plot and the Invention of Western Narrative*, Cambridge, Cambridge University Press, 2000, esp. pp. 157–87. Relevant essays in *Narrators, Narratees, and Narratives in Ancient Greek Literature*, eds. I.J.F. de Jong, R. Nünlist, and A. Bowie, Brill, Boston, MA, 2004, offer a helpful narratological account. One conclusion: story-driven tragedy does not fit well with the pastiche of the post-modern.

6 Although ancient Greek was accented by pitch and not stress, we get a rough sense of the way common speech fits into metrical forms with a colloquial American expression, 'I'd like a coke, a burger, and a shake.' The sentence scans as iambic pentametre, the standard blank-verse line in Shakespeare. Greek tragic characters occasionally speak in trochaic tetrametre catalectic, consisting of a line scanned ‾ ˘ ‾ ˘ / ‾ ˘ ‾ ˘ / ‾ ˘ ‾ ˘ / ‾ ˘ ‾ / (‾ is long, ˘ is short), where two short syllables can be substituted for any long syllable. For example, during the argument between Iris and Lyssa in Euripides' *Heracles*, Iris suddenly shifts from normal dialogue trimetre to the tetrametre line, the change indicating an imminent crisis, when talk gives way to action. See also Chapters 6 and 9.

7 Cf. P. Wilson's claim: 'Ancient Greek theatre was a fundamentally musical experience … Tragedy was much closer to what we might term "choral opera" than "theatre."' In Easterling and Hall, op. cit. (Chapter 3, n. 14) p. 39. However, roughly 70 per cent of the lines in extant tragedy are in dialogue metre, spoken without instrumental accompaniment. A more theatrically valid approach emphasizes the *interplay between two distinct modes*, rhetoric and lyric, that the

tragedians could transform by having an actor join choral lyric, or sing a solo monody, or (far less often) having a chorus member make a speech.

8 See F. Jouan, 'Réflexions sur le rôle du protagoniste tragique', in *Théâtres et spectacles dans l'antiquité: Actes du Colloque de Strasbourg*, Leiden, Brill, 1983, pp. 63–80, and Rehm, op. cit 2002 (Chapter 4, n. 5), pp. 133–35, 150–52, 174–75.

9 The phrase is from J. Jones, *On Aristotle and Greek Tragedy*, London, Chatto & Windus, 1962, p. 278. He reminds us that 'the meaning of the ancient drama for ourselves is best fostered by our mustering what awareness we can of its near-inaccessibility'.

10 See B. Vickers, *Towards Greek Tragedy*, London, Longman, 1973, pp. 438–94.

11 See P.E. Easterling, 'Anachronism in Greek Tragedy', *Journal of Hellenic Studies* 105, 1985, pp. 1–10.

12 M. McLuhan, *Understanding Media*, 2nd edn, New York, McGraw-Hill, 1964, pp. 36–45, 259–68, explains his somewhat contradictory model of a hot medium (radio) vs. a cool medium (television). For problems with McLuhan, see K. Burke, *Language as Symbolic Action*, Berkeley, University of California Press, 1966, pp. 410–18.

13 The idea of 'acts' in Greek tragedy has no ancient support; emptying the stage of actors as a structuring principle derives from Shakespearean criticism; see Taplin, op. cit. (Chapter 3, n. 10), pp. 49–60.

14 See D.S. Raven, *Greek Metre*, 2nd edn, London, Faber & Faber, 1968; also articles on tragic metre, chorus, and dance in Dale, op. cit. (Chapter 4, n. 9).

15 See J. Gould, 'Tragedy and Collective Experience', in *Tragedy and the Tragic: Greek Theatre and Beyond*, ed. M. Silk, Oxford, Clarendon Press, 1996, pp. 217–43; also H. Foley, 'Choral Identity in Greek Tragedy', *Classical Philology* 98, 2003, pp. 1–30.

16 The appearance of a secondary or 'shadow' chorus is the exception. Here, the playwright introduces a clearly defined subsidiary group, such as the secondary chorus that escorts the Eumenides at the close of Aeschylus' *Oresteia*, or the sons of the fallen Argive heroes who mourn with the female chorus (the heroes' mothers) in Euripides' *Suppliant Women*.

17 A. Henrichs, '"Why Should I Dance?" Choral Self-Referentiality in Greek Tragedy', *Arion* 3.1, 1995, pp. 56–111; B. Kowalzig, '"And Now All the World Shall Dance!" (Eur. *Bacch*. 114): Dionysus' Choroi Between Drama and Ritual', in *The Origins of Theater in Ancient Greece and Beyond: From Ritual to Drama*, eds E. Csapo and M.C. Miller, Cambridge, Cambridge University Press, 2008, pp. 221–54, quotation p. 236.

18 Herington, op. cit. (Chapter 1, n. 10), p. 75, who notes that such mixing of genres would have sounded to the archaic ear 'as disconcerting as ... the intervention of a trombone in a string quartet' (p. 74). See also W. Allan, ed. and comm., *Euripides, 'Helen'*, Cambridge, Cambridge University Press, 2008, pp. 38–45.

19 Kowalzig, op. cit (above n. 17), p. 226. See also Csapo and Miller, op cit. (above n. 17), pp. 4–7, 31–2; and A. Bierl in, *Choral Mediations in Greek Tragedy*, eds R. Gagne and M.G. Hopman, Cambridge, Cambridge University Press, 2013, pp. 211–26.

20 Seaford, op. cit. 1994 (Chapter 2, n. 1), pp. 240–3; generally, *Dithyramb in Context*, eds. B. Kowalzig and P. Wilson, Oxford, Oxford University Press, 2013. On theatrical references in *Bacchae*, see Segal, op. cit. 1997 (Chapter 2, n. 2), and H. Foley, 'The Masque of Dionysus', *Transactions of the American Philological Association* 110, 1980, pp. 107–37.

21 Kowalzig, op. cit. (above n. 17), p. 245.

22 For tragic singing, see E. Hall, 'Singing Roles in Tragedy' in op. cit. 2006 (Chapter 1, n. 6), pp. 288–320. Particularly fond of monodies, Euripides has *two* characters (played by different actors) sing significant lyric passages in *Alcestis* (Alcestis and her son Eumelos), *Andromache* (Andromache and Peleus), *Ion* (Ion and Creusa), and *Trojan Women* (Cassandra and Hecuba).

23 The unrecognized Old Tutor in Sophocles' *Electra* presents himself as a messenger from Delphi, and he delivers a false report of Orestes' death (*El.* 660–803); however, the audience is aware of his deception. The same applies in *Philoctetes* (*Ph.* 123–32, 542–627), when Odysseus tells Neoptolemus that he will send a scout disguised as a merchant captain with a false message to put Philoctetes under Neoptolemus' power, and this transpires. On messenger speeches generally, see I.J.F. de Jong, *Narrative in Drama: The Art of the Euripidean Messenger-Speech*, Leiden, Brill, 1991, and J. Barrett, *Staged Narrative: Poetics and the Messenger in Greek Tragedy*, Berkeley, University of California Press, 2002.

24 See, for example, M. Esslin, 'Beckett and the Art of Broadcasting', in his *Mediations*, Baton Rouge, Louisiana State University Press, 1980, pp. 131–32.

25 'The tragic question', in the view of J.-P. Vernant, 'Greek Tragedy: Problems of Interpretation', in *The Structuralist Controversy*, eds R. Macksey and E. Donato, Baltimore, MD, Johns Hopkins University Press, 1972, pp. 285–87. See also R. Lattimore, *Story Patterns in Greek Tragedy*, Ann Arbor, University of Michigan, 1969, pp. 28–35, and R. Rehm, *Radical Theatre: Greek Tragedy and the Modern World*, London, Duckworth 2003, pp. 65–86.

26 See M. Lloyd, *The* Agon *in Euripides*, Oxford, Clarendon Press, 1992; J. Duchemin, *L'Agon dans la tragédie grecque*, 2nd edn, Paris, Les Belles Lettres, 1968; and H. Strohm, *Euripides*, Zetemata 15, Munich, C.H. Beck, 1957, pp. 1–49.

27 Many people today experience similar frustration at what passes for political 'debate' on national security, climate change, economic inequality, nuclear disarmament, and human rights. As in tragedy, the rhetoric often begins by purposefully missing the point.

28 See, generally, J. Fletcher, *Performing Oaths in Classical Greek Drama*, Cambridge, Cambridge University Press, 2012.

29 Seaford, tr. and comm., *Euripides, Bacchae*, Warminster, Aris & Phillips, 1996, line 833. For theatrical costuming generally (including design, construction, and materials), see R. Wyles, *Costume in Greek Tragedy*, London, Bristol Classical Press, 2011.

30 See B.M.W. Knox, 'Euripidean Comedy' (org. 1970), in his *Word and Action*, Baltimore, MD, Johns Hopkins University Press, 1979, pp. 250–74.

31 D. Seale, *Vision and Stagecraft in Sophocles*, London, Croom Helm, 1982, pp. 144–50, presents a valuable account of this scene, and many others in Sophocles.

32 Other double prologues (two separate scenes, marked with characters entering and exiting, before the arrival of the chorus) occur in Euripides' *Hippolytus, Iphigenia among the Taurians, Phoenician Women*, and *Iphigenia in Aulis*. In *Eumenides*, Aeschylus presents *three* such scenes before the chorus of Furies sing.

33 Aristotle (*Poetics* 1454a.37–1454b.2) faults the end of *Medea* for depending on the machine and not the plot. Mastronarde op. cit. (Chapter 4, n. 12) offers in-depth treatment of the convention. On closure generally, see F.M. Dunn, *Tragedy's End: Closure and Innovation in Euripidean Drama*, Oxford, Oxford University Press, 1996.

34 See B.M.W. Knox, 'The *Hippolytus* of Euripides' (org. 1952), in op. cit. (above n. 30), pp. 205–30.

35 See the fragments of *Niobe* in *Sophocles* III, pp. 227–35.

36 As far as we know, satyr plays did not follow *all* tragic performances, only those at the City Dionysia, The Lenaia (which featured three to five comedies and two pairs of tragedies, each pair by a different tragedian) did not include satyr plays. Deme festivals may have done so, but the evidence is uncertain.

37 See generally M. Griffith, *Greek Satyr Play, Five Studies*, Berkeley, California Classical Studies, 2015. I. C. Storey, 'But Comedy Has Satyrs Too,' in *Satyr Drama Tragedy at Play*, ed. G.W.M. Harrison, Swansea, The Classical Press of Wales, 2005, pp. 201–18, points out that satyrs appear in at least eight (lost) Greek comedies. See also P. O'Sullivan and C. Collard, ed, *Cyclops and Major Fragments of Greek Satyric Drama*, Oxford, Oxbow Books, 2013.

38 Griffith, op. cit., p. 125.

39 Hall, op. cit. 2006 (Chapter 1, n. 6), p. 10, summarizes: 'At a deep psychosocial level, the satyr play functioned to affirm a group identity founded in homo-social laughter and the libidinal awareness of its male, citizen audience.' See also Griffith, op. cit. pp. 46–57.

Part II
Exemplary plays

6   Aeschylus' *Oresteia* trilogy

At the City Dionysia of 458 BC, two years before his death, Aeschylus presented his dramatization of the myth of the house of Atreus. Later known as the *Oresteia* ('the story of Orestes'), Aeschylus' version takes the form of a connected trilogy that unfolds in chronological sequence, with continuity of subject-matter, imagery, characters, and story-line. *Agamemnon* tells of the title figure's return after conquering Troy, and his murder (along with his Trojan concubine Cassandra) at the hands of his wife Clytemnestra, who seizes power with her lover Aegisthus. Her exiled son Orestes returns to avenge his father's death, murdering Clytemnestra and Aegisthus with the help of Electra and the slave-women of the house, who give the second play its name, *Choephori* (*Libation Bearers*). After the matricide, Orestes is pursued by the Furies, spirits who take vengeance on those who shed kindred blood, tracking him first to Delphi and then to Athens. There Athena establishes a court to try cases of homicide, and the goddess breaks the jury's deadlock by voting to free Orestes. She calms the Furies' anger, persuading them to reside in Athens as spirits of marriage and fertility, transformed into 'kindly ones' or *Eumenides*, the title of the third play. Following the trilogy, Aeschylus' satyr play *Proteus* (now lost) told the escapades of Menelaus, Agamemnon's brother and husband of Helen, shipwrecked in Egypt on his way home from Troy.

To understand how the trilogy works requires a double focus. We must remain alert to the overall unity of the piece and the various ways that Aeschylus achieves it, developing a rich poetic text without sacrificing dramatic momentum. But we also must attend to the differences that operate from play to play, for the triadic structure means that each tragedy establishes its own relationship to the audience. With this double focus we engage the moment-to-moment unfolding of events, even as we place them in the larger pattern of history and chronology that the trilogy encompasses.

In *Agamemnon* ambiguity and *double entendre*, dark prophecy and deceptive hopes create an atmosphere of troubled uncertainty. Events and emotions keep turning into their opposites – affirmation leads to denial, good news presages disaster, victory breeds defeat, beauty gives rise to destruction – and the triumphant return of the king proves but a prelude to his murder. In contrast to *Agamemnon*, the action of *Choephori* is tightly focused, unfolding with precision and clarity, almost claustrophobic in its effect. Aeschylus radically alters the dynamic between stage and auditorium by drawing the spectators into the murder plot as co-conspirators, committed to the plan and its success. The audience's response to the dramatic events shifts again in *Eumenides*, as the play leaves the mythical world of Orestes for the story of Athens and the foundation of her civic, ritual, and legal customs. Here the fifth-century audience approximated the jurors at Orestes' trial, arriving at a specific verdict and yet aware of the crucial role that the case plays in the virtual history of their legal system.

The trilogy works via a progressive movement towards the audience – from obscurity to clarity, from past to present, from monarchy to tyranny to democracy, from retributive to collective justice, from ancient Argos to near-contemporary Athens. We see the theatrical embodiment of this process in the transformation of verbal imagery into dramatic action, the realization of the world implicit in the word, as language literally 'takes the stage'. Pivotal images and figures of speech assume a visual and physical life, until the institutions of the city where the play was performed are created before the audience's eyes, and with their help.

Agamemnon

The *Oresteia* begins with one of the great opening monologues in the theatre. An unassuming Watchman lies on the roof of the house, waiting for the beacon fire that will bring news of Troy's fall (*Ag.* 1–39). With his first word 'Gods!', he begs the higher powers to release him from the pain of a year's watch. He speaks of the great cycle of stars, doubtful that in such a panoply a single torchlight could appear. Nonetheless, he obeys 'the command / of a woman who thinks like a man' (10–11). The sudden appearance of the beacon turns his fears for the house to joy, the fire-signal gleaming like the dawn of a new day. Before the Watchman leaves to wake Clytemnestra and 'start the dance' (31), he recovers some of his early guardedness, refusing to divulge what he knows, but calling on the house to tell its own story.

Like all well-written dramatic characters, the Watchman has something specific to do – stay awake, keep watch, spread the news if the beacon announces Agamemnon's return. His monologue has a natural ring to it, as if he were welcoming the audience into the play. But the prologue also presents a tightly wrapped bundle of proleptic themes and images that will be played out over the next four and a half hours in the theatre – the gods, sickness and pain, night and day, sleeping and wakefulness, women and men, good news and conquest, speech and silence.

The Watchman's desire to 'start the dance' sets the stage for the entrance of the chorus, old men of the city left behind when the army sailed for Troy. The *parodos* opens with an anapaestic prelude (40–82) that moves back ten years, when the brothers Agamemnon and Menelaus first 'brought suit against Priam' (41), a legal euphemism for the Trojan War. Priam's son Paris had abducted Helen, the wife of his Greek host Menelaus and sister of Agamemnon's wife Clytemnestra. In so doing, Paris violated the Greek code of hospitality, *xenia*, guaranteed by the god Zeus, who sends the two sons of Atreus and a thousand ships to win Helen back. The chorus call the war-dead 'a first offering' (literally, a 'preliminary sacrifice', 65), the word referring to the sacrifice before a wedding, presumably that of Paris and Helen. The perversion of a marriage ceremony is the first of many such maimed rituals in the trilogy, linking weddings with death.

The chorus emphasize their old age ('fallen leaves that crumble', 79–80) and powerlessness ('we wander, a dream through the daylight', 82), and yet find themselves animated by the sacrifices that burn through the city. Addressing their absent queen, they wonder whether the burnt offerings mean that good news has come from Troy. The very thought of Clytemnestra and the prospects of victory energize their reflections, serving as the catalyst for their shift from anapaests into full lyric.

Characteristic of the play, the same impulse that drives the action forward takes us back in time to the port at Aulis before the Greek army sailed for Troy. In the complex lyric that follows, a series of narrative vignettes – what we might call 'choral events' – stands out. The chorus recall the eagles that appeared as portents of military success, until 'swooping down / on a pregnant hare big with young, / they tore and feasted' (118–20). The chorus try to reverse the pattern of good omens turning bad by sounding a refrain they will repeat two more times in the course of the *parodos*: 'Sing sorrow, sorrow, but may good win out in the end' (121).

The chorus re-enact the prophet Calchas' interpretation of the oracle, perhaps with a single chorus member delivering Calchas' lines, a technique that could operate later in the ode when they recreate Agamemnon's sacrifice of his daughter. The prophet predicts triumph, but prays that no god 'darken the bit / you forge on Troy' (131–32), leading the chorus to repeat their refrain of sorrow that hopes for victory. The group then turn their thoughts to the ships held at Aulis by contrary winds, a delay that leads to a more ominous sacrifice than that of the pregnant hare, and to strife that (literally) 'lies in wait, terrible, ready to break out again, / keeping house with deceit, a child-avenging wrath that never forgets' (154–55). The piling-up of adjectives gives some sense of the complexity of Aeschylean lyric. The two lines evoke the sacrifice of Iphigenia at Aulis and of Agamemnon at Argos, and the feast of Thyestes in the previous generation, but the references are muted and jumbled, waiting for the play to elucidate them.

As if voicing the audience's desire for clarity, the chorus sing for the last time their refrain that sorrow might achieve some ultimate good. They then utter a desperate prayer to Zeus, the god 'who sets men on the path / to learn by suffering. / … / Against our will comes wisdom, / the grace of god by force' (176–82). The chorus consider the Greek army at Aulis an example of this cosmic lesson. Angry that the eagles' devour the pregnant hare, the goddess Artemis sends contrary winds to keep the ships from sailing. With the soldiers growing restless, their commander-in-chief Agamemnon must sacrifice his daughter to assuage the goddess or abandon the expedition. Presumably a single chorus member takes on the role of the tortured king, debating with himself (still in lyric) as he realizes there is no way without evil. The group then describes how Agamemnon 'put on the yoke of necessity' (218), a paradox that emphasizes both his individual choice and the way that fate necessitates it. We might say that Agamemnon freely chooses to do what he, in fact, has to do, a situation re-enacted later in the play when he walks on the red tapestries.

The climax to this extraordinary *parodos* is the re-creation of the sacrifice of Iphigenia (228–47), an innocent girl whose blood is shed so that more blood can flow. Through the vivid language and choral movement, we see her pray to her father for mercy while the soldiers shout for war. Bound and gagged, lifted like a goat over the altar, Iphigenia strikes each of her killers with her gaze, like a picture straining to speak. The images are striking, unforgettable – a twisted sacrifice, the perversion of paternal love in the face of the cry for war, the death of innocence, the waste of a young life. On the verge of the fatal blow, the chorus stop short and refuse to say what happened. Their unexpected reticence reminds us of the Watchman at the end of the prologue, who also refuses to divulge everything he knows.

Suddenly the chorus-leader shifts into iambic trimetres and greets Clytemnestra, who enters from the palace. Her first words cap the opening movement of the play: 'Good news! as the saying goes, / when dawn is born from her mother night. / Joy beyond your greatest hopes — / the Greeks have seized Troy' (264–67). The confirmation of triumph coincides with her appearance, and Clytemnestra will dominate the play both rhetorically and dramatically for most of the play.

In her famous Fire speech, Clytemnestra describes the beacon signals that announce Agamemnon's victory in a series of stunning similes – torches like a relay race, bonfires that rise up like the sun and then break through the clouds like a full moon, flames racing like ships across the water and dancing in the clear mirror of the sea. Even as the language dazzles, it draws the worlds of Argos and Troy together, bound by a chain of fire. The news that arrives at the house of Atreus is a blaze descended from the holocaust of Troy.

Clytemnestra further explores the relationship between the Greek victors and their Trojan victims in her next speech, imagining the chaos of a fallen city. Psychically attuned to the victims, she creates the pathetic scene of Trojans falling on the bodies of their dead, of women weeping for their husbands, of children clutching at the legs of the old men. The Greek conquerors, on the other hand, roam the city freely and sleep 'like happy men, / a night when no guard stands watch' (336–37). Implying their defences have fallen too quickly, Clytemnestra fears that the Greek army may be 'conquered by what they have won' (342). They still must return home, where 'the anger of the slaughtered may wake, / and evil break out again' (346–47). With these two extraordinary speeches, Clytemnestra forces us to see the fate of Troy and of Argos inextricably bound together. With her poetic and rhetorical power, she takes control of the play, and as she re-enters the palace we know she is the force to reckon with.

Alone in the orchestra, the chorus celebrate the victory in their first stasimon, returning to their view that Zeus guarantees the rights of hospitality (*xenia*), punishing mortals who 'trample untouchable things' (371). They move from the general idea of human excess to the specific example of Paris, who came as a guest to Menelaus' home and stole his wife. The chorus also consider Helen, who brought to Troy a 'dowry of death' (406), as well as her husband, abandoned back in Sparta. There, the household laments the royal bed and the fading print of Helen's body. Menelaus finds no respite in sleep, for the dreams of his lost wife slip through his arms (410–19).

As in the *parodos*, the chorus leap quite naturally across space and time, alternating between victory and loss, between human actions and their divine underpinnings. Changing focus again, they leave the royal palaces for the hearth of an average Greek home, where a lone woman confronts the deadly commerce of war:

> War is a moneychanger of bodies;
> his balance rests on the point of a spear.
> From the fires of Troy,
> he sends dust that weighs heavy.
> Packed in the hold
> urns swollen with powder
> take the place of a man.
>
> (*Ag.* 437–44)

The blow of Zeus, so clearly marked in the fate of Paris and the fall of Troy, also operates on the Greeks who conquered the city. Popular anger swells against Agamemnon and Menelaus, and the stasimon ends in a mood far different from the jubilation with which it began. A great victory has turned into a series of defeats, and collective joy at the sack of a city gives way to individual grief. The shift is so complete that the chorus begin to doubt the news of victory, wondering whether the beacon-story was simply Clytemnestra's dream, a woman-inspired rumour, swift to spread and swift to die (486–87).

A bedraggled figure enters the orchestra through one of the *eisodoi*, not the spectacular return of a triumphant Agamemnon but the homecoming of an ordinary soldier. The chorus leave the lyric mode to welcome him in regular iambic trimetres, a human who will confirm or deny the wordless message of the beacon.[1] Instead of news of victory, however, the Herald expresses his amazement that he has come back at all, 'with all my hopes shattered except one – / … that I might / die here, and be buried with my loved ones' (505–07). After enumerating the simple pleasures of survival – the earth, the sunlight, the sight of home, the presence of protecting divinities – the Herald finally celebrates victory:

> Digging up the soil of Troy,
> he [Agamemnon] worked it with the pick-axe of Zeus—
> altars smashed, temples rubble,
> the seed of the land destroyed.
>
> (525–28)

Agamemnon has 'yoked' Troy, paying Paris back for the rape of Helen that 'harvested' only death for his country (529–36). The reversals are complete – the natural world is uprooted and the places of the gods obliterated. Clytemnestra's warning that the Greeks let 'no passion make them / ravage what they should not' (341–42) has gone unheeded.

A strange stichomythic exchange follows, the first real dialogue in the play, and yet one that brings very little to light. The chorus-leader adumbrates that those at home also suffered during the army's absence, but he refuses to elaborate, preferring silence as his 'long-practised remedy from harm' (548). For the third time in the play, the dark side of the past is hinted at, only to be covered up by the refusal to say more. As the Herald tries to understand the veiled hints, he finds himself pulled back to the war – the blazing sun on the decks of the ships, the dank heat and sweat of their berths, the worm-eaten rations, the fear of camping near the walls of the enemy, the steady drizzle, the slow rot of their clothes, the teeming lice, the winter cold sweeping down from Mt Ida. After his graphic account of the realities of war, the Herald desperately tries to resurrect the joy of conquest:

> But why count the dead?
> Have we lived only to think of them?
> Must their wounds break out again?
> No! I say good-bye to disaster. /... /
> It is good to boast in the light of the sun,
> my words soaring over all land and sea,
> "Troy has fallen!..."
>
> (*Ag.* 570–77)

In spite of the Herald's triumphant tone, his language seems forced, as if the horrors at Troy have spoiled any simple sense of victory.

Suddenly Clytemnestra appears at the threshold, upstaging the Herald and the chorus. From her position controlling the entrance to the palace, she tells the Herald to return to her husband and urge him to hurry back 'like a lover to his city'. For a woman, 'no light shines brighter than her man / when she opens wide the gates and welcomes him home' (601–5). The language is daring, an erotic voice interrupting the war-talk of the Herald, and no less dangerous. Clytemnestra returns to the palace after once again reasserting her dominance.

With the queen's departure, the chorus turn their attention to Menelaus and learn that his ship was lost from sight. The Herald's secret is out: a storm at sea destroyed the fleet on its return.[2] In a *tour de force*, the Herald recreates the catastrophe. Fire and water (lightning and sea) joined forces against the Greek ships, like a crazed shepherd driving his flock to doom. After the storm, 'when the shining light of the sun rose up, / we saw the Aegean flower with corpses' (658–59). As elsewhere in the play, the sun – with its promise of renewal – rises on desolation. The oxymoron 'flower with corpses' has a similar effect, a symbol of beauty and growth that turns into its opposite. The poetic imagery reflects the structure of the scene, for the report of victory that the Herald has brought becomes, in the telling, news of disaster.

Having brought the war and its aftermath wrenchingly to life, the Herald departs, one of the great secondary roles in Greek tragedy. In a mood markedly different from that which started their previous stasimon, the chorus burst into lyric with an attack on Helen, the paragon of beauty who spread only ruin: 'Helen – / hell for ships, hell for men, hell / for cities' (688–90). Aeschylus puns on the word *hele*, a form of the verb 'to destroy', as if Helen's name encapsulates the fate of anyone drawn into her orbit. Developing the idea that she and Paris made a marriage to death, the chorus describe her as 'a spear-bride fought over by both sides', who abandoned the 'gentle veils' of Sparta, perhaps suggesting the bridal veil worn at a Greek wedding. The 'marriage hymn' that the Trojans sing when Helen arrives in their city turns into a funeral dirge, and the nuptial-bed becomes a 'bed of death' (705–14). These 'bitter rites of marriage' reveal her as 'the bridal-weeping Fury' (745–49), the noun 'Fury' ringing out as the final word of the strophe. The conflation of weddings and funerals brings home to the audience the depths of the violence unleashed at Troy, and also links Helen to her sister Clytemnestra, who (as we shall see) has fatally destroyed the sanctity of her own marriage.

In this stasimon Aeschylus exploits the freedom of lyric to incorporate material unbounded by strict logical and psychological constraints. In the story of the lion cub, for example (716–36), the chorus introduce a dramatic image so vivid that it assumes a life of its own. Raised in the home, the young animal reveals its true nature over time, turning from cuddly pet into savage killer. With no simile at work, the relevance to Helen (or Clytemnestra or Agamemnon) remains unclear. We find it puzzling when the chorus shift abruptly from the havoc wreaked by the lion to the day of 'windless calm' that brought Helen to Troy (737–40). The peaceful arrival seems far removed from the violence and bloodshed of the beast grown wild, until we learn that the bride proves to be a Fury, unleashing untold death (744–49).

At the end of the stasimon, the chorus shift to anapaests to welcome Agamemnon, their formal address capturing the paradox that defines him: 'King, who ravaged Troy, / offspring of Atreus … (783–84). As the leader who destroyed a city, Agamemnon bears responsibility for his actions; as the child of Atreus, an heir to a past over which he has no control, Agamemnon is guiltless. The double edge of human circumstance, so briefly but tellingly marked here, emerges time and again in the trilogy and provides much of its vitalizing tension.

Driving his cart into the orchestra, Agamemnon symbolically brings the Trojan War with him. At his side, unnamed but visible to all, stands his war-prize, the Trojan princess and prophetess Cassandra. A wagon in which a man and woman appear together reflects fifth-century wedding iconography on Attic vases depicting a newlywed couple. The confusion of weddings with war in the previous stasimon (the destructive marriage of Paris and Helen) now takes concrete visual form with the arrival home of Agamemnon and his 'war-bride'.

Agamemnon greets his city and then describes the gods who helped him to victory:

> Shield-bearing young of a wooden horse
> timed their birth to the setting stars. A lion
> leapt the walls and gorged on a frightened city,
> lapping up the blood of kings.

(Ag. 825–28)

In this disturbing metaphor, we hear echoes of the omen at Aulis, where eagles devoured the young of the pregnant hare, but here the newborn do the feasting. The army becomes a lion feeding on the blood of a great city, like the cub in the second stasimon that grows to destroy the house. Given the poetic richness of the *Oresteia*, language can implicate a character in a way he or she does not intend. Here, Agamemnon's description triggers a complex set of responses that take the audience back to events preceding the war, particularly those leading to the sacrifice of Iphigenia.

For the third time in the play, Clytemnestra appears at the threshold, and the situation turns electric. She delivers a riveting speech that merges public with private, intimacy with boldness, and culminates in the play's famous dramatic action, the spreading of the dark-red tapestries to welcome Agamemnon home. Significantly, Clytemnestra begins by addressing the chorus, not Agamemnon, a *gestus* of her alienation from her husband. In a domestic version of the Herald's speech on the hardships of war, Clytemnestra describes her loneliness at home when rumour broke around her like a plague. Fear was her sole companion, as she heard reports of Agamemnon wounded and even killed, driving her to thoughts of suicide. At this rhetorical highpoint, Clytemnestra shifts gears and addresses her husband obliquely: 'So your child is not here, as it should be, / the living proof of our love for each other, / Orestes' (877–79). By holding off the child's name, Clytemnestra leaves open the possibility that she has Iphigenia in mind, and the effect in the theatre is palpable.

Having spent many wakeful nights waiting for the beacon, and having endured the nightmares when sleep did come, Clytemnestra at last can welcome her husband home:

> I call on my husband – sheepdog of the flock;
> mainstay and mast of a warship; central pillar
> of a great hall; a father's only son;
> land to the sailor lost at sea;
> calm after a night of storm;
> spring water to the parched traveller.
>
> (*Ag.* 896–901)

The verbal hyperbole generates its theatrical counterpart, when the queen orders her slaves to spread the tapestries for Agamemnon so that 'justice may lead him to the home / he never hoped to see' (911).

For a long moment the talking stops, as the servants lay out the lush red fabric for Agamemnon to walk on. Do they flow out of the palace to suggest the bloodshed that lies ahead, and the past violence that has stained the house of Atreus? Or are the tapestries spread out from Agamemnon's chariot leading up to the palace, as if the blood spilt at Aulis and Troy symbolically floods the orchestra? Or are they strewn from both ends, linking the fates of Troy and Argos, binding the past to the present? However the scene was staged, the tapestries sliced the orchestra with a dark-red path, a striking visual field that draws together the various images of bloodshed in the play.

Fearing that trampling such wealth might arouse the gods' envy, Agamemnon rejects the oriental excess and obsequiousness of his wife's welcome. Clytemnestra initiates a rapid stichomythic dialogue with her husband, and after an exchange of only 14 lines Agamemnon yields. Critics have tried to glean the rational basis for his change of heart, but in performance the crucial shift is less a question of argument and deliberation than of momentum – Agamemnon is swept up by Clytemnestra's verbal pace and energy. Put in psychological terms, tragic stichomythia respects the mystery of decision-making without trying to explain it away, acknowledging that men and women often pretend to rational choice while really taking a stab in the dark.

Before stepping down from the cart, Agamemnon introduces Cassandra and orders his wife to welcome her as a new slave into the house. But Cassandra is forgotten as soon as Agamemnon begins to 'trample down the dark-red path' (957). The king's action is not sacrilegious (the cloth possesses no sacred qualities), but it does symbolize Agamemnon's destruction of the wealth of the house. Clytemnestra enforces that interpretation as she vows to drain the sea for the dyes needed to colour endless fabric, 'worth more than silver' (959). She is ready 'to lay out all the bounty of the house to be trampled, / ... / weaving the strands that bring this life home' (963–65).

Clytemnestra's verbal excess matches the boldness of her plan, and as her husband reaches the palace, she utters a final prayer that seems to signal his imminent death: 'Zeus, Zeus, harvester! Ripen my prayers. / Turn your mind to the harvest at hand' (973–74). She follows Agamemnon inside, leaving the chorus to consider what has happened, and what lies ahead.

In the agitated ode that follows, the elders admit that the king has returned safely, but they cannot silence this 'dirge of the Furies' that sings within them (991). Try as they may, the chorus cannot calm their fears or quench the fire 'that burns in the mind' (1034). We fully expect the off-stage death-cries of Agamemnon to resolve their uncertainties, but suddenly Clytemnestra enters from the palace. Both she and the chorus have forgotten Cassandra.

Clytemnestra alternately cajoles and commands the Trojan prophetess to follow her inside and stand by altar for the sacrifice she has prepared for Agamemnon's homecoming. But Cassandra refuses to respond, and her silence could not prove more eloquent or effective. For the first and only time in the play, Clytemnestra and her verbal pyrotechnics do not control the action. When her last strident threat fails, the queen beats a sullen retreat into the palace, and all eyes turn to Cassandra, the solitary figure still standing in the war-cart. What will she say?

On-stage and mute for some 250 lines (the last three of which focus directly on her *refusal* to speak), Cassandra finally breaks her silence. But she does not speak; she sings. Letting out a heart-rending cry, Cassandra identifies her destroyer, the god Apollo. After each of her lyric utterances, the chorus respond with two lines of spoken dialogue, inverting the normal pattern in which the chorus use lyric metres and the actor speaks. This 'cross-over' gives the lyric dialogue exceptional power, and Aeschylus exploits its dramatic possibilities. Eventually the chorus adopt Cassandra's lyric mode, swept up in the events that the prophetess conjures in her song and dance.

Raped by Apollo, Cassandra refused to bear the god a child, so he cursed her with the gift of prophetic insight that no one would believe (1202–12).[3] A victim of multiple manifestations of male violence, Cassandra finds herself bound to Agamemnon, the commander of the army that destroyed her family and razed her city. She foresees his death, and her own, at the hands of Clytemnestra, a woman too much like a man.[4] Powerless before a past and future she can see but cannot control, Cassandra recognizes other victims of bloodshed in the house, the children of Thyestes who were served in a feast to their father (1095–97). The fate of the slaughtered children suggests the sacrifice of another innocent youth, Iphigenia, whose death forges an important link that binds Cassandra to her new home.

Turning from the past to the present, Cassandra reveals Clytemnestra's plan to kill 'the husband who shares her bed' (1108), the very event taking place off-stage. At the precise moment that Cassandra envisions the netting of Agamemnon in the bath, the chorus leave the rhetoric of dialogue and move into the dance, shifting from iambic trimetres to lyric dochmiacs (1121). They exclaim that Cassandra's 'prophecy does not make us happy', a phrase that literally means 'your word does not cleanse me'. Unconsciously the chorus echo Cassandra's description of Clytemnestra 'washing her husband clean in the bath' (1109), caught up in her image and mode of expression. Metaphorically netted in a *kommos*, the chorus now alternate with Cassandra in lyric as she evokes Agamemnon's off-stage murder, the fate of Troy, and her own 'sacrifice' at the side of the Argive king.

We should linger a moment over the importance of the bath as the place of Agamemnon's death. Commentaries on the play emphasize the Homeric practice of a wife bathing her husband (an anachronism in fifth-century Athens), but they often fail to appreciate the contemporary relevance of a wife dutifully (if ironically) washing her husband's body before burial, one of the responsibilities of women in Greek funeral ritual.[5] There is a hint of nuptial bathing as well – Clytemnestra is Agamemnon's 'bedmate' (1116), suggesting a twisted version of the ritual bath that took place as part of the Athenian wedding. We already have seen how the play masterfully confuses weddings and funerals: the 'preliminary offering' of the corpses of Greek and Trojan soldiers at the wedding of Paris and Helen (65); the wedding song that turns into a dirge when Helen arrives at Troy (705–16); Cassandra driven to her new home like a bride, only to 'die together' (1139) with Agamemnon.

Cassandra's lament reminds the chorus of the nightingale's plaintive song (1142–46), referring to the myth of Procne and her sister Philomela. Procne's husband Tereus raped Philomela, and then cut out her tongue.[6] When she communicates the deed in her weaving, the two sisters take their revenge by killing Tereus' son, Itys. Transformed into a nightingale, Procne forever sings for her dead child; turned into a swallow, the speechless Philomela sings an inarticulate melody, which the ancients associated with the swallow's song. Comparing Cassandra to Procne is apt: she is raped by Apollo, forced to 'marry' Agamemnon, and finally sings a lament for the loss of her family and city. Cassandra also takes on the other voice of the myth, that of Philomela, for earlier Clytemnestra likens the prophetess to a swallow who sings incomprehensibly (1050–51). Aeschylus exploits both aspects of Cassandra's persona, the lyrical and the inarticulate, finding an appropriate myth to elicit the audience's double sympathy.

These connections of myth, ritual, and character should not be dismissed as recondite or irrelevant to the stage. A modern production of the *Oresteia* could costume Cassandra to suggest a twisted wedding, and the actress could use the bridal imagery as a way to grapple with the character's inner visions. The movement and the music accompanying her song could suggest, alternately, a marriage hymn and a funeral dirge, perhaps echoing the recreation of Helen's arrival at Troy in the second stasimon. The bird imagery – from the eagles in the *parodos* to the swallow and nightingale associated with Cassandra – could be linked by dance and gesture to signal both the innocence and the ultimate power of nature. Encoded in Aeschylus' language, these theatrical ideas should be given their due in a modern production (or in the mind of a contemporary reader) that wishes to tap the trilogy's rich poetic resources.

After this unprecedented exchange, Cassandra moves into speech to 'talk through' what she and the chorus have just experienced. She untangles the strands in the web of past, present, and future, but only after she has swept the chorus and audience up in them. Her first words in dialogue metre clarify the nuptial motifs scattered through the lyric: 'No more like a newly wedded bride / will my prophecies peek out from under veils' (1178–79). Fifth-century art often represents bridal veiling and unveiling, an important aspect of the Greek wedding that occurs at crucial moments in other tragedies. In Euripides' *Alcestis*, for instance, the climactic return of Admetus' wife takes the form of a bride unveiling before her husband. Earlier in *Agamemnon* Helen left the 'delicate veils' of her marriage-bed in Sparta for a disastrous wedding at Troy (690–92), and now Cassandra throws off her metaphorical veil before she enters the palace at Argos.

With her visionary insight, Cassandra sees a chorus of Furies who never leave the house, a band of revellers who 'sing their hymn as they besiege the chambers' (1186–91). The original audience may have imagined the group of Furies as symposiasts at a drinking party, or more likely as the celebrants who accompany the nuptial procession and sing an epithalamium outside the newlyweds' chamber. Instead of praising the bride and groom, however, their hymn denounces the betrayal of a wedding, 'a brother's bed and the man who trampled it' (1193). The reference is to Thyestes' fatal seduction of Atreus' wife that prompted Atreus to prepare a feast of Thyestes' own children. The 'trampled' (*patounti*) bed carries undertones of the twisted marriage of Paris, who abducted Menelaus' wife Helen and so 'trampled (*patoith'*) untouchable things' (372). It also suggests the adultery of Helen's sister Clytemnestra, whose unnatural liaison with Aegisthus links her to Thyestes' only surviving child. Finally the image of trampling recalls Agamemnon's exit down the dark-red tapestries. He 'tramples' the cloth (*patôn* 957, *patêsmon* 963), just as Cassandra will 'trample' her way into the palace (*pateis* 1298).

The chorus are amazed at Cassandra's resolution, walking to her death 'like a god-driven / bull to the altar' (1297–98). The sacrificial imagery links Cassandra to Iphigenia, whose sacrifice features so prominently in the *parodos*. The young girl's death at Aulis served as a 'preliminary offering' for the ships (*proteleia* 227), the same word used for the first casualties at Troy, offered for the wedding of Paris and Helen (60–67). Cassandra views her own death as a sacrifice, but not for a marriage – her warm blood will sanctify the funeral of Agamemnon (1278). Iphigenia once sang paeans at her father's table (242–46), only to provide a silent offering when she is gagged like an animal wearing a bit (234–46). Clytemnestra berates Cassandra for *refusing* to wear the bit (1066), and the prophetess sings inauspicious lamentations to Apollo rather than the customary paeans to the god (1074–75, 1078–79). Through poetic image and situation, the death of Cassandra reduplicates the sacrifice of Iphigenia, the blood of innocent women fertilizing the ground for new acts of bloodshed.

Unlike Agamemnon who blindly walks the red tapestries to his death, Cassandra sees clearly what lies in store for her, and her last words reveal a tragic nobility in the face of death. She proclaims that life is at best a shadow, and, at worst, as ephemeral as a picture erased by a wet sponge. In language that echoes the unveiling image with which she began her speech, Cassandra prays 'that the blow is sure ... and I close my eyes at last' (1294). Only with the fall of the sacrificial blade will this unveiled bride escape the horrors that her prophetic visions have forced her to see.

After her extraordinary scene with the chorus, Cassandra finally enters the palace, and we expect to hear the off-stage death-cries, just as we did after Agamemnon's exit. Once again our expectations appear to be frustrated, for the chorus begin to chant in anapaests (1331–42), the steady rhythm that introduced the *parodos* (40–103) and the first stasimon (355–66). The metre leads us to expect that a full choral ode is gathering steam, when suddenly we hear the blood-curdling cry of Agamemnon from behind the façade. Thanks to Aeschylus' manipulation of lyric metres, the long anticipated murder of Agamemnon comes as a surprise.

At the king's outcry, the chorus fracture into twelve voices (1348–71), their tone varying from impassioned anger to utter timidity. Some call for immediate intervention in the palace: 'I cast my vote / for action' and 'Better to die than live under tyrants.' Others advise caution: 'From the evidence of cries alone / are we to prophesy that he is dead?' 'It is one thing to guess, another to know.' The last speaker adopts the wait-and-see attitude: 'I add my vote for that opinion.' The chorus split down the middle, six for delay, six for action. Although no one in the audience is counting, the division of the chorus foreshadows that of the jury in *Eumenides*. The stage-picture in the orchestra – a chorus divided over Agamemnon's murder – may have been mirrored in the final play, when the jury's vote is split over Orestes' guilt.

The appearance of Clytemnestra with the corpses of her two victims dispels any doubts.[7] In a ferocious speech, Clytemnestra recounts the murder of her husband, shifting to the present tense when she describes the deathblows. Classicists write somewhat dismissively of the 'historical' present tense without appreciating the powerful clue it offers the actor. It is as if Clytemnestra's emotional memory works so strongly that she actually relives the crucial moments. She revels in Agamemnon's blood as if it were rain that falls on the crops in the spring, infusing the seeds with life (1389–92).

Not only does she confuse death blood with life-giving rain, but Clytemnestra assaults the ritual order of the city as well. She speaks of Agamemnon's blood as the third offering that honours 'Zeus below the earth, the saviour (*sôter*) of corpses' (1387), conflating the ritual offerings to the dead with those poured at a banquet, where the third libation traditionally went to Zeus *Sôtêr*. Clytemnestra also appropriates Agamemnon's funeral rites to herself, denying the chorus the right to lament the corpse and supervise the interment (1551–54). With grisly irony, Clytemnestra already has given her husband his funeral bath, and now he lies in public view, a perverse laying-out of the body wrapped in its net-cum-funeral shroud. In these ritual inversions, the original audience saw before them a powerful image of their world gone awry.

Responding in dochmiacs, the chorus alternately attack the queen's brazenness and mourn the dead king. Clytemnestra defends her actions by pointing to Agamemnon's sacrifice of their daughter, Iphigenia. We have observed the close ties between Iphigenia and Cassandra, and now Clytemnestra implicitly brings them together, remembering Agamemnon's sacrificial victim while standing over the corpse of the young princess she has slaughtered. United by imagery and circumstance, the two innocent females personify the destruction caused by Agamemnon and Clytemnestra. The king had to die, in no small part because of the sacrifice of his daughter Iphigenia, and Clytemnestra's murder of Cassandra, perhaps more than the slaying of her husband, distances her from the audience and makes her death seem dramatically right.

As Cassandra predicts (1326–29), the chorus bewail Agamemnon without mentioning her, but Clytemnestra cannot get the Trojan prophetess out of her mind. After alluding to her own adulterous liaison with Aegisthus, Clytemnestra derides the dead Cassandra as the whore of the Greek army, boasting that her death 'brings added relish to my bed' (1447). Clytemnestra's distorted view of her victim blinds her to what she has done, slaughtering an innocent woman, a second Iphigenia. We feel Cassandra's death personally, having witnessed her long and moving scene with the chorus before her murder.

The chorus answer each speech of Clytemnestra with a lyric outburst, mainly in dochmiacs, increasing their pressure until the queen finally leaves the metres of speech and meets the chorus half way in anapaests. The dramatic effect is that of two opposed parties battering their way towards a precarious cease-fire. In the process, major themes and characters reappear with striking vividness: Helen, Clytemnestra's crazed sister who brought death to so many at Troy; the bloodthirsty curse, an avenging force that works in the house; the role of Zeus, both cause and fulfiller; the wounds of the past that break out again; the king Agamemnon, caught in the web of a spider; his sacrifice, and the sacrifice of Iphigenia; Thyestes' feast on his own murdered children; the *lex talionis* that blow must answer blow, and that whoever acts must suffer. At the end of the Clytemnestra-chorus exchange, a provisional resolution seems within reach. The emotionally drained queen prays for a pact with the demon in the race, to leave things as they are if only the madness and bloodshed would cease.

Suddenly Aegisthus enters down an *eisodos* and shatters the mood in the theatre:

> Light of dawn, break on this day of justice.
> The gods bring vengeance,
> they look down on the sins of men.
> I know when I see this man at my feet,
> tangled in the robes of the Furies.
> It brings me joy ...
>
> (*Ag.* 1577–82)

It is as if Aegisthus enters in the wrong mode, with the wrong energy, into the wrong play. Coming after the lyric exchange between the chorus and Clytemnestra, his speech upsets the precarious balance that has been achieved, renewing the drive towards vengeance and propelling us into the next play of the trilogy.

Aegisthus recounts the story of his father Thyestes, who ruled Argos with his brother Atreus until rivalries led to Thyestes' banishment. Atreus later welcomed his brother home with a banquet made of the cooked flesh of his own children, and in horror Thyestes cursed the house. The sole surviving son of Thyestes, Aegisthus boasts that the curse still lives, for now he stands over the corpse of Atreus' son, Agamemnon. The gruesome banquet, referred to earlier by Cassandra and the chorus, lies behind the other images of slaughter and eating in the play – the eagles devouring the pregnant hare, the lion cub that grows to feed on the household flock, the Greek army that drinks Trojan blood like a ravenous lion. By clarifying the archetype of perverted feasting in the last scene of the play, Aeschylus prepares for the re-emergence of the motif in *Choephori* and *Eumenides*, where Clytemnestra dreams of a snake that drinks her blood, and the Furies hope to feed on the living Orestes.

The chorus treat Aegisthus with open hostility, berating his cowardice and decrying his seizure of political power in Argos. When they raise the spectre of Orestes' return from exile to exact vengeance and claim the throne, Aegisthus calls out his armed bodyguards, whose arrival confirms that a tyrant rules the city. The play began with the distant war at Troy, and now chaos has come home to Greece in the form of political repression and civil discord.

Silent since her anapaests with the chorus, Clytemnestra intervenes firmly and decisively. She reminds her new husband of the bitter harvest they have reaped already and the blood they have shed, and she urges the chorus to disperse to their homes. Instead of leaving *en masse*, which is usual at the end of a tragedy, the chorus break into small groups and each has a final, shrill exchange with Aegisthus before exiting from the theatre. The vitriolic departure of the chorus gives the visual and verbal lie to Clytemnestra's wish for herself and Aegisthus: 'You and I shall rule / and make the house well again' (1672–73). The final scene of *Agamemnon* makes it clear that more bloodshed and a new cycle of violence must be unleashed before there is any hope of cure.

Choephori

Agamemnon begins with waiting; *Choephori* opens with arrival. Two young men enter the empty orchestra, and we learn that Orestes has returned from exile with his friend Pylades. He offers belated funeral rites for his father, cutting off a lock of hair and laying it on the grave, a ritual act that establishes the place and dramatic circumstance. Whether or not a portable stone marker was put in place between the plays, Orestes' words and actions 'create' the tomb in the centre of the orchestra. As well as establishing his filial piety, the ritual gesture signals Orestes' new maturity, for Athenian youths dedicated locks of hair on reaching manhood. The activities at the grave cease with the sudden arrival of the chorus of women, and Orestes and Pylades withdraw unseen to observe these new visitors at the tomb.

In this brief prologue, Aeschylus differentiates *Choephori* from *Agamemnon* in several essential respects. The protagonist (Orestes) appears at the outset, moving the story into a new generation. He shifts the focus from the palace-façade at the back to the tomb of Agamemnon in the centre of the orchestra, meaning that the palace must be 'thought away' by characters and audience alike until Orestes arrives there at line 652 to begin the revenge plot. In dynamic terms, the action moves out towards the audience for the first half of the play, and then pulls back to the façade for the murders. The fact that Orestes and Pylades withdraw to watch the new arrivals presents us with a mirror image of the audience's relationship to the play. Like Orestes, we are onlookers and we share his perspective, especially when Electra discovers the offerings he made at the grave – we know who left them, and we know he is looking on. As the plot unfolds, our position as spectators shifts from fellow-observers to 'accessories before the fact', accomplices who watch with full knowledge the entrapment and murder of Aegisthus and Clytemnestra. Contrast our relationship to *Agamemnon*, where we know that something untoward is happening, but the details are not revealed until the Cassandra scene, and then from the point of view of the victim and not the perpetrator.

Dressed in black, singing threnodies, and bearing libations to the grave, the chorus (accompanied by the silent Electra) continue the funeral motifs begun by Orestes. In response to a terrifying nightmare, Clytemnestra has sent her slave-women with offerings to calm the spirit of her dead husband. The chorus know their libations provide no remedy: 'no stream can wash away / blood that stains the hand'. The earth is so clotted with gore that 'no liquids can flow' (*Cho.* 66–75). In a play that focuses on murder, Aeschylus emphasizes at the start the revulsion of nature at human bloodshed. After the *parodos*, Electra asks the chorus for help as she pours Clytemnestra's offerings. In a short dialogue, the women demand murder for murder, and they convince her to alter the designated prayer and call instead for the death of Aegisthus and Clytemnestra. As Electra prays for vengeance, the chorus crown their libations with a lament that brings the play's first movement to a close.

Aeschylus has set the stage beautifully for the emergence of Orestes from hiding. Electra spies a lock of hair at the tomb and concludes that her brother has returned, only to reject the thought as impossible. Like the chorus in *Agamemnon* unsure of the beacon fire, Electra needs a human voice to answer her doubts. The sight of footprints adds to her mental anguish, and the appearance of Orestes in person compounds it. In a quick stichomythic exchange, she asks the stranger 'Why do you wind me in this net?' and Orestes responds, 'It traps me as well' (*Cho.* 220–21). The reunion of brother and sister takes the form of mutual entrapment, the alternating lines of dialogue articulating the strands of the net. The imagery reveals that the world of *Agamemnon* – the net thrown on Troy, the snare that traps the returning king – still lives in the next generation.

The recognition scene works through the idea of germination, the small and insignificant generating the large and momentous. We see Orestes plant the dramatic seed by leaving a lock of hair, and we watch it burst into life when Electra seizes on it. Knowing that a 'vast trunk can grow from the smallest seed' (204), Electra welcomes her brother as a 'seed of hope, watered by tears' (236). We recall from the first play that Agamemnon uprooted the city of Troy, only to have his own blood fall like spring rain on the newly planted seeds (*Ag.* 1388–92). Now the renewing acts of homecoming and recognition take place at his tomb, where the metaphors of birth and growth are harnessed to death, generating fresh plans for bloodshed.

Orestes describes the forces that drive him to vengeance, chief among them Apollo's oracle prophesying what he would suffer if he failed to avenge his father and regain his patrimony. The principle of retributive justice provides the impulse for the long lyric *kommos* that follows, lying at the heart of the trilogy. The chorus, Orestes, and Electra steel themselves to the task ahead, calling for support from the spirit of Agamemnon and various deities above and below the earth. Critics have argued long and hard over the dramatic purpose of this complex interchange, the longest lyric passage in extant tragedy. Does the *kommos* convert Orestes from a hesitant to a single-minded avenger? Or is the energy directed primarily at the spirit of Agamemnon? Or does it focus on the audience, a gathering of dramatic forces (both seen and unseen) that convert the theatre itself into a place of vengeance?

Beginning in anapaests, the chorus call Orestes and Electra to the inexorable demands of the *lex talionis*. In the lyric sections that follow – strophic pairs with intermezzi, alternating Orestes–chorus–Electra–chorus – the siblings mourn their father's fate, while the women sustain the refrain that blood must pay for blood. The pattern of speakers, metre, and responsion changes when the chorus and Electra recount the aftermath of Agamemnon's murder, driving Orestes to deliver his strongest cry for vengeance. All three parties summon Agamemnon's spirit to join them, completing the transformation of the offerings sent by Clytemnestra to calm Agamemnon's anger. Just as Electra altered her prayer when pouring the libations over the grave, now she and Orestes follow the chorus's lead in rousing Agamemnon's spirit to action.

As Cassandra does in *Agamemnon*, so Orestes and Electra 'talk through' the events of the lyric in regular speech, a formal reiteration of the essential issues of the *kommos*. In the brief exchange with Orestes that follows, the chorus recount Clytemnestra's nightmare that led her to send libations to Agamemnon's tomb. Although editors commonly attribute these lines to the chorus-leader, they may have been divided among the individual members of the group. The voices coming from around the orchestra would give the sense that Orestes was surrounded and trapped by the very dream that terrified his mother – he is the snake born to Clytemnestra that feeds at her breast and drains her lifeblood along with her milk.

With the attention now focused on him alone, Orestes outlines his plan for revenge. Disguised as foreign travellers, he and Pylades will approach the palace, ask for hospitality, and, once inside, kill Aegisthus. Orestes makes no mention of Clytemnestra. He advises the chorus to be silent when appropriate, and to speak when the time is ripe, setting up their intervention with the Nurse later in the play. Electra exits through one *eisodos* (and out of the play, for she never returns), Pylades and Orestes depart via the other, and the chorus are left alone for the first time.

Functioning as a true 'act-dividing song', the lyric snaps the moorings of locale and setting, as the chorus sing of strange beasts from the earth and sea, of celestial terrors made of air (hurricanes) and fire (thunderbolts), all four elements of early Greek cosmology. However, these natural prodigies prove no match for the human monster, illustrated by three myths and epitomized by Clytemnestra's murder of her husband.[8] The last image in the stasimon is of a *new* murder returning home, the child of former murders, and the final word is 'Furies'. At that moment Orestes appears from an *eisodos*, fulfilling in the flesh the chorus's description, and he demands entry into the palace. A young Fury has come home to perpetrate a crime that is the offspring of prior bloodshed in the race.

The second arrival of Orestes and Pylades introduces the play's second act, and its opening scene could be called 'getting inside'. Orestes knocks at the palace door and calls impatiently for a servant, an odd set of actions for a tragic hero but a scenario recognizable from Greek comedy, where rousing a servant to open the door is a stock routine. Orestes announces that he brings news to the rulers of the house, more fitting for a man to hear than a woman. We are surprised, therefore, when Clytemnestra appears at the doorway instead of Aegisthus. She promises the strangers all due hospitality, including 'a warm bath and soft bed to soothe you' (*Cho.* 670). Given the welcome to her husband in *Agamemnon*, Clytemnestra's offer of a bath is almost grotesque. However, the irony here operates totally at her expense, and its edge sharpens when the unrecognized young man claims that he brings news of Orestes' death, adding disingenuously 'But perhaps / I am speaking to those who are not concerned. / I do think his father should be told' (688–90).[9]

Why does Aeschylus throw such strange shadows over the action – the comedic door knocking, Clytemnestra's unwitting *double entendre*, and Orestes' conscious irony delivered from the safe distance of disguise? The answer may lie in the relationship that these elements help to forge with the audience. The incongruous tone binds us even faster to the revenge plot, for the prior knowledge that allows us to laugh to ourselves also fortifies our complicity in, and commitment to, the impending deed. The audience are 'in' on the joke, just as we are 'in' on the plans for murder.

Clytemnestra reacts to the news with a cry of grief, prompting some critics to conclude that she can manufacture any and all emotions at will. A more interesting approach to her character, however, would take these moments of strong feeling at face value. I find it far more powerful and disturbing if we assume that Clytemnestra wants her husband home when she says she does in *Agamemnon*, and that she considers him worthy of the praise she bestows – or at least she can imagine a time when she once did, a tragic form of wish fulfilment. Now she cries out instinctively when she learns that another child of hers has been taken: 'Stripped of my loved ones, / and now Orestes. He did well to keep his distance / and not step near this morass of death' (695–97). The 'actor' in this scenario is not Clytemnestra, but Orestes himself, biding his time before he adds his mother's blood to the quagmire. Orestes asks that his hosts not stint their welcome because of the news he brings, an appeal to the guest–host relationship that resonates uneasily, for we know that Orestes will violate its sanctity just as Paris did with Menelaus. The ploy works, and Clytemnestra welcomes Orestes and Pylades inside. Agamemnon's son has accomplished the task set for the scene in the space of only sixty lines.

Alone in the orchestra for the second time, the chorus call on various powers to join the battle and guide Orestes' sword. They repeat the word 'now!' four times in as many lines (723–26), giving the impression that the murder of Clytemnestra is at hand. Suddenly the chorus-leader spots the figure of the Nurse, Cilissa, bustling from the palace, sent by Clytemnestra to fetch Aegisthus. Even more surprising than her appearance is the speech she delivers, a disarming account of her sorrow at the news of Orestes' death. She relates in unabashed terms what her life was like as the wet nurse for the baby Orestes. Waking in the middle of the night to nurse 'the little beast' (753), she tried to guess his needs, but ended up washing nappies:

> Young insides are a law unto themselves;
> you just have to guess. Like a prophet I was,
> but many's the time I guessed wrong ...
> Washwoman and child nurse, they're one and the same.
>
> (*Cho.* 757–60)

The Nurse's speech intensifies the tragedy, for we imagine Orestes as an infant, connected like everyone at that age to basic bodily functions. *This* is the man who now waits in the palace to commit murder, and we wonder again at the complex weave of events that could lead from the instinctual cries of a baby to the deceit of a matricide. We might recall the lion-cub lyric in *Agamemnon* – eventually 'time shows its nature', and the savage adult lion wreaks havoc in the house.

In some respects the Nurse represents an alternative maternal figure to Clytemnestra. Her manner of expression and conscious self-irony ('like a prophet I was') contrast with the rhetoric of the queen, and her commitment to the baby Orestes puts in relief Clytemnestra's claims to feel a mother's concern. The humorous 'prophecies' of the Nurse years ago also recall the dire prophecies earlier in the trilogy (Kalchas, Cassandra), and we realize that Aeschylus' humour has a double edge. Finally, however, we enjoy the Nurse's account because we know that the object of her care and love is still very much alive.

With typical tragic economy, Aeschylus now makes the unknowing Cilissa a linchpin in the plot. The chorus convince her to alter the message she brings to Aegisthus, so that he will come without his customary body-guards, the thugs introduced at the end of *Agamemnon*. The intervention of the women here demonstrates the falseness of the oft-repeated rubric that the tragic chorus never materially affect the action. Sensing that better news might lie ahead, the Nurse leaves to do as her fellow-slaves suggest.

With the stage empty, the chorus embark on their second act-dividing song, three strophic pairs with a mesode between each strophe and antistrophe (a—mesode 1—a' / b—mesode 2—b' / c—mesode 3—c'). The tripartite structure – itself built on triads – links the divine world to that of the human characters, foreshadowing the ultimate resolution of the trilogy where gods and humans stand together in common purpose. Praying for Orestes' victory, the chorus appeal to Zeus, the household divinities (perhaps implying the Furies who live in the race), Apollo at Delphi, and Hermes who leads souls to the underworld. In the final triad they turn to the mortal agents, imagining Orestes in the palace face to face with Clytemnestra: 'When she cries, "Son!" / say to her "My father's!" / and drive death home' (828–30).

Given the chorus's emphasis on the fatal meeting between mother and son, the audience once again expect a death-cry from the palace. Instead, Aegisthus enters briskly down an *eisodos*, barely concealing his delight at the news from the Nurse. The chorus play their part to perfection, flattering the tyrant's vanity by urging him to find out the truth for himself, man to man. Eager to cross-examine the Messenger, Aegisthus exits into the palace with self-assurance bordering on the ludicrous, proclaiming with his last words that the stranger 'cannot trick a man whose eyes are open' (854). Aegisthus' sole appearance in *Choephori* is so incongruous, and his dispatch so rapid (the entire scene takes twenty lines), that he almost makes a comic impact. His arrogant confidence that his 'eyes are open' when he walks into the trap brings to mind his rival Agamemnon, who walked blindly to his death through the same door in the previous play.

The pace accelerates as the chorus shift to lyric anapaests, again praying for Orestes' victory. As soon as they hear Aegisthus' death-cries, however, they pull back from the murder: 'Stand back till the verdict is in / and we will seem guiltless' (872–73). The women who transformed Electra's opening libation into an offering for vengeance, who urged Orestes to bloodshed in the *kommos*, who intercepted the Nurse and changed her message, who guided Aegisthus to his doom – these very women now distance themselves from the outcome. Following this stasimon, exits and entrances continue apace. A servant rushes from the palace crying that Aegisthus has been slain, the queen enters to ask the reason for the alarm, and she learns that 'He who is dead has killed the living' (886). The servant then exits after an on-stage life of only twelve lines, followed almost immediately by the appearance of Orestes and Pylades at the palace doors. The confrontation between mother and son has finally come to pass.

This spate of entrances and exits, unprecedented in tragedy, shatters Clytemnestra's control of the threshold. The effect would be lost if there were another entrance into the palace. There must be only one, a single passageway that Orestes penetrates. Ironically, his initial success in doing so unleashes a scurry of comings and goings, finally leading to the matricide that drives Orestes *away* from his home even as he reclaims his rightful place in it.

In their crucial scene together, Clytemnestra reminds Orestes that by killing her he will be stabbing the breast that nurtured him. For a moment the thought chills Orestes, and he turns to Pylades, asking his friend the central tragic question (discussed in Chapter 5), *ti drasô*, 'What shall I do?' (899). In a three-line response (his only words in the play), Pylades tells Orestes to follow the oracle of Apollo, preferring the enmity of mortals to the anger of the gods. The tragic situation could not be etched more clearly. A heretofore silent character, one who has loomed in the background as a symbol of Orestes' exile and alienation from his natal family, steps forward and speaks for the matricide. Short of a *deus ex machina*, Aeschylus could not have introduced a more compelling voice than that of Pylades, emanating from both inside and outside the action, and Orestes 'judges' in his friend's favour (903).

Clytemnestra initiates a stichomythic exchange (908–30) that propels the scene to its climax. Pleading for her life, she threatens Orestes with 'the bloodhounds of a mother's curse', a vivid periphrasis for the Furies.

She finds her son no more approachable than a tomb, and in a flash of insight realizes that he is the snake she bore in her dream. Orestes drags Clytemnestra off-stage to kill her over the corpse of Aegisthus: 'You killed whom you should not, now suffer what should not be' (930).

With that paradox still echoing in the theatre, the chorus-leader introduces the third and final stasimon with a four-line speech, noteworthy for the sympathy it shows Orestes' victims: 'I feel sorry even for these two, and their double doom' (931). The ode proper constitutes the victory song the chorus referred to earlier, the form similar to that of the previous stasimon, with a mesode intervening between each strophe and antistrophe. However, Aeschylus tempers the note of triumph by the predominance of dochmiacs, the agitated metre associated with the Furies at several points in the trilogy. The tension between the drive to resolution (the repeated phrase 'it has come', 935, 937, 946), and the unsettling rhythm with which it is expressed, underlines the moral ambiguity of Orestes' action.

Orestes returns from the palace with the bodies of Clytemnestra and Aegisthus, and the stage-picture recalls the scene in *Agamemnon* where Clytemnestra exults over the corpses of her husband and *his* lover.[10] In both plays, the victims lie wedded to death, while the killer conjures images of the adultery that helped motivate the murder. For all the dramatic differences between *Agamemnon* and *Choephori*, the two plays confirm that the cycle of violence will continue. Bloodshed engenders future bloodshed as inexorably as one generation follows the next.

Along with the two bodies, Orestes displays the robe that trapped Agamemnon in the bath, and he struggles to find the right name for it: a hunting net, bath-curtains, a death shroud, a brigand's trap (997–1004). Returning to the funereal mode with which the play began, he delivers a eulogy for his father, but then shifts almost immediately to mourn 'the act, the suffering, the whole race, / since I win no glory but wear the stain of victory' (1016–17). Like Agamemnon before him, Orestes has returned a conqueror, but unlike his father he realizes how compromised his conquest is.

Sensing that he is losing the reins, Orestes takes hold of an olive bough garlanded with cotton, the traditional sign of a suppliant. Facing exile for killing his mother, Orestes will return to Delphi in supplication, as Apollo advised. The chorus reassure him that by 'killing the vipers you freed the land of Argos' (1046–47), but the young man cries out in terror. The vipers he sees are not lying at his feet but writhing in the hair of women who approach him, clad in black, dripping blood from their eyes, 'the bloodhounds of a mother's curse' (1054). Orestes describes his visions in a stichomythic dialogue with the chorus, the strict form encapsulating the madness even as it underlines the growing chasm between the hero and the group. With the hallucinatory power of a nightmare, it is as if the black-clad chorus women have metamorphosed into Furies, the snakes in their hair recalling the viper of Clytemnestra's dream that has grown up to be Orestes himself.

Isolated by his encroaching madness, Orestes flees from the theatre, armed only with his suppliant wand. The fact that he cannot withdraw inside the palace makes it clear that the cycle of bloodshed must be stopped elsewhere, in a new dramatic world. Alone in the orchestra for the last time, the chorus shift to anapaests to describe the generational storms that have struck the house: first, the feast of slaughtered children, referring to Thyestes' horrible banquet; second, the death of a husband, king, and commander-in-chief, killed by his wife in the bath; third, Orestes' murder of Clytemnestra, an act that may restore the house or bring on its doom. It is fitting that the chorus close the play with a question: 'Where will it end? / When will it sleep, this force of ruin?' (*Cho.* 1075–76). The destructive energies that have worked their way through *Agamemnon* and *Choephori* remain to be dealt with, and they call out for the final play.

Eumenides

The last act of the trilogy opens at Apollo's temple in Delphi, the most important oracular site in the Greek world. At the centre of the orchestra, where the tomb of Agamemnon was located in *Choephori*, stands the *omphalos* or navel stone of the earth, marking the inner sanctum of Apollo's shrine. In a cancelled entry, Orestes takes his suppliant's position at the *omphalos*, and the chorus of Furies (perhaps covering their masks with their cloaks to hide them from the audience) scatter on the orchestra floor, asleep. To begin the action, the priestess of Apollo delivers her prologue back by the façade, unaware of what lies at the centre of the orchestra, which represents the 'interior' of the temple.[11]

The Pythia's speech outlines the devolution of prophetic power at Delphi, moving peacefully through a series of female deities until control of the shrine is conferred on the god Apollo. The priestess prays in orderly fashion to a string of deities, articulating a careful hierarchy that culminates with Zeus, the 'Fulfiller' or 'Harvester' (*Eum.* 28). Because the audience can see what the Pythia does not – namely that the monstrous Furies surround the bloodstained Orestes at the *omphalos* – we maintain an ironic distance from her opening genealogies and formulaic prayers. The audience's 'split' vision infuses the Pythia's prologue with the tension it otherwise lacks, when compared to the inherently dramatic situations facing the Watchman in *Agamemnon* and Orestes in *Choephori*.

At the conclusion of her prayer, the priestess 'enters' the temple by walking downstage, towards the centre of the orchestra. At the unexpected sight of Orestes and the Furies, however, she scrambles away in terror on her hands and knees (*Eum.* 34–38). The Pythia describes in vivid terms Orestes at the altar and the Furies surrounding him, a tableau still present before the audience but as yet unanimated. She portrays the Furies much as Orestes imagines them at the end of *Choephori*, first as women, then as gorgons, then harpies without wings, dressed in black, noses dripping, eyes oozing vile liquid, defiling the temple. The precision of the Pythia's verbal picture fills in what most of the audience could make out only vaguely, given the size of the theatre of Dionysus. Once again, it is the words working on the audience's imagination, along with the graphic masks and costumes, that create the sleeping Furies and their prey in the orchestra.

Leaving the problem of the temple's pollution to Apollo, the Pythia exits out one *eisodos*, even as the god himself enters down the other. The overlapping entrance and exit give the impression that events have reached a stage where divine interference is required. Promising his suppliant release from the Furies, Apollo advises Orestes to flee to Athens and take refuge at Athena's cult-statue. There the goddess will find 'judges for your case, / and words that cast a calming spell, the means / to rid you forever of this pain' (81–83). Apollo calls on Hermes to protect the traveller, and the god's role as intermediary between the earth and the underworld suggests that Orestes' flight to Athens is like a journey back into life. Although Hermes' physical presence is not necessary, the god (played by a mute) may have entered with Apollo and led Orestes off at the end of the scene.

As Apollo and Orestes exit out one *eisodos*, the ghost of Clytemnestra (yet unnamed) enters down the other. This second 'flowing' exit and entrance reinforce the rhythm of flight and pursuit, introducing the murder victim who demands vengeance on the living. Moving among the sleeping Furies, she rouses them to pursue Orestes, who, like a fawn, has escaped their net. The physical manifestation of the Furies – sleeping, waking, dancing, hunting, tracking – strengthens the sense that they represent a natural force, and their outrage at kindred bloodshed demands a primal respect. In perhaps the strangest dialogue in tragedy, each of Clytemnestra's exhortations is followed by a groan or whimper from the chorus, one of the few ancient stage directions that has survived.[12] The Furies 'chase the prey in a dream, / like howling dogs that never leave the track' (131–32). Goaded by Clytemnestra, they finally wake to vengeance and pursuit, rising from the orchestra floor to begin the *parodos* as the dream-ghost disappears.

The stage picture of Clytemnestra waking the Furies recalls the *kommos* of *Choephori*, in which Orestes, Electra, and the chorus wake the spirit of Agamemnon. If Agamemnon's tomb and the *omphalos* at Delphi both were located orchestra-centre, then Clytemnestra's effort to rouse the forces of vengeance would mirror the *kommos* in subject and staging. At the end of *Eumenides*, Athena 'replaces' Clytemnestra's ghost in the centre of the orchestra (both parts were played by the same actor), reversing the energy unleashed at the start by putting the anger of the Furies to sleep and converting them to beneficent spirits.

The *parodos* proper begins with the chorus already in the orchestra, where they perform three strophic pairs in a mixture of iambic and dochmiac metres, the agitated rhythm reinforcing their anger that the prey has 'slipped from the snare' (147). In the last four lines of the second strophe and antistrophe, the metrical correspondence is more than exact – word-breaks occur at precisely the same place, and several phonetic and syntactic echoes are heard. The lyric effectively binds together the Furies' drive for vengeance with the stain that Orestes has spread at the navel of the earth. Accusing Apollo of polluting his own temple, the chorus vow to track Orestes down even if he flees to the underworld.

Taking his cue, Apollo bursts back into the orchestra to drive the Furies out of his sanctuary. In a clash of irreconcilable opposites, the beautiful, gold-clad Olympian assaults the blood-dripping, subterranean daughters of Night. He associates them solely with torture and mutilation, rejecting their ancient office of bringing to justice those killers who shed kindred blood. Apollo argues that the bond between husband and wife surpasses ties of birth and kinship, and so, by not pursuing Clytemnestra when she killed her husband, the Furies have dishonoured the sanctity of marriage. The chorus respond instinctively, vowing they will never let Orestes go, and they leave the orchestra 'driven by a mother's blood / to track and hunt him down. We go for Justice' (230–31).

Apollo follows them out through an *eisodos* vowing to help Orestes. With the orchestra now empty, that very man arrives down the other *eisodos* to take refuge at the altar of Athena. This last 'flowing' exit and entrance effect the transition from Delphi to Athens. Orestes establishes that the orchestra now represents the interior of the temple of Athena by addressing the cult-statue of the goddess at the centre-point (*Eum.* 235–43). Given the flexibility of the Greek stage and the power of language to create location, it is likely that the marker used earlier for the *omphalos* at Apollo's temple now represents the ancient, aniconic image of the goddess.[13] Orestes makes his appeal to Athena at the same place he called on Apollo for help, and where he and his sister prayed to their murdered father in *Choephori*.

His prayers are answered not by Olympian intervention but by the arrival of the Furies, one of the most powerful entrances on the Greek stage. Performing a second *parodos*, the chorus fill the orchestra with images of the hunt, moving like dogs tracking a wounded fawn or cowering hare (244–53). The simile recalls the pregnant hare in the *parodos* of *Agamemnon*, killed by eagles who feasted on her unborn children. That act of bloodshed led to the sacrifice of Orestes' sister, Iphigenia, and now Orestes himself must give the Furies his blood to drink as payment for the matricide.

Surrounded by these manifestations of the force of vengeance, Orestes clings to the goddess's image and cries out again for Athena to save him. Here Aeschylus subtly shifts from the strange world of the Furies towards the recognizable world of fifth-century Athens. Orestes calls on Athena in Libya, where Athens recently had sent a large expedition to support a local revolt against Persian rule, and he promises Argive loyalty in the future if she will help him, a reference to the treaty between Argos and Athens, concluded only a few years before the *Oresteia*'s premiere in 458.[14] As *Eumenides* unfolds, Aeschylus relates the dramatic situation more and more directly to the audience and the city where the play now takes place.

Although the specific Athenian references mean nothing to us, they do point the way for a production that wishes to explore and establish comparable equivalents for a contemporary audience.

Once again, the only response to Orestes' appeal to Athena comes from the Furies. Binding Orestes 'in the chains of their song' (306), they too move towards the recognizably contemporary, casting a spell on their victim that mimics the Athenian practice of depositing curse tablets before a trial, pre-emptory magic aimed at silencing an adversary when he comes to testify. The Furies modulate from speech to anapaests and then into lyric proper – three strophic pairs interspersed with mesodes in an intricate structure, followed by a final strophe and antistrophe with no mesodic interruption. The changing rhythms and interlocking patterns mark a progression from outrage to assertive clarity. The third mesode contains particularly violent dance-rhythms, reinforcing the way the Furies spring and bring down their human victims, but the cadences grow calmer in the closing stanzas, as the chorus claim that their rights were spun out by the Fates and are part of the make-up of the universe.

At last Athena appears, probably at orchestra level, since her strategy throughout is to insist on parity and work towards inclusion. Although surprised to see the Furies in her temple, she treats them and the suppliant Orestes with equal consideration. In a stichomythic dialogue, Athena questions the Furies and gains a major concession when they grant her authority to judge the issue by trial. She next questions Orestes, who responds with his longest speech in the play, recapitulating the action of *Agamemnon* and *Choephori*. The slower pace allows Athena and the audience to realize the full dilemma before them – how to choose between a suppliant who brings no harm to the city, and the Furies whose ancient offices must be honoured. If they leave without victory, the goddess predicts 'the poison in them will seep / over this land, an endless plague' (478–79). To resolve the crisis, Athena establishes a court to try the case, and she leaves to gather the jury, 'the best people of my city' (487).

In the stasimon that follows, the Furies consider the broader context, in which Orestes serves as one example. If Athena's court overturns the *lex talionis* and frees Orestes, then the human urge to commit crimes will run unchecked. The imperative verbs and second person pronouns (526–28, 538, 542) suggest that the Furies are addressing the audience, appealing to the Athenians' sense of justice. They present themselves as the guarantors of social order conceived in terms of fifth-century popular morality. Euripides uses a similar strategy in his *Bacchae*, produced some fifty years after the *Oresteia*, when the chorus of Bacchantes – who represent wild and foreign forces at the outset of the play – uphold the middle ground of conventional Athenian morality (*Ba.* 386–401). The change in *Bacchae* is temporary, for the horrific violence unleashed later in the play undermines any claim to moderation. The shift in *Eumenides*, however, serves a more integrative function, for the Furies embody complex forces that demand both fear and respect. They remind us of the fragility of the human family and the restraint needed to keep chaotic tendencies from bursting the bonds of community.

The merging of play and spectator gathers momentum when Athena returns with a herald, a trumpeter, and twelve Athenian jurors, a kind of surrogate audience brought on-stage. Athena directs the Herald to call the trial to order, and he uses the audience in the theatre as the crowd he must quiet. The trumpeter sounds his call, the only time in an extant tragedy that that instrument was heard. According to ancient sources, a trumpet blast signalled the start of dramatic performances at the City Dionysia, serving as the cue to begin a new play. By using the sound here to open the trial, Aeschylus links the dramatic action to the theatrical festival in which it is a part, suggesting that the trial represents a fresh start, a new way of dealing with the trilogy's intractable dilemmas.[15]

While Athena promises to teach the city her new ordinances, Apollo enters unexpectedly and interrupts her 'founder's speech'. Normally in Greek tragedy someone on-stage announces a new arrival, or the character identifies himself when he or she first appears. Aeschylus observes neither convention here, highlighting the anomaly of the god's entrance. Surprised by his appearance, Athena asks Apollo what business he has in the case and then postpones her speech on the future of the court, declaring the trial open.

Although the physical set-up is uncertain, an appropriate staging would leave Orestes in the centre of the orchestra, Apollo on one side, the Furies on the other, and Athena standing upstage-centre between the two voting urns brought on by the jurors, who take their seats near (or perhaps even in) the audience. This arrangement allows the prosecution and defence to avoid upstaging themselves when they make their arguments, and encourages the audience to view themselves as the extension of the jury come to judge the case. In rapid-fire stichomythia, the Furies cross-examine Orestes, who justifies the matricide as revenge for the death of his father and Clytemnestra's husband. Because the Furies privilege the murder of a mother, related by blood, over that of a husband, Orestes' plea makes little impact on them. Taking up Orestes' defence, Apollo points to his oracle commanding Orestes to avenge his father's murder, and then advances the specious argument that no blood tie exists between a mother and her offspring anyway. According to Apollo, the mother of a child is not really a parent at all, and therefore the Furies have no business pursuing Orestes.

This notorious speech (657–73) deserves comment, for it often is quoted as evidence of Aeschylean misogyny and proof that the *Oresteia* encodes and legitimizes the repression of women. The politics of gender in the trilogy (and the society that produced it) is more complex than often admitted, and the assumption that Apollo acts as the mouthpiece for the poet should be rejected as naïve and simplistic. Among other things, such an interpretation neglects the dramatic context in which the god appears in the trilogy. Recall the strong negative associations of Apollo in the Cassandra scene in

Agamemnon, and the god's dismissive arrogance towards the Furies at the opening of *Eumenides*. The contrast with Athena, who protects the suppliant Orestes without driving the Furies away, could not be more pronounced, and the goddess herself reinforces the difference by reminding Apollo that he may do what he likes in Delphi but not in Athens.

This background strongly colours the audience's response to Apollo's speech, where he argues in sophistic fashion that the father is the mother of the child. The god offers as proof the strange birth of Athena, who sprang fully formed from the head of Zeus. According to Apollo, women are not really parents, but merely the nurturers of the seed that the father generates. Therefore Orestes' murder of his mother is not as unnatural as it appears, because there is no real blood connection between a mother and her child.

Of course the position that women were not really parents was neither the popular nor the legal view in the fifth century. The Periclean citizenship law of 451/450 limited Athenian citizenship to individuals both of whose parents were Athenian. We also know that the marriage of *homometric* siblings was forbidden as incestuous, while a man could marry a sister by the same father as long as they had different mothers. Besides the counterintuitive nature of Apollo's argument, the most telling reason for the audience to reject it derives from their experience of the trilogy in the theatre. If a mother is not a parent, then why does Aeschylus highlight the image of the pregnant hare devoured with her unborn children, or use it as a means of foreshadowing the destruction of the Trojan War in *Agamemnon*, where the 'shield-bearing young of a wooden horse/ time their birth to the setting stars' (825–26)? If Apollo is right, then Orestes' murder of Clytemnestra raises no serious questions about blood ties, pollution, and matricide; the Furies have no business haunting Orestes, nor has Orestes any reason to feel haunted; and the dramatic heart of the trilogy – the *Choephori* – suffers cardiac arrest.

Apollo further compromises his position by offering a bribe to Athena and her city (667–73), something against which Athena specifically warns her people (693–95, 704). Aeschylus also suggests the shady side of Apollo by failing to give the god a clear exit when he slips off-stage at some point after the jury casts its vote. Apollo neither speaks nor is spoken to, an anomaly in the ancient theatre, as if his argument had little significance in a court where mortal agents make the difficult decisions. Viewed in the full dramatic context, Apollo's speech denying that women are parents of their own children radiates with something less than the pure white light of Aeschylean approval.

Athena follows Apollo's defence with a plea that her city continue to honour the homicide court down through the ages. Three times in her charter speech she addresses the Athenians of the future, as if to remind her citizens in the audience that the trial scene acts out their own, ongoing history. At her instruction, the jury rise from their seats to vote, moving to the urns (probably large and freestanding), placing a hand into each, but dropping a white pebble in only one.[16] In *Agamemnon* the conquering king describes the fall of Troy in similar terms:

> Hearing no pleas for justice
> the gods made their verdict clear.
> An urn of blood filled with votes
> for manslaughter and the death of Troy.
> At the other urn, the shadow
> of hope, her hand wavered ...
> now smoke holds that city.

(Ag. 814–19)

That imaginative vision of the gods' destruction in the first play is redeemed through the actual process of voting in the last. Human jurors decide the murder trial, moving between Apollo and the Furies who remain in their fixed positions on opposite sides of Orestes. As they file across the orchestra, the Athenian jury symbolize the freedom and responsibility of democratic justice.

After the last juror returns to his seat, Athena steps forward to speak, perhaps taking her stand between the two urns. She announces that, if the votes are equal, she will cast the tie-breaker for Orestes. Born without a mother, Athena champions the male principle in all things and so refuses to honour the death of a woman more than a man. It seems at first that the goddess simply parrots Apollo, but she complicates her position (and vote) by adding that her respect for the masculine does not extend to marriage.[17] The ballots are counted and found to be equal, an image of deadlock that – thanks to Athena's intervention – allows Orestes to go free. In a long speech of gratitude, Orestes expands his earlier vow to Athena upon arriving at her temple. He promises that Argos (the home city to which he returns) will join in a non-aggression pact with Athens, an alliance he will guarantee even from the grave. In *Choephori*, the tomb of Agamemnon was the locus for vengeance; the tomb of his son, Orestes, will be the source of a different kind of energy, uniting cities and honouring the role of Athens in establishing a new mode of justice.

As Orestes exits via the *eisodos*, Aeschylus' story of the house of Atreus draws to a close. But the play does not, for *Eumenides* continues another three hundred lines, almost a third of its length. The Furies and Athena remain in the orchestra, two female forces locked in the most important conflict of the trilogy. Their confrontation shapes up as a battle between two contending modes of expression – lyric and rhetoric – that proved so important in *Agamemnon*. Enraged at Athena's verdict, the Furies explode into lyric, threatening to release a plague on Athens and her people. Each of their lyric outbursts is matched by a speech from Athena, who tries to persuade them that their defeat is, in fact, a victory. After four such lyric eruptions from the chorus and spoken responses from the goddess (*Eum.* 778–891), the Furies finally agree to 'put the black wave of bitter anger to sleep' (832), leaving the dance and joining Athena in regular speech. Describing their conversion as 'falling under a spell' (900), the Furies accept the position of honour and authority in the city that Athena offers. The scene ends with the chorus lying on the orchestra floor and Athena standing over them, recounting the blessings they are to sing for their new home.

The metamorphosis of the chorus into Eumenides ('kindly spirits') reverses the dynamic at the start of the play, when the ghost of Clytemnestra roused the sleeping Furies to vengeance. Instead of waking them to anger, Athena calms their rage, moving among them in a mirror image of that earlier scene, enhanced by the fact that the same actor played both Athena and Clytemnestra. The visual parallels take us back to the *kommos* of *Choephori*, where the chorus, Orestes, and Electra wake the spirit of the dead Agamemnon to help them exact vengeance. But the seeds of these enactments of sleeping and waking are planted in *Agamemnon*, when the Watchman struggles to stay awake, afraid to close his eyes, and the chorus sing of Zeus leaving the memory of pain in place of sleep (*Ag.* 179–80). Clytemnestra imagines the victorious Greeks at Troy, sleeping with no guard on watch and unaware that the anger of the slaughtered may wake against them. The Herald describes the sea dozing in the heat of summer, and the terrors of sleeping beneath an enemy's wall. The chorus tell Cassandra to put her prophecies to sleep (*Ag.* 1247), and they protest after Agamemnon's cry that the murderers' hands are wide awake (*Ag.* 1357). From its poetic genesis in the first play, the actions of sleeping and waking culminate in the final transformation of the Furies who 'awaken' from their vengeful anger and rise from the orchestra floor to bless the city of Athens.

By persuading the Furies to remain, Athena redeems another pattern central to the trilogy, that of homecoming. The opening play dramatizes the return of Agamemnon and his fatal entrance into the palace. *Choephori* also features a homecoming, one not fatal to the returning party (Orestes) but to the rulers of the house. However, the son comes back from exile only to flee again, haunted by his crime of matricide. *Eumenides* continues the pattern, opening with the flight of the Pythia from her temple, followed by Orestes' departure for Athens, pursued by the chorus of Furies. After his acquittal, Orestes returns to his patrimony in Argos, while Athena persuades the Furies *not* to leave, but to make their home in Athens. When the chorus do exit from the orchestra at the end of the play, it is to take up residence in their new city as permanent honoured guests.

The crowning action of *Eumenides*, the Furies' 'departure to remain' fulfils the theatrical possibilities suggested earlier in the trilogy. After the spell of persuasion cast by Athena, the chorus wake to bless the city and her people, and the goddess joins their song (at least halfway), by moving into lyric anapaests. A similar metrical scheme operates after the murder of Agamemnon, when the chorus confront Clytemnestra in lyric and she responds in regular speech, a pattern that repeats until she finally shifts to anapaests. At the end of the trilogy, Athena moves into the mode of the chorus to reflect a basic harmony with them, although there are intriguing contrapuntal motifs. While the chorus abandon their retributive tones for the blessings of Eumenides, Athena sounds increasingly like the Furies earlier in the play, emphasizing the need for the old laws and respect for ties of blood.

A subsidiary chorus of women, the attendants of Athena's temple, enter to escort the Eumenides to their new homes. The women bring torches, sacrificial animals, and purple robes that the chorus put on, and they sing a final song in praise of the new residents of their city. The entire company including Athena parades out of the theatre, mirroring two great processions of Athens – the Panathenaic festival, which celebrated Athena as patron goddess of the city, and the City Dionysia, of which the performance of the *Oresteia* itself was a part.[18]

But we needn't look outside the play for the relevance of the costumes and visual detail. The chorus's dark-red robes re-introduce the colour of the tapestries on which Agamemnon walked. Once a symbol of bloodshed, the colour now celebrates the peaceful inclusion of the Furies into the city. The torch-led procession takes the audience back to the opening scene of the trilogy, where a lone watchman struggled to see the beacon flames under the panoply of stars. The fiery message of conquest broke out like the sun at dawn, only to rise over a scene of destruction. Now, the torches signal a different kind of victory, one in which the city truly wins, and the defeated party shares in the triumph and is essential to it.

The Furies exit from the theatre, not as a departure but as a homecoming, marked with blessings of fertility, health, prosperity, and hope. Transformed into spirits of birth and regeneration, the Eumenides reunite the animating forces of nature with life-producing marriage, a synthesis that seemed hopelessly shattered in *Agamemnon*. However, the promise of civil concord, of men and women finding their way together, remains only a promise. No secure solution could follow the acts of bloodshed in *Agamemnon* and *Choephori* without trivializing the plays and ignoring the complex network that made the murders necessary. Looking at the Furies, Athena proclaims 'from their terrible faces / I see great gain for my people' (990–91). Although their bodies are covered in robes of respectability, the frightening masks remain. The visual dialectic is essential to the *Oresteia*, where good news turns to defeat, homecoming leads to death, and the forces of vengeance and justice are inextricably linked. As the dramatic workings of the *Oresteia* make clear, Aeschylus' trilogy offers at best a provisional resolution, one that must be fought for again and again in the theatre and in the society that produces it.

Notes

1 Some editors assign the announcement of the Herald's arrival (489–500) to Clytemnestra, arguing that she reappears from the palace at this point. Because manuscripts do not indicate entrances and exits per se, and rarely name a new speaker, editors must make such determinations from the surrounding dialogue and their sense of the play. Does a production gain by having Clytemnestra present and silent during the Herald's speech, or by having her appear suddenly and seize control of the scene after he has finished? The latter seems the better choice; the claim that Clytemnestra must be on-stage to learn that her husband has returned reflects a theatrical realism foreign to Greek tragedy.

2 The question of Menelaus' whereabouts sets up the satyr-play *Proteus* that followed the end of trilogy, telling of Menelaus' shipwreck in Egypt. For possible reconstructions (based on the surviving one and a half lines, and a great deal of scholarly ingenuity), see Griffith, op. cit. (Chapter 5, n. 37), pp. 57–74.

3 We meet Apollo the rapist again in Euripides' *Ion*, discussed in Chapter 9.

4 The Watchman refers to Clytemnestra as 'like a man in thought' (*Ag.* 11).

5 R. Seaford, 'The Last Bath of Agamemnon', *Classical Quarterly* 34, 1984, pp. 247–54.

6 In *Titus Andronicus* Shakespeare draws heavily on Ovid's treatment of the same myth.

7 Assuming the *ekkyklêma* was used, the platform with the bodies of Agamemnon and Cassandra was rolled out, with Clytemnestra standing above them. If the device was not yet available (some think it was introduced later in the fifth century), then servants carried out the bodies and placed them on the ground, while Clytemnestra took up her position behind them. See Taplin, op. cit. 1977 (Chapter 3, n. 10), pp. 325–27, 442–43.

8 See A.F. Garvie, ed. and comm., *Aeschylus, Choephori*, Oxford, Clarendon Press, 1988, pp. 201–23, for an analysis of the stasimon and discussion of the poetic form called a priamel, where a series of examples are used as a foil for the point of particular interest.

9 The Greek word is 'parent', but the masculine article implies the father.

10 I assume Aeschylus used the *ekkyklêma*, as in *Agamemnon*. See above, note 7.

11 The staging of the opening section has generated endless controversy. The scenario adopted here avoids obvious problems: how to get 12 to 15 furies surrounding Orestes at the *omphalos* onto the *ekkyklêma*, and how to solve the subsequent problems that result if Orestes is back by the façade. Aeschylus would have taken advantage of the orchestra area to forge strong visual links with other key moments in the play and in the trilogy as a whole. See Rehm, op. cit. 1988 (Chapter 4, n. 14), pp. 290–301.

12 Greek tragedies include many *implied* stage directions – indications in the dialogue of actions, gestures, emotional states, costume and appearance, tone of voice, etc.

13 To have a stagehand carry on a separate piece of stage furniture to represent the cult-statue of Athena would disrupt an otherwise smooth transition from Delphi to Athens – the Furies exit at 231, Apollo leaves at 234, Orestes arrives at 235. Those who believe that Aeschylus used the *ekkyklêma* for the *omphalos* (above n. 10) and for Athena's cult-statue fail to consider the theatrically disastrous upstaging that would result. Everyone addressing Orestes would have to face away from the audience, a non-starter for masked actors in a large outdoor theatre. The Furies could not surround Orestes at the start of the play, or in their binding song, greatly reducing the impact of their dance.

14 A.J. Podlecki (ed.), *Aeschylus, Eumenides*, Warminster, Aris & Phillips, 1989, pp. 17–21, and A.H. Sommerstein (ed.), *Aeschylus, Eumenides*, Cambridge,

Cambridge University Press, 1989, pp. 25–32, offer clear and persuasive accounts.

15 The idea that a crowd of spectators, in addition to the jurors, came on-stage is dramatically redundant, given the presence of thousands of Athenians in the audience. On the trumpet sounding the start of each contest, see Pickard-Cambridge op. cit. 1988 (Chapter 2 n. 9), p. 67.

16 Sommerstein, op. cit., pp. 184–85, imagines smaller urns on a table, but these might not register in the spacious theatre of Dionysus. Also, a table would arrest the movement of the jurors when they came to vote; it would be more effective if the jurors stopped between two large, free-standing urns, voted, and then passed through, suggesting the democratic legal process in motion.

17 As a virgin goddess, Athena never subjects herself to sexual domination, a qualification that compromises her apparent subordination to the masculine point of view. R.P. Winnington-Ingram, 'Clytemnestra and the Vote of Athena' (org. 1949), in his *Studies in Aeschylus*, Cambridge, Cambridge University Press, 1983, pp. 124–31, and S. Goldhill, *Language, Sexuality, Narrative: The Oresteia*, Cambridge, Cambridge University Press, 1984, pp. 258–59, offer interesting analyses of Athena's complex character.

18 Athena's prominence indicates that the primary association was the Panathenaia, but resident aliens, referred to as 'metics' (as are the Furies at *Eum.* 1011), wore purple robes at both festivals.

7 Sophocles' *Oedipus Tyrannus*

Long considered the 'classic' Greek tragedy, Sophocles' *Oedipus Tyrannus* holds a special place in the history of Western theatre. In some respects the notoriety of the play helps it work on the contemporary stage, because most audiences know the outline of the story. Compare the lack of familiarity with Aeschylus' *Seven Against Thebes*, or Euripides' *Phoenician Women*, which also deal with the house of Laius. However, exposure to the Oedipus myth has its drawbacks as well, for much modern fascination with the play derives from Freud's use of the story as the paradigm for a psychoanalytic account of a young child's sexual desire and its successful resolution through gender identification with the same sex parent. There is no denying the importance of the Oedipal complex as a psychological and interpretive model, but it sheds little light on the play Sophocles wrote and, when applied to a production, leads the audience down a theatrical blind alley.

So, too, does the application of psychological realism to the play, epitomized by questions such as 'Once he heard the oracle, why did Oedipus marry anyone old enough to be his mother?' *Oedipus Tyrannus* is not a cautionary tale of crime and punishment, where the audience are meant to think that Oedipus and Jocasta should have known better. The issue held no dramatic interest for Sophocles, who never hints at it in the text.

A more insidious form of theatrical reductionism arises from the mistaken belief that the characters in the play are simply puppets in the hands of the gods. Although Oedipus is born to doom, everything he does on-stage he freely chooses. Even when he matches his life to the terrible fate prescribed for him, Oedipus continues to act autonomously, following the best information available. Thinking himself the son of Polybus and Merope, he strives to avoid the pollution of parricide and incest by fleeing Corinth; as political leader of Thebes, he struggles to rid his city of the plague by tracking down the killer of Laius; and, when the opportunity arises, he applies his energies relentlessly to untangle the riddle of his own identity.[1]

This last effort, the most compelling in the play, returns Oedipus to the riddle of the Sphinx on which his earlier fame rests. The answer to the question 'What creature goes on two, three, and four feet?' is man. Oedipus himself personifies the enigma, a tragic figure who is more than one (terrible) thing at a time. For all his lack of self-knowledge (in a deep sense), Oedipus manifests no moral failing or 'tragic flaw', a mistranslation of Aristotle's term *hamartia*. The word implies practical failure rather than moral deficiency, and its verbal form is used when an archer 'misses the mark' by not hitting the bull's-eye.[2] Oedipus errs through simple ignorance of the material facts of his birth. Out of that situation Sophocles crafts a play that is both keenly particular (Oedipus is like no man) and broadly universal. Do any of us know who we really are, what we are doing, the full consequence of our actions?

The audience's familiarity with the story operates to best advantage in the play's ubiquitous ironies. As Oedipus drives towards the truth, he unwittingly participates in a remarkable series of puns, nowhere more striking than on his own name. Meaning 'swollen-footed', a reference to the pierced ankles he suffered when exposed as a child, 'Oedipus' contains the Greek word *oida* meaning 'I know', literally, 'I have seen'. The prophet Teiresias taunts Oedipus with 'not knowing / your own, who live with you' (*OT* 337–38), prompting the retort 'but I came along, / the one who knows nothing, Oedipus, and stopped the Sphinx' (396–97). The verbal play, more prominent in the Greek than in most English translations, suggests that Oedipus' name signals his destiny. A man of intellect, whose rational gaze saw through the riddle of the Sphinx, gradually comes to realize how flawed his vision and understanding have been. His self-blinding adds further irony to his name, 'Oedipus – the one who has seen'. He stabs his eye-sockets (Greek *arthra*, *OT* 1270), the same word for ankle-joints (*arthra* 718) that were pierced as a child. As he stumbles forth in his blindness at the end of the play, Oedipus embodies the terrible ironies that have made up his life.

The audience in the theatre resemble the gods who foresee Oedipus' destination, but we are ignorant of its precise course. That is, we know in general terms where the play is going, and we watch galvanized as Oedipus leads himself (and us) to recognize what always has been present. Critics from Aristotle onwards have marvelled at the working of the plot, unwinding with the precision of a perfectly balanced watch spring. But formalist criteria cannot account for the fact that Oedipus' struggle draws us into the emotional turmoil of his situation, gradually undermining our god-like position as ironic observers until, by the end of the play, we are less sure of the future than Oedipus is.

That Oedipus will lead us through the drama is manifest in the opening scene. Before any dialogue takes place, a group of suppliants have gathered at the altar (a pre-set prop placed orchestra centre, as in Aeschylus' *Choephori* and *Eumenides*). They include small children, young adults ('the unmarried youth', 19–20), and older men (probably the chorus itself), the entire assembly led by an old Priest.[3] If the three age-groups represent the three ages of man from the riddle of the Sphinx, then the stage-picture points to Oedipus' past success as well as his present challenge, the task of saving the city once again. Emerging from the palace, Oedipus addresses the suppliants as 'children' (the first word in the play), establishing his paternal responsibilities as ruler and hinting at the underlying cause of the plague that ravages the city – the child who killed his own father, and then fathered children by his own mother.

The Priest describes the wasted earth of Thebes, the dying flocks, the cries of women after stillborn labour, the teeming house of death, the city like a storm-tossed ship swamped in a sea of blood. Looking to Oedipus for guidance, the Priest does not consider him 'equal to the gods' (31), but first among men, and Oedipus accepts the challenge, declaring to the crowd that 'no one /among you can make his sickness equal to my own' (60–61). Metaphors of 'making equal', of number, sum, and balance, recur throughout the play, ironically suggesting the equilibrium that Thebes has lost and the hidden truth that Oedipus is 'equal to himself' in horrifying ways. Slowly the numbers turn on him, until the notorious place where three roads meet will reveal him to be equal to his father's killer.

These figures of speech, and the verbal play on ones, twos, and threes, find their theatrical correlative in the organization of actors in successive scenes. Sophocles masterfully exploits symmetry and imbalance in each dramatic encounter, shifting from one-, two-, and three-actor scenes as the play drives towards its climax. At the outset, for example, Oedipus' entrance balances the Priest and suppliants who have gathered in silence, until the arrival of the third actor, playing Creon, tips the action in a new direction. Apparently symmetrical scenes, such as that between Oedipus and the prophet Teiresias, end in discord, and the play's masterfully written triangular scenes – each involving the protagonist and two other characters – eventually reveal Oedipus as the perpetrator of the very deeds he has tried to avoid. He stands alone as the paradoxical still-point where the imbalances of the play – the plague, the murder, the oracles, the three roads – all come together.

When the Priest begs him to help with the plague, Oedipus announces that he already has sent Creon to consult Apollo's oracle at Delphi. With perfect timing, Creon returns with the prophetic response, one of many juxtapositions that keep the play moving at speed. Learning that the plague arises from the unsolved murder of Laius, Oedipus vows to find the criminal and 'drive off the pollution / for no absent loved ones, but for my own sake, and self' (137–38). He means that he will make his rule more secure by finding the killer of the previous king, but the audience hears the unintended irony that twists Oedipus' proclamation back on himself.

In the lyric that follows, the chorus graphically evoke the plague that sweeps the city. At one point (190–94), they link the sickness to Ares, the god of war, not the normal Greek divinity associated with disease. Most scholars agree that Sophocles intended the epidemic ruining Thebes to call to mind the great plague that ravaged Athens in the early years of the Peloponnesian War (429, and again in 427–26), around the time of

Oedipus' first production.[4] The predominant dactylic metre, with several lines in full hexametre, also points to Apollo's oracle, because prophetic responses at Delphi took that metrical form. The horrific description of the plague and the desperate search for some remedy carried specific contemporary relevance for the audience.

After the *parodos*, Oedipus returns to the stage and vows to track down the killer of Laius 'as if this man were my father' (264). Standing alone before the chorus and the audience, Oedipus curses the murderer and brands him a pariah. The next time Oedipus stands as the sole actor on-stage follows his self-blinding, when he is caught in the curse that he now unknowingly pronounces on himself. The chorus advise Oedipus to consult Apollo's prophet Teiresias, only to find that Oedipus has sent for him already. As with Creon's return from Delphi, Teiresias arrives almost as soon as he is mentioned, adding to the feeling of irrepressible momentum. Holding a staff for support, the blind prophet makes his way into the orchestra led by a child, a memorable image that foreshadows Oedipus at the end of the play, clinging to his children and clutching a blind-man's stick.

Oedipus begs Teiresias to save the city that lies in supplication before him (326–27). Unlike the suppliant scene at the opening of the play, however, this appeal to community and civic responsibility falls on deaf ears. A far cry from the gentle English vicar that classicists once imagined, Teiresias comes across as uncompromising, shrill, unpleasant, inaccessible. He happens to know the truth and prefers not to share it. Teiresias' intransigence in the face of desperate public need strikes Oedipus as treasonous, and he suspects collusion between Apollo's prophet and Creon who brought word from Apollo's oracle. The accusation of treachery leads Teiresias to denounce Oedipus himself as the city's pollution, the very murderer he seeks to find. The dramatic pitch has risen so quickly, and the prophet's claim seems so outlandish, that Oedipus hears nothing but mockery and abuse, and the scene degenerates into invective and diatribe. Oedipus taunts Teiresias with blindness and failure to solve the riddle of the Sphinx. The prophet counters by predicting the blinding insight that awaits Oedipus, the revelations that will 'make you equal to your own children' (425).

The paired speeches give way to a short stichomythic exchange, allowing a real question to surface out of the virulent recriminations. Provoked by a comment about his background, Oedipus asks Teiresias about his parents, and again the prophet answers enigmatically: 'This day will give you birth and ruin' (438). Oedipus responds that his personal fate is of little consequence 'so long as I save the city' (443). Unmoved, Teiresias calls his young attendant to lead him off. The prophet's final speech comes somewhat unexpectedly, and it may well be that he delivers it out to the audience while Oedipus stands behind him, back by the palace door. The words ring out with terrible clarity, but not to the man for whom they are intended:

That man [Laius' murderer] is here, present:
a foreigner by name, but he will show himself
born a Theban, a great occasion, but it will not
make him happy. A blind man after seeing,
a beggar after being king, he will feel the ground
before him with a stick as he makes his way.
And he will show himself to be both
father and brother to his own children;
to the woman who bore him, both son and husband;
a fellow-sower with his father, and his killer.

(*OT* 451–60)

This daring summation of the truth, revealed so early in the play, reminds us that Sophocles has not written a detective story or murder mystery. Rather, his dramatic technique involves the projection of an overriding pattern, guaranteed by the oracle and grounded in the myth, but one that his protagonist cannot see. Acting on his best instincts, Oedipus must uncover the truth on his own, and the audience watches riveted as he discovers what has always been there.

After Teiresias and Oedipus exit, the chorus perform the first stasimon (463–511). They imagine the killer of Laius roaming the wilds, breaking through the timbers like a mountain bull hunted down by the prophetic voice from Delphi. For the audience, the description of the desperate fugitive applies to Oedipus, his plight all the more pitiable given that he plays the role of the hunter as well as the hunted. Twice (at line 483) the chorus call the charges levelled by Teiresias *deina*, an untranslatable word that occurs often in the play, meaning 'terrible', 'strange', 'clever', 'awful', and 'wonderful', in the sense of awe-inspiring, full of wonder, something that surpasses, or violates, the norm.[5] The chorus distinguish between the gods who remain beyond question and their human interpreters (such as Teiresias) who do not. They reconfirm the civic priorities with which the play began, refusing to believe that the prophet's accusations convict the man who once saved the city from the Sphinx.

Creon enters from an *eisodos* to answer the charges against him, charges that he, too, labels *deina* (513). He reminds the chorus that his life is bound up with theirs, that he considers nothing worse than to be called evil by the city he loves. Time and again Creon describes Oedipus as not thinking or seeing straight, the figure of speech suggesting the underlying twistings of the truth that prompted the charge of treason. Oedipus confirms Creon's assessment when he bursts onto the stage, accusing his brother-in-law of suborning the prophet and plotting against the throne. Creon mounts a strong defence in a speech that became a *locus classicus* for the disadvantages of holding power. He prefers the status and sway of second-in-command to the responsibilities of a ruler. Reasonable, cautious, sober, well intentioned, Creon reveals the gulf that separates him from Oedipus, who acts impulsively, driven by duty and circumstance to press beyond where a reasonable man would go.

Creon points out that Oedipus rules in Thebes with 'power equal to Jocasta' (Creon's sister and Oedipus' wife), and that he himself is 'equal with a third share' (579, 581), possessing the advantages of kingship without the worries. The image of Oedipus as first among three equals takes theatrical shape when Jocasta enters from the palace as the third party, diffusing the tension between the other two. She shames the men for 'stirring up / private quarrels when the country is diseased' (635–36). Although she frames her commands as questions, Jocasta effectively takes charge, telling her husband to go inside and ordering her brother home. The only female in the play, Jocasta restores temporary sanity to the proceedings, and the chorus help by initiating a *kommos* with Oedipus, persuading him to let Creon live. After her brother's departure, Jocasta joins the chorus and Oedipus in the *kommos* as she tries to find out what led to this altercation. The lyric ends with an image of order restored, the ship of state with Oedipus at the helm, guiding the city through the present storm.

Jocasta's forceful entrance, coupled with the *kommos* that follows, marks the key transition in the play. The first half of the lyric ushers Creon out of the action, and the second half recalls the situation facing the city and Oedipus' role in leading her to safety. When the lyric dies away, we are in a different dramatic world. Gone are the public pronouncements to the city, gone too the heated encounters between Oedipus and the men he suspects of treason. In their place, Sophocles presents an intimate, even confessional scene between husband and wife.

By disclosing a long-buried story from her past, Jocasta tries to calm Oedipus' fears of a conspiracy stemming from the Delphic oracle. Her husband Laius had received an oracle that he would die at the hand of his own son, but brigands slew him where the three roads meet. As for the child, mother and father pierced his ankles and left him to die on Mt Kithairon. Based on personal experience, Jocasta concludes that the gods can make the future clear, but their human intermediaries – prophets, oracles, and seers – should not be trusted.

One of several accounts of the murder of Laius in the play, Jocasta's story reveals a single detail so surprising to Oedipus that he fails to hear anything else she says. Deaf to her account of the exposed child, he zeros in on the fact that the murder took place where three roads meet. Oedipus begins to cross-examine Jocasta in stichomythia, driven to fit together the pieces of his past. The intensity is palpable, a kind of white heat that takes the play to a deeper dramatic level. Matching Jocasta's confessional tones, Oedipus then tells his wife of his youth in Corinth, the insult at a banquet that led him to wonder if he was a bastard, his trip to Delphi where he heard an oracle that he would kill his father and sleep with his mother, and – most critically for the moment – his fatal encounter with an old man at a place where three roads meet (798–813).

Oedipus relives that meeting in vivid detail, a masterful description of spare, stark moments that culminate in a brief flurry of violence: the party tries to drive him off the road, he protests, the old man strikes him like a beast, he kills them all. If that man was Laius, then Oedipus stands self-cursed and condemned to exile. In the face of so terrible a prospect, Oedipus fears something else even more. No matter what happens to him at Thebes, he vows never to return to Corinth where he would risk killing his father Polybus and marrying his mother Merope, as the oracle foretold. The implicit reminder to the audience that worse discoveries lie ahead for Oedipus confirms the truth of his observation: 'Someone who judged that these things came against me from a raw, savage god, / would he not speak in a straight line?' (828–29).

A slim hope survives that the shepherd who survived the attack will confirm the initial report that several brigands and not a single agent committed the murder. Oedipus sends for the old man: 'If he still says / that *they* killed him, the same number, then I didn't. / No, it's not possible for *one* to equal *many*' (843–45). Again, Oedipus finds himself in a numbers game where incommensurates come out equal. Jocasta insists that no matter what the shepherd says, the oracle did not come true, for Laius was not killed by his own son. In the cruel world of the play, she takes comfort from the fact that her baby, 'that poor, wretched thing' (855), died long before. Oedipus and Jocasta withdraw together into the palace, a wounded couple striving to make the best of their broken past. The audience see how ragged their hopes are, for their very union is the knotted curse they cannot escape.

Against this dramatic backdrop, the chorus dance out their sense of the sacred, the divine laws that order the world: '... No / mortal nature, no man / gave them birth, never will forgetting / lull them to sleep. / A god is great in them, does not grow old' (868–72). The chorus then consider how humans drive towards self-destructive excess, moving from the killer of Laius to any mortal who acts irreverently and 'touches untouchable things' (an echo of Aeschylus' *Agamemnon*). If these men prosper and their actions are honoured, the chorus wonder, 'Why should we perform the dance?' (896). Self-reflexive in the extreme, the question challenges the *raison d'être* of the tragic chorus, and asks the audience to examine their own presence in the theatre. If no divine force supports the world, if it is 'best to live at random as best one can' as Jocasta claims later (979), then why bother to participate in dramatic festivals and attend the theatre? Why gather to watch the story of Oedipus?

Before we dismiss the question as too much for any play to ask of itself, recall that fifth-century tragedy was no mere entertainment or celebration of individual expression, but rather a means of engaging the city in a process of self-questioning, self-correction, and self-definition. If someone literally gets away with murder, as the killer of Laius seems to have done, if one can toy with the world, profit from injustice, trample the sacred with impunity, then on what meaningful basis can the theatre – and the society that produces it – exist? Sophocles' answer is radically simple and humanly complex: tragedy can neither justify nor sustain itself if the world is as random as it appears to the chorus at this moment in the play. The order behind the apparent chaos may prove unpleasant and discomfiting; indeed, the play reveals a truth uncompromising and cruel. Nonetheless, it takes on meaning and significance in the very process by which a character such as Oedipus exposes it, and then finds the strength to stare it in the face.

For all its broad implications, the question arises from the dramatic situation, the chorus's considered response to the turmoil of the play. The crosscurrents batter them as well as the main characters, and in the final antistrophe they threaten to abandon Delphi and the other sacred shrines 'unless these things fit together, / pointing the way for all men' (901–02). Recalling Jocasta's view that oracles may go unheeded, the chorus fear that 'the things of the gods have passed away' (910). The physical anguish caused by the plague, vividly present in the prologue and *parodos*, has metamorphosed into a fundamental, existential fear. The nature of that fear emerges in the last line of each strophe and antistrophe, moving from faith to disbelief: 'A god is great in them [the sacred laws] and does not grow old' (872); 'I will never stop considering the god as my protector' (882); 'Why should we perform the dance?' (896); 'The things of the gods have passed away' (910). Until Oedipus is found out, the gods and their oracles *must* seem false. Until the murderer is discovered, the civic and religious institutions that make up the *polis* remain under attack.

The very moment the chorus fear that worship of the gods has left the city, Jocasta leaves the palace and makes her way to the altar of Apollo, bearing a suppliant's wand and offerings to the god. Jocasta's striking about-face underlines the deep insecurity that affects her and everyone in the play. The queen prays to Apollo to 'untie the knot and make us clean' (921), desperate for her husband who now fears he is Laius' murderer and remains haunted by the oracle that he will kill his father and sleep with his mother. As if answering her prayer, a messenger from Corinth arrives unexpectedly, bearing the news that Polybus has died and the Corinthians have proclaimed Oedipus their new king. In the face of this extraordinary news, Jocasta calls her husband from the palace, overjoyed that the part of the prophecy involving parricide now lies in the grave.

Normally a father's death would be met with grief and lamentation, but the world into which Oedipus and Jocasta have been thrown reverses such natural reactions, and they rejoice at the news. Learning that Oedipus still fears he will sleep with his mother, the Corinthian Messenger happily lifts that burden by informing him that Polybus and Merope were not his natural parents. Oedipus learns that he was found as a baby on Mt Kithairon and handed over to the very man now speaking, who pulled the pins out of his ankle-sockets and named him Oedipus, 'swollen foot'. The Corinthian received the baby from an old shepherd, the same man Oedipus sent for at the close of the previous scene, the sole surviving witness to Laius' murder.

Throughout the stichomythic exchange between the two men, Jocasta says nothing, but the audience knows that her worst nightmare is coming true. Sophocles exploits the potential of the three-handed scene with keen precision, as the spotlight turns inexorably back on the figure who had dropped out of the dialogue. Jocasta finds herself caught by the very workings of chance that she hoped would free her husband from divine prediction. The principle of living at random reveals the world (and the oracles) making brutal, all-too-coherent sense, and she begs Oedipus to stop: 'If you have any care for, any love of your own life, / don't track this down. My disease is enough' (1060–61). The plague that afflicts Thebes now finds its source in Jocasta, who sees the truth, and in Oedipus, who does not. He knows that he is on its trail, however, and no one will sidetrack him, not even his wife. Jocasta races into the palace keeping the horrible knowledge to herself, behaviour that strikes Oedipus as the vanity of a woman who fears she married beneath her. Ironically, Oedipus now adopts Jocasta's principle, valorizing the randomness of his own birth: 'I consider myself a child of Chance [or 'Fortune'] / ... / ... Such is my nature / and I would never wish to be otherwise' (1080, 1084–85).

Oedipus and the Corinthian Messenger remain on-stage during the lyric celebration of the chorus, who praise Mt Kithairon as the mother, nurse, and native land of Oedipus, a child of Fortune. Did some god beget him – Pan dallying on the slopes? Or Apollo lying with a nymph? Hermes? Or Dionysus cavorting in the meadows? Following Jocatsta's ominous departure, this outburst in honour of Oedipus and his mountain-mother seems shockingly out of place. The audience may compare this surge of lyric eroticism and fertility to the opening plague chorus that described the stillborn labours of the Theban women. In the previous stasimon the chorus had asked 'Why should we perform the dance?' Now they seem to answer the question with a dance for Mt Kithairon, and we realize that something is terribly wrong. Whatever 'chance' and 'fortune' are, whatever Mt Kithairon symbolizes, they do not represent the order on which the life and health of the city rest. The abrupt shift in choral mood underlines the instability at the heart of the play, as the dramatic pendulum swings back and forth with increasing violence.

Into the imaginary world of Mt Kithairon, this sexual playground for gods and mortals, enters a real dweller of the place, the mountain Shepherd whom Oedipus summoned earlier as a witness to Laius' murder. His arrival begins the final three-handed scene, drawing together the separate strands of Thebes, Corinth, and Kithairon. As before, Sophocles couples the speakers in different combinations. Oedipus interviews the Shepherd; the Messenger takes up the questioning, pressing the old man about the child he handed over years before; and Oedipus resumes the interrogation when the old Shepherd grows reticent, threatening him with torture if he does not divulge the truth. At this point, neither Oedipus nor the play can tolerate delay:

| *Shepherd*: | Ahhh! I am on the verge of it, of saying it—*deina*. |
| *Oedipus*: | And I on the verge of hearing it. It must be heard. |

(*OT* 1169–70)

The child was Laius' son, whom the Shepherd took from Jocasta with orders to kill it because of a fearful prophecy. Feeling pity, the Shepherd disobeyed and gave the baby to the Corinthian to raise far from Thebes. Now, years later, the same three parties stand together, reunited, confronting what that original meeting has led to.

With ruthless honesty, Sophocles shows that the noble intentions and simple instincts of men and women have wreaked havoc on Oedipus. The Shepherd responded with pity and saved the baby Oedipus; the Corinthian felt sympathy and took the infant to Corinth; the childless king Polybus and queen Merope adopted the orphan as their own, lovingly raising him as heir to the throne; the Corinthian as Messenger brought the good news that Oedipus had become king of Corinth, and then removed his fear regarding his Corinthian 'parents'. As for Oedipus, he strove to avoid the parricide and incest he learned of at Delphi, only to bring about the very predictions he tried so hard to escape.

The three parties who originally came together on the mountain years before now go their separate ways. The Shepherd and the Corinthian leave via the two *eisodoi*, and Oedipus returns to the palace. For the first and only time in the play, all three passages are used simultaneously, a powerful visual image of the various triads that have led Oedipus to self-knowledge, in particular the three roads that brought him, blindly, face to face with his destiny.

Left alone in the orchestra, where the three theatrical paths converge, the chorus sing a moving tribute to their king. They recount the mutability of all human fortune, where joy and accomplishment vanish like a dream, where success and honour turn to agony and shame. From general observations that mankind is 'numbered equal to nothing' (1188), the chorus turn to the paradigm of Oedipus himself, who surpassed all men, defeated the Sphinx, saved the city single-handedly. In the second strophe they consider that his fall 'into the marriage-bed / of both son and father' (1209–10) marks Oedipus' undying infamy. Time, the agent that brings all things to light, has judged Oedipus' and Jocasta's marriage no marriage at all, revealing breeder and child as one and the same. At the close of the stasimon, the chorus adopt a more personal mode. They wish they had never seen Oedipus, they mourn his fate as if lamenting the dead: 'You close my eyes in a sleep of death' (1222).

The images of light, darkness, revelation, and shuttered vision foreshadow the news that the Messenger brings from the palace. He tells his audience they have been spared much of the horror, because they did not have to view it with their own eyes. This incessant focus on eyesight and seeing does more than anticipate Oedipus' self-blinding. Via the chorus and the Messenger, Sophocles encourages the audience to adopt Oedipus' new mode of perception, to 'close our eyes and see', allowing the Messenger's words to create the dreadful events that have taken place off-stage and out of sight.

We hear first of Jocasta's suicide, and because it is her choice, it cannot be Oedipus'.[6] Having dismissed Jocasta's earlier pleas to stop his search, he now rejects her response to what that search has revealed. Instead of ending his life, Oedipus chooses to make literal what was figuratively true of him, and he blinds himself. The Messenger's vivid account of the self-blinding suggests that Oedipus begins the first in a series of confrontations with his past. We hear how he smashes through the bolted bedroom doors, cuts down Jocasta who has hung herself over the bed, and then repeats an action he had performed for so many years. He undresses his wife, taking out the pins that hold her dress, but now he uses them against himself:

> ... again and again, not just once
> he stabbed and spitted his eyes. Each time the gore
> from the sockets soaked down his cheeks,
> not spurting out drop by drop, but in a gush
> like a black cloud of hail, till the blood softened his face.
>
> (OT 1275–79)

With the specificity of a sexual nightmare, the final meeting of Oedipus and Jocasta, of son and mother, becomes a telling re-enactment of the physical relationship they enjoyed as man and wife. Gouging out his eyes beside Jocasta's corpse, Oedipus confronts the person with whom he has been most intimate and most ruinously unaware. With that encounter behind him, Oedipus is prepared to return to the stage and face the public.

The palace doors open to reveal the blind hero, and the chorus find the sight *deina* (1297), most *deina* (1298), a judgement they repeat later (1312, 1327) in the *kommos* they share with Oedipus. Out of the heightened intensity of the lyric, Oedipus expresses an almost Beckettian amazement that even a disembodied trace of his life remains: 'My voice, / where does it fly, / where does it carry me?' (1308–10). He knows the world around him only by sound: 'though all is shadow, I recognize your voice' (1326). Wishing he had died on Mt Kithairon, Oedipus curses the Theban Shepherd for saving his life, and the chorus take his comments to their logical conclusion. Leaving the lyric for regular speech, they state that Oedipus would have done better to kill himself rather than to live as a blind man.

Their pronouncement has an immediate effect, for Oedipus follows the chorus into iambic trimetres, delivering a speech that begins unequivocally: 'What I did was done for the best. / Don't instruct or advise me' (1369–70). He vehemently defends his action as the harsher and more fitting punishment. By living blind, Oedipus has cut himself off from all society, fulfilling the curse he pronounced on the killer of Laius earlier in the play. Blindness will free him from gazing upon the father he killed when they meet in the underworld, and he will never have to look his incestuous children in the eye.

The competing tensions within Oedipus give his speech exceptional power, and the actor playing the part must convey the desire both to close off the past and to remember it; to terminate experience and to prolong it; to give up and to fight on. The details carved in Oedipus' memory provide their own paradoxical rationale for continuing the struggle: 'Three roads and a hidden glen, / the oaks closing in where the three ways join – / you drank my father's blood, and my own, shed by / these hands of mine – do you still remember me?' (1398–1401). The last question reveals something of the depth of Oedipus' character, a man who earlier wanted to 'wall off the ears / and dam up the flowing stream of sound, / close it all off ... / and dwell outside all reminders of evil' (1386–90). Oedipus cannot help but remember, to the point of wondering whether the defining places in his life remember him.

Oedipus' need to resurrect and reiterate the past reflects what one critic has called a 'definitional fondling of the truth'.[7] By confronting his prior life so forcefully, Oedipus emerges from the chorus and takes the stage on his own. In the final step of his orchestrated return to full strength, he steels himself for a scene with another actor, facing again the drama of dialogue and conflict. As Creon enters, Oedipus recalls their earlier encounter when he wrongly accused his brother-in-law of plotting to seize power. The reversals of the play are such that Creon, who had no desire for the throne, now stands as the new ruler with Oedipus at his mercy.

Sophocles wastes no time in making the audience aware of how different their experience in the theatre would have been if the play were *Creon Tyrannus*. Although he himself brought word from the Delphic oracle declaring that the murderer of Laius should be exiled, Creon decides to send someone back to Delphi to make sure. Oedipus instinctively knows that his exile is best for the city (1449–58), and the audience agrees that the blind man's rightful place is the slopes of Mt Kithairon, a prophetic voice at home in the wilderness. But the new king insists on caution, refusing to allow the play the closure it has earned.

Although deprived of his political and physical powers, Oedipus asks the questions, makes the demands, and drives the action forward. Sophocles gives us a verbal *gestus* of the situation: 'And you [Creon], I command you – and I beg you ...' (1446). The shift mid-sentence reflects Oedipus' awareness of his weak position, and yet he admits to no diminished authority. Although we recognize moments of abject self-pity, the basic tone of Oedipus' speech remains one of natural dominance, so much so that Creon must remind the blind man of his true situation: 'Don't think you can rule always. / You have survived, but not your power', Creon's final words in the play (1522–23).

Nowhere is Oedipus' indomitable spirit more evident than in the meeting with his young daughters, whom he begs to hold in his arms one last time. That these previously unseen and unnamed children make the final entrance of the play is a daring piece of dramaturgy. The image of a polluted father embracing his daughters/half-sisters would have seemed monstrous and indecorous to the original audience, something to be kept out of sight. Perhaps for this very reason, their brief scene of reunion achieves a kind of redemption. For the first time since he came to self-knowledge, Oedipus does not focus on himself but on others. His kingdom has shrunk from the great city of Thebes – whom he addressed as his children in the opening line of the play – to two small, incestuous daughters. Yet he remains *their* leader, predicting the bitter future that awaits them and imploring Creon to help: 'Do not make them equal to my own evil' (1507). Earlier Oedipus claimed that the sight of his children would bring him no pleasure, that he wished he had died on Mt Kithairon, that he would like to cut off all sensory experience. Now he clings to his daughters and acknowledges in their embrace the tangled web of his own life:

> Children, if you were old enough, if you had understanding,
> the things I would tell you … But now, I pray only
> that you may live where occasion allows, that you find a life
> better than that of the father who brought you into it.
>
> (OT 1511–14)

Thinking back over the play's dénouement, we realize that Sophocles has recapitulated Oedipus' life, presenting a series of encounters between the protagonist and the major players in his past – Jocasta (as reported by the Messenger), the chorus (in the *kommos*), Creon (in their scene together), and his own daughters. Although there is no literal second meeting with Teiresias, Oedipus himself evokes the seer's presence. Groping for his daughters, he resembles the blind prophet led on and off the stage by a small child. Oedipus adopts a prophetic voice, prophesying what lies in store for his children and for himself: 'I know this much – no disease, / no natural cause will kill me, nothing. For I never / would have been saved from death except for something strange [*deina*] and terrible' (1455–57). And yet, for all their similarities, Oedipus remains essentially different from Teiresias. Oedipus vowed to save the city no matter what the personal cost, but when he and Thebes turned to Teiresias, the prophet turned away. Huddling with his wretched family in the orchestra, Oedipus again manifests the commitment to human society that separates him from the self-contained prophet of Apollo.

For the first three-quarters of the play the audience know what lies in store for Oedipus, and yet we marvel at the way the inevitable falls into place. The precise dovetailing of the plot, the collusion of fate and mortal choice, the dynamics of language and action draw us into the experience of the protagonist as he goes from ignorance to knowledge. After the blinding, however, Sophocles has Oedipus lead us in another direction, where the boundaries are not marked so clearly. With no riddle to solve, no blinding flash of insight to signal the climax, a humbled mortal struggles to live with the truth, and slowly recovers his strength of purpose and need for human contact. There is no softening here, no sentimental concessions or surrender to heart-warming fellow-feeling. The play ends with Creon separating Oedipus from his children and forcing him back into the palace.[8] And yet the audience has rediscovered the Oedipus who was always there before them – accursed, wilful, inquisitive, courageous, inspiring. Ultimately, Sophocles' play appeals to the theatrical imagination not because of Freud, or fate, or human folly, but because it presents a compelling and fully tragic drama, one in which man is not destroyed, but found.

Notes

1 For valuable discussions of this aspect of the play, see E.R. Dodds, 'On Misunderstanding the *Oedipus Rex*', *Greece and Rome*, 1966, vol. 13, pp. 37–49; G. Gellie, *Sophocles: A Reading*, Melbourne, Melbourne University Press, 1972, pp. 79–105, 201–08; R.P. Winnington-Ingram, *Sophocles: An Interpretation*, Cambridge, Cambridge University Press, 1980, pp. 150–204; B.M.W. Knox, 'Introduction' to R. Fagles (trans.), *Sophocles: The Three Theban Plays*, New York, Viking, 1982, pp. 131–53; and C. Segal, *Oedipus Tyrannus: Tragic Heroism and the Limits of Knowledge*, 2nd edn, Oxford and New York, Oxford University Press, 2001.

2 The chorus in Sophocles' *Ajax* (154–55) use the term in precisely this sense: 'Point your arrow at a noble spirit / and you won't miss'. Standard editions of Aristotle's *Poetics* correctly translate *hamartia* as 'error' or 'mistake', not 'tragic flaw'.

3 Many ideas have been proposed for the staging of the opening scene. An interesting alternative has *no* suppliants accompany the old Priest; the chorus would enter later in a traditional *parodos*. The Priest and Oedipus both use the theatre audience as the crowd who seek relief from the plague, linking the epidemic to the one in Athens near the time of the play's production (see following note). However, we know that the Priest orders at least some of the suppliants to leave with him (*OT* 142–44), indicating that he is not alone onstage. See P.D. Arnott, *Public and Performance in the Greek Theatre*, London, Routledge, 1989, pp. 21–22.

4 On this basis (Thucydides, 2.47–55), and the parodic references to the play in Aristophanes' comedies of 425 and 424, scholars date *Oedipus Tyrannus* between 429 and 425. For the play's relationship to the contemporary Athenian situation, see V. Ehrenberg, *Sophocles and Pericles*, Oxford, Blackwell, 1954.

5 Sophocles uses the same word *deina* to open his famous Ode to Man chorus in *Antigone* (332–33): 'There are many things *deina*, / but nothing more *deina* than man'.

6 So, too, the suicide of Lady Macbeth makes it dramatically impossible for her husband to do the same in *Macbeth*, and Svidrigailov's suicide in *Crime and Punishment* tells the reader that Raskolnikov must follow a different path.

7 Jones, op. cit. (Chapter 5, n. 9), p. 203, who finds that the process, 'far from being morbid, is the means to restoration, and almost an act of peace'.

8 The chorus' closing lines (1524–30) point to Oedipus as once having epitomized good fortune, but now providing the proof that no mortal can be sure of his happiness until his life is over. As with the closing 'choral tags' of other tragedies, the lines may be spurious.

8   Euripides' *Suppliant Women*

If there is something forlorn about an unperformed play, as Jonathan Miller puts it, then Euripides' *Suppliant Women* cries out with particular eloquence to be reclaimed by the living stage. Set at Eleusis, home of the famous Eleusinian Mysteries, the action juxtaposes the promise of spiritual rebirth with the basic human drive to bury the dead. Not one, but two choruses – the suppliant women of the title and a secondary group of their grandsons – occupy the stage before the action begins. Later in the play, a funeral cortège of corpses fills the orchestra, only to be followed by a *second* procession following the cremation, bearing the urns of ashes. In between these spectacles of the dead, a distraught wife enters unexpectedly high above the orchestra and leaps into the funeral pyre of her husband. With great theatrical daring, Euripides explores the compulsions to violence and the costs of war in this neglected masterpiece.

Suppliant Women opens with Aethra, the mother of the Athenian leader Theseus, making offerings before the temple of Demeter and Persephone at Eleusis. The rite she performs, the Proerosia, was intended to guarantee fertile sowing and bountiful harvests for Attica, sharing with the Mysteries a focus on rebirth and regeneration – the first agricultural, the second personal.[1] Aethra takes her position in a cancelled entry, surrounded by suppliant women from Argos, who 'bind her' to the altar with suppliant wands (*Supp.* 32). They have come to beg Athens to recover the corpses of their sons, the famous Seven against Thebes, who have been denied burial by the Thebans. In addition to the cluster of women around the altar, the Argive leader Adrastus lies prostrate before the entrance to the temple, and near him stands a secondary boys' chorus representing the sons of the Seven.

Throughout the long opening scene the Eleusinian setting would appear to dominate. With the temple façade behind her, Aethra addresses the altar (33–34, 291), calling it 'the holy hearth of the twin goddesses, Demeter and Kore' (another name for Persephone). And yet the chorus have come to consign corpses to the underworld, to 'bury the dead' (173–74), a phrase that rings out like a leitmotiv throughout the play. Their request sounds inappropriate at Eleusis, for the Mysteries celebrate the initiates' symbolic victory over death. And yet the word 'corpse' occurs as the first or last word of the trimetre line *eighteen times* in the play. The contrast with the Mysteries and the Proerosia is striking – a tragedy overwhelmed with the dead set against rituals of rebirth and regeneration.

The opening tableau distinguishes two groups – the women around the altar nearer to the audience, the old man and young boys back by the façade – and the dramatic focus alternates between them. The play begins with Aethra's prologue followed by the lyric of the Argive mothers, who have surrounded her in the orchestra (*Supp.* 1–86). Following Theseus' entrance, the action moves upstage for an exchange between the men, until Theseus finally rejects Adrastus' pleas and the Argive supplication (110–262). The women regain the initiative with the second lyric section and Aethra's long speech urging her son to change his mind (263–333). The scene closes with Theseus' acquiescence, his decision to seek Athenian support on the suppliant's behalf, and the freeing of his mother from the altar (334–64).

Euripides mirrors the alternation between male and female points of view in the stage movement, and it is helpful to work out the blocking. Theseus makes the first proper entrance in the play at line 87 via one of the *eisodoi*, setting the pattern for *all* subsequent entrances and exits (except Evadne and Athena who appear on the *theologeion*). The door in the temple façade is never used. After an introductory five lines to cover his arrival, Theseus notices his mother surrounded at the altar and continues downstage while speaking to her, stopping on the same axis to one side of the altar. At line 104, the groaning of Adrastus directs Theseus' (and the audience's) attention away from Aethra, and Theseus crosses upstage to the old man who lies near the façade. He persuades Adrastus to uncover his veiled head and stand (110–12), and from that position the two men play out a scene of some 150 lines.

Setting the Theseus–Adrastus exchange in the upstage area near the façade maintains the thematic blocking that separates men from women. At the outset of the play, a silent group of males (Adrastus and the boys' chorus) observes the activity of Aethra and the suppliant women; now a silent group of women watches as two male representatives make their respective cases regarding the supplication. Because the altar is sufficiently downstage of the backdrop, the audience views the Theseus–Adrastus dialogue through the 'filter' of the women. Although they take no part in the actual debate, Aethra and the Argive mothers occupy the visual foreground, an arrangement that suggests their ultimate importance in Theseus' decision. Most likely the chorus sit or kneel on the ground (indicated at 10, 44, 271–72), and Aethra sits at the altar as she did earlier (93). Because almost all of the spectators in the theatre of Dionysus sit above the orchestra, the group at the altar does not obstruct the scene that takes place behind them.

At the conclusion of their debate, Theseus rejects Adrastus' request that Athens help recover the corpses, and the dejected Argive leader instructs the chorus to leave their suppliant wands and depart. Instead of exiting, the women take their appeal directly to Theseus, first in iambics (263–70) and then in dactylic hexametres (271–85). They divide into two half-choruses, allowing the non-singing contingent of each section to perform the movements demanded by the text while the other group sings. Taking Theseus by his knees, chin, and hand, the women re-enact the supplication of the opening tableau but move it upstage, leaving Aethra alone at the altar for the first time. The stage-picture is as follows: the supplementary boys' chorus stand with Adrastus back at the façade; Theseus stands in the upstage part of the orchestra surrounded by the Argive women on their knees; and Aethra remains kneeling at the altar in the middle of the orchestra.

From this position, Theseus and Aethra are on the same vertical axis running from the orchestra altar back to the façade; this alignment allows Theseus suddenly 'to see' his mother again, having neither spoken nor referred to her since line 108. Instead of responding to the chorus' emotional appeal (they have literally fallen at his feet), Theseus addresses Aethra: 'Mother, why are you weeping, covering your eyes / with your robe?' (*Supp.* 286–87). In a striking visual echo, Aethra's veiling and collapse at the altar (286–90) recall the gesture and posture of Adrastus earlier (110–12), who also covered his head in shame and lay on the ground. Urging his mother to raise her head and throw off her veil, Theseus crosses down to her at the altar, reversing the upstage move he made to Adrastus when he encouraged the old man to stand and speak.

If this reconstructed blocking is correct, then Euripides has carefully brought together mother and son for what proves to be the crucial exchange of the opening section. By having the chorus leave the altar to bring their supplication to Theseus, Euripides frees the central acting area in the theatre, allowing the two Athenian principals to stand together 'downstage centre'. The stage is set for the colloquy that Aethra passed up earlier when she deferred to Adrastus, and mother and son are now the focus of the audience seated before them and the Argives (all together for the first time) standing behind them.

The gender differences that guided the initial blocking now give way to a grouping by bloodline and city, the two Athenians (mother and son) at the altar, the Argive suppliants (father, mothers, and grandsons) back at the façade. The change gives dramatic impetus to Aethra (299–300), who speaks out strongly for the good of her son and her city: Athens should stand up for the pan-Hellenic norm of burying the dead, and Theseus should adopt the Argive cause as his own. Aethra abandons the idea with which she ended her prologue – 'For women who are wise / it is right to act through men in all things' (40–41) – and she sets the stage for more powerful forms of female expression later in the play.

Aethra does more than change Theseus' mind, for her words provoke the first of several overtly political speeches in the play. Speaking to the theatre audience from his position at the centre of the orchestra (the Argive group stand well behind him), Theseus describes the democratic self-government of his city (349–56). Taking Adrastus with him, he will address the

Athenian Assembly and present the case for intervention on behalf of the Argives. Theseus then calls on the chorus to remove the suppliant wands that bind Aethra to the altar (359–60). Mother and son exit via one of the *eisodoi*, followed by Adrastus and the sons of the Seven, and the opening act of *Suppliant Women* comes to a close.

Euripides carefully works out the possibilities that follow from the cancelled entry at the start of the play, integrating the movement of principals, chorus, and secondary chorus to clarify important themes. As we have seen, these include the relationship between men and women in both private and public spheres, the difference in their access to public discourse and their manner of experiencing loss, the nature of civic responsibility *vis-à-vis* foreigners. Prompted by Aethra, Theseus converts the theatre of Dionysus into a political space for exploring democratic practice.

After the others exit for Athens, the chorus perform the first stasimon. They praise the Greek custom of burying the dead and pray that Theseus' help may lead to a future alliance between Athens and Argos. The women's short sixteen-line lyric – two strophes and antistrophes of only four lines each – provides a hiatus that spans an extraordinarily long interval. We are to understand that Theseus and the Argive males travel to Athens, meet with the Assembly, persuade the city to undertake the task, and make their way back. As discussed in previous chapters, Greek tragedy exploits a flexible notion of space and time, and here Euripides gives the impression that Athens and Eleusis have merged, that the political space of Theseus' Athens is co-extensive with the stage.

Adrastus and Theseus return with a plan to recover the corpses, but before Theseus can dispatch his emissary to Thebes, a Theban Herald arrives and assails their audacity. He rails at the arrogance of the original Argive expedition against his city, symbolized by Capaneus whom Zeus himself struck with lightning. The Herald then launches a debate on the relative merits of monarchy vs. democracy, referring to the Athenian system as mob rule. In spite of his abrasive tone, the Herald mounts a telling critique of democracy-in-action, stressing the influence that self-serving demagogues exert on the majority. The common man does not have time to inform himself on issues, and so he gives his vote to the most persuasive speaker (412–25). Democracy only appears to be the rule of the people; more accurately, it is power wielded by a few who manipulate the many through clever rhetoric.[2]

The Herald's most compelling indictment involves the patriotic fervour aroused in a citizen body that blinds it to the costs of war:

> When a people vote to make war,
> no one considers that he himself might die
> but turns that harsh fate on to another.
> But if death was *there to behold* when the votes were cast,
> war-crazed Greece would never destroy itself.
>
> (*Supp.* 481–85, my italics)[3]

Theseus counters by praising the advantages of democratic rule. He singles out the annual rotation of officers, a distinctive feature of Athenian political practice (406–07), and he echoes the phrase that opened each meeting of the Assembly: 'Who here has a good proposal / and wants to put it before the city?' (438–39). Following his mother's lead, Theseus emphasizes the humanitarian aspects of burying the dead, one of the unwritten laws that characterize a civilized people. Following their verbal *agôn*, the scene ends with a bitter stichomythic exchange, and the Herald departs for Thebes to prepare for war. Confident that the gods will side with Athens, Theseus exits to make ready his attack, pointedly leaving Adrastus behind. The upcoming battle has nothing to do with the hatred between Argos and Thebes, arising from a war that even Adrastus has admitted his city never should have started (156–62). Athens fights only to recover the bodies and uphold the principle of burying the dead.

As they did earlier in their appeal to Theseus, the chorus divide into two groups, but this time they engage in an anxious dialogue with one another. Having lost sons in a foreign adventure, and wary of bloodshed to come, the mothers hope that a 'compromise through discussion' (602) might eventuate, leaving Thebes and Athens at peace. However, their anguish over the upcoming battle soon gives way to their demand for their sons' burial: 'Justice calls for Justice, and blood for blood' (614). Caught between the wish to avoid conflict and the appeal of battle as a necessary 'equalizer', the women are both the victims of war and one of the reasons it breaks out again.

As in the previous stasimon, the lyric covers an enormous passage of dramatic time, the Athenian invasion of Thebes and the battle to recover the bodies. A Messenger arrives with news of Athens' victory, and he emphasizes Theseus' remarkable self-control at the height of his triumph. With the Theban enemy defeated and the city open to plunder, Theseus refuses to press his advantage, proclaiming that 'he did not come / to sack the town, but only to take back the dead' (724–25). The Messenger praise of Theseus' moderation had particular relevance to the war-torn Athenians in 423 BC, when the play premiered:

> Best to pick such a military leader [*stratêgos*]
> who provides in times of trouble the surest defence,
> for he hates the popular tendency towards violent overreaching
>   when someone does well,
> who then tries to climb to the top of the ladder (*klimakôn*)
> and so destroys the prosperity he had at his command.
>
> (*Supp.* 726–30)

The term *stratêgos* is the same one used for the annually elected military leaders of Athens, discussed in Chapter 2. The Messenger's image of climbing too high brings to mind Capaneus, one of the Argive Seven, who tried to scale the walls of Thebes by ladder (*klimakôn*) and was blasted by the lightning bolt of Zeus (496–99).[4] Capaneus' rise and fall epitomizes the entire Argive expedition, whose arrogant violence called down the punishment of the gods. On hearing of Theseus' victory, Adrastus admits again the foolhardiness of the original invasion, for Thebes had offered a peaceful and fair resolution, which the Argives rejected (739–41). Adrastus sees his own city's error replicated by the Thebans, who refused to give back the bodies and 'fell victim to their own violent overreaching' (743). He echoes the judgement of the Argive women that cities should strive to resolve disputes by words, and not by bloodshed (744–49).

Theseus emerges as a model of control in warfare, unafraid of combat but committed to the specific goals for which he fights. His behaviour following the victory proves no less exemplary. The Messenger describes how, after recovering the bodies, Theseus initiated funeral rites. He washed the corpses with his own hands and readied the funeral biers, rituals normally reserved for the mothers of the dead (762–68). Adrastus is incredulous that Theseus – a man, a general, a political leader – would demean himself by performing these rites for rotting corpses long exposed to the elements. Even slaves, Adrastus adds, would approach this task 'with abhorrence' (762), 'an awful business, full of shame' (767). We recall that earlier Theseus took his mother Aethra's advice on a question of policy, reversing his initial decision to deny the Argives help in recovering their dead (293–341). Now we hear of his willingness to assume a female's role, caring for the bodies as if they were his own kin. We witness further evidence of Theseus' humility when he returns to the stage not as a triumphant general, but as part of a procession bearing the corpses for cremation and burial.

As the pallbearers carry the bodies of the Seven into the theatre, the longest funeral sequence in Greek tragedy begins (798–954). The orchestra fills with lamentation, featuring a *kommos* shared by Adrastus and the mothers. Theseus then enjoins Adrastus to deliver a funeral oration for the instruction of 'the young men of the city' (843), modelled on the great funeral address (*epitaphios logos*) delivered annually in Athens to honour soldiers who fell in battle that year and received burial at public expense. The theatre audience would have listened attentively because the scene onstage echoed the public discourse of their city, most famously in Pericles' funeral oration of 431/30.[5]

We can imagine their consternation when Adrastus gainsays the lessons he has learned: the Argive expedition was unnecessary and vainglorious; the deaths could have been avoided; the gods themselves punished the Seven for excessive pride. In a blatant case of 'mythifying' the past, Adrastus re-creates Capaneus as a moderate aristocrat. Gone is the violent man struck down by Zeus' lightning, the epitome of violent overreaching (495–99). In his place, Adrastus describes a hero who 'was no prouder than a poor man' (862–63), one for whom 'the mean was enough' (866). To speak of the blasphemous Capaneus as affable and moderate defies belief, and Adrastus compounds his double-speak with an excursus on education. He views teaching as a process of providing models of behaviour for the young, even if 'they don't fully understand them. / Whatever someone learns that way will stay with them / until they grow old. So teach your children well' (915–17). Adrastus' funeral oration turns into a call for the fifth-century equivalent of brain-washing, and the audience are not fooled. As a modern critic asks, 'Could an Athenian citizen really take seriously the advice to bring up his children to be a Capaneus?'[6]

By staging a semblance of the Athenian funeral oration, Euripides probes its potential for misuse. Although Theseus says nothing to counter Adrastus' rewriting of history, the mothers of the dead draw no comfort from it, responding to his platitudes with expressions of grief and despair (918–24). Theseus and Adrastus lead the bodies out of the orchestra for cremation, and the women sing a formally balanced ode of mourning, with strophe, antistrophe, and epode (955–89). The play seems to have reached a still point, and perhaps a time for reflection.

Suddenly the chorus spot Evadne, the wife of Capaneus, climbing the rocks above the shrine. From her commanding position on high, she sings an emotionally charged monody, and then, after a brief exchange with her father, who has come from Argos to dissuade her, she leaps to her death on her husband's funeral pyre. Nothing like this ever took place in fifth-century tragedy before or after *Suppliant Women*, and we would be hard pressed to find a more theatrically daring moment in the history of the stage. The opera heroine Tosca plummets to her death when she discovers that Cavadarossi has been executed, but Puccini doesn't introduce her for the first time only moments before.

With shocking immediacy Evadne interrupts the ritual mourning for the Argive Seven, determined to perform her own ceremony of grief. She mounts the *theologeion* on the roof of the skene so that all can see.[7] Wearing her wedding dress, she prepares for a marriage to the dead, singing a monody that conflates erotic and funereal motifs: 'I will mingle in love my body with my husband's, / melting in the radiant flames, / my skin touching his skin' (1019–21). When her father Iphis arrives to stop her, Evadne rejects his pleas, preferring to lie with her husband in death.

Significant for the play's Eleusinian setting, Evadne frames her suicide in terms of the Demeter–Persephone myth, for she hopes to arrive at 'the marriage chamber of Persephone' (1022). Evadne re-enacts that mythic marriage to Hades as if in a parabolic mirror. In place of Persephone's ascent into the light and reunion with her mother, Evadne leaps down into the fire to merge wholly and indissolubly with her dead husband. Leaving her father heart-broken. Evadne's Eleusinian journey denies the hope of recovery and rebirth intrinsic to the myth of Demeter and her daughter, the heart of the Eleusinian Mysteries.

Why does Euripides include this *coup de théâtre* at this point in the play? As we noted above, *Suppliant Women* is heavy-laden with death. The unburied corpses of the Argive Seven dominate the play, and their funeral rites are supplicated for, debated about, fought over, and finally achieved. With Evadne's self-immolation, the waste of death becomes palpable – someone living stands before our eyes, and suddenly that someone is gone. Death is, as it were, *animated*, revealing itself as an action, as dying and kill-ing, rather than something mourned as a fact (the lament over dead bodies) or reported as a distant event (the Messenger's account of Theseus' victory at Thebes). The progression from death to dying proves particularly disturb-ing when the victim is a non-combatant, one who freely chooses to leave a world already awash with militarized bloodshed.

Evadne does not consider her suicide a private act of grief. When she announces that she will leap to her death, her father Iphis begs her not to 'say such things before a crowd' (1066). Evadne responds that she wants 'all the Argives to learn' (1067). No less than Adrastus' funeral oration, her dying represents a public act, and Euripides asks us to compare the lessons she teaches with those offered by the Argive leader. Recall that Adrastus praised instilling the values of patriotic militarism from an early age, so that the young would hold onto them until they grew old. Perhaps this accounts for Euripides' decision to stage Evadne's suicide – only something excessive and shocking can shake an audience free from the education towards war they have received from youth. With inspired theatricality, Evadne sets off a dramatic explosion that brings home to the audience what the other char-acters on-stage only talk about, and then forget.

Broken by his daughter's suicide, Iphis leaves the orchestra hoping that his own death will come soon. 'Old age', he muses, 'should make way for the young' (1113). It does so literally, for the secondary chorus of children, bearing urns holding the ashes of their fathers, enter as the old man leaves. Euripides has primed us to attend to the lessons learned by the younger generation, and what we hear is ominous. Joining the grieving women's chorus in a *kommos*, the boys sing of their orphaned status (1134). One son expresses the hope that as 'shield bearer' he will avenge his father's death (1142–44); another prays that the gods help him secure 'justice for my father' (1145–46); a third imagines himself leading a new Argive assault on Thebes (1149–51). Their cries for vengeance produce a troubled response from the chorus, the boys' grandmothers: 'And this evil still does not sleep. / Terrible things! Too much lamentation, / too much grief comes at me' (1146–48). Holding the ashes of their fathers who fell in an unnecessary and avoidable battle, the sons resolutely sow the seeds of future conflict.

At this point we should consider the special relevance to the play of one of the pre-performance ceremonies at the City Dionysia, outlined in Chapter 2. Orphaned sons of Athenians who had fallen in battle were reared at pub-lic expense, and when they reached the age of 18 the young men marched through the orchestra dressed in hoplite armour provided by the city, a gift with which they were expected to defend their benefactress.[8] In the closing section of the play, Euripides masterfully evokes this ceremony. Orphaned boys process through the orchestra holding the cremated remains of their fathers, men who had just received a funeral oration, much as the fathers of the Athenian orphans would have done at their public burial in Athens. The Argive youths long to bear a shield and avenge their war-slain fathers, just as their Athenian counterparts bore the city's gift of armour (including a hoplite shield) in honour of their forbears.

The unexpected arrival of Athena as *dea ex machina* on the skene-roof adds fuel to the fire. Insisting on formalizing a defensive alliance between her city and Argos (*Supp.* 1183–1212), the goddess gives her blessing to a second Argive assault on Thebes and guarantees its success (1213–26). She exhorts the orphans to lead a 'bronze-clad' army against Thebes when their 'beards begin to shadow' (1219–20), again recalling the Athenian orphans who, having come of age, also come into arms. As we have seen, contemporary references run through the play, involving not only Athenian political practices, but also the devastating Peloponnesian war with Sparta and her allies. Theseus' battle with Thebes over the corpses probably reflects the refusal of the Thebans to relinquish the Athenian dead after a military campaign in November of 424.[9] The Argive–Athenian defensive alliance that Athena demands anticipates the actual agreement achieved in 420, following the Peace of Nicias that ended the first part of the Peloponnesian War in 421.

If the play were first produced in 423, as many scholars believe, then the original performance took place only *a few days before* the Athenian Assembly met to vote on a year-long armistice with Sparta, an early effort to halt the devastating war. It is likely that the Peloponnesian delegates had arrived for discussion with the Council before the City Dionysia began and actually were in attendance at the theatre, along with citizens of Athens who would vote on the agreement.[10] They saw dramatized before them two broad, but clearly opposed, scenarios for their city: to fight – but only as a last resort – in defence of laws and customs that were pan-Hellenic in nature, as Theseus does; or to surrender to the instincts of violence and vengeance, a temptation to which the orphans succumb and Athena encourages.

I find it hard to believe (although many critics do) that Athena speaks *for* Euripides when she encourages a fresh outbreak of military violence.[11] Recall the Theban Herald's observation that 'if death was *there to behold* when the votes were cast, / war-crazed Greece would never destroy itself' (484–85). Viewing the end of the play with those words in mind, we appreciate the dramatic measures Euripides has taken to present us with images of death 'there to behold'. In the array of corpses that dominate the second half of the play, and, above all, in the suicide of Evadne, Euripides makes every effort to preclude a failure of imagination on the part of his audience, keeping war-generated death forcefully, and shockingly, before us.

With the return of the sons of the dead bearing the urns of ashes, the terrible cycle of violence begins anew. The ripples spread out to the contemporary world when the Theban orphans, eager to arm for war, begin to resemble their Athenian counterparts, outfitted as hoplites and paraded in the orchestra before the performance. Gone are the offerings to Demeter for bountiful harvest that began the play, as well as the wise mother, Aethra, who made them. Gone, too, is the hope of return from death and the under-world symbolized by the figure of Persephone, and institutionalized by the Mysteries in her honour. In their place we have a gathering of ashes, an orchestra full of mourners and future warriors, the patron goddess of the city in her characteristic armour, and, still present as an after-image, the stark and forbidding memory of a wife leaping to join her husband – a the-atrical world, in short, firmly wedded to war and death. Whether that will also be the world of the audience is, I think, the question of the play.

Notes

1 On the Proerosia, see Parker op. cit. (Chapter 2, n. 16), pp. 195–203, who also explores the ritual's connection with marriage, of relevance to *Suppliant Women*.

2 Euripides returns to this issue in *Orestes* (902–30, 944–45). Aristophanes exploits its comic possibilities in *Acharnians* (esp. 631–35) and *Wasps* (698–705, 719–21), and in his running attack on Cleon in *Knights* (41–70, 486–91, 710–809, 1111–20). See also L.B. Carter, *The Quiet Athenian*, Oxford, Clarendon Press, 1986, pp. 82–98; and R.K. Sinclair, *Democracy and Participation in Athens*, Cambridge, Cambridge University Press, 1988, pp. 203–08. In his account of Athenian democracy, Ober op. cit. (Chapter 1, n. 4), pp. 112–18, admits the elite status of public speakers in the Assembly.

3 A not uncommon ploy in Greek poetry, difficult truths come out of the mouth of an unsympathetic character, and later events vindicate them. In the *Iliad*, the hunchback Thersites' verbal assault on Agamemnon earns him a thrashing (*Il.* 2.225–77), but his words ring true when Achilles repeats them in the embassy scene (9.315–37, 369–77).

4 The event is referred to obliquely elsewhere in the play (639, 860–61, 934, 1010–11), described in the *parodos* of *Antigone* (127–33), and developed in greater detail in Euripides' *Phoenician Women* (1172–86). A ladder identifies Capaneus in the art of the period; the Messenger's reference to the proud man on his ladder would have brought Capaneus immediately to the audience's mind.

5 Thucydides 2.34–47. See the classic study by F. Jacoby, '*Patrios Nomos*', *Journal of Hellenic Studies* 64, 1944, pp. 37–66; also W.K Pritchett, *The Greek State at War*, vol. 4, Berkeley, University of California Press, 1985, pp. 94–124, 249–50; and N. Loraux, *The Invention of Athens*, A. Sheridan (transl.), Cambridge, MA, Harvard University Press, 1986, pp. 28–30, 56–72.

6 J.W. Fitton, 'The *Suppliant Women* and the *Herakleidai* of Euripides', *Hermes* 89, 1961, pp. 438–39.

7 Some commentators think that Evadne climbed up a special structure (rising behind the temple façade) painted to appear like the crags of Eleusis. Such a construction would eliminate the surprise of Evadne's appearance, because the audience would expect to see it used. Evadne could appear on the *theologeion*, as Athena does as the *dea ex machina* at the end of the play, providing a mean-ingful contrast between the overwrought young woman dressed for her wedding and the militaristic goddess with her traditional helmet and shield. However, the possibility that Evadne used the seating banks or hillside – perhaps leaping off the eastern side wall that supported the slope where the audience sat after

the construction of the Odeion of Pericles – would allow the actor to be seen climbing ever higher as the chorus indicate she does (*Supp.* 989), impossible on the *theologeion*. Using a non-traditional area seems a fitting scenario for an unprecedented scene.

8 For a summary of what we know about public support for war orphans, see R.S. Stroud, 'Theozotides and the Athenian Orphans', *Hesperia* 40, 1971, pp. 288–93.

9 For the play's date, see C. Collard, ed. and comm., *Euripides, Supplices*, vol. 1, Groningen, Bouma's Boekhuis, 1975, pp. 8–14. V. Di Benedetto, *Euripide: teatro e societá*, Torino, G. Einaudi, 1971, pp. 158–62, discusses the political events surrounding the production; see also G.M.A. Grube, *The Drama of Euripides*, London, Methuen, 1941, p. 242; D.J. Conacher, 'Religious and Ethical Attitudes in Euripides' *Suppliants*', *Transactions of the American Philological Association* 87, 1956, p. 26; R.B. Gamble, 'Euripides' *Suppliant Women*', *Hermes* 98, 1970, pp. 404–05.

10 See Thucydides 4.117.1–120.1 for the Assembly vote; also A.W. Gomme, *A Historical Commentary on Thucydides*, vol. 3, Oxford, Clarendon Press, 1956, p. 603.

11 For a valuable discussion of this and many other aspects of the play, see I.C. Storey, *Euripides: 'Suppliant Women'*, London, Duckworth, 2008.

9 Euripides' *Ion*

Ion is hardly a 'tragedy' in the popular sense of the word. The play treats of recovery and reunion, no one is killed, a foundling finds his real mother, a foreigner learns he was born to the throne. Critics often label *Ion* (along with Euripides' *Helen* and *Iphigenia among the Taurians*) a 'romance', and the story seems like a fairy-tale version of Sophocles' *Oedipus Tyrannus*.[1] In place of the perfectly hinged turning point of Sophocles' tragedy, however, *Ion* requires *three* dramatic reversals to keep the play on track – a dove who drinks the poison meant for Ion, the Priestess who appears in the nick of time to stop him from killing his mother Creusa, and Athena who arrives as a *dea ex machina* to halt future disclosures at the end. The energy and invention required to achieve the 'happy ending' serve to complicate our response to it, as do the experiences of the mother and child who are tossed in the play's shifting currents.

Ion himself suggests the problem with a romantic or comic approach to the play when he rejects the apparent advantages of leaving Delphi for Athens: 'Things seen close up are not the same / seen far away' (*Ion* 585–86). His simple insight mirrors that of the audience, whose perspective on the dramatic events alters as the play draws them into sympathy with the characters caught up in unpredictable and radical change. By juxtaposing humorous with deadly elements, Euripides keeps the tone of the play ambiguous and unsettling, forcing the audience to look beyond the façade of the ending arranged by Apollo into the darker recesses of what that ending might wish to hide.

The play opens with a prologue delivered by Hermes, the 'lackey of the gods' (*Ion* 4), who provides the background to the story. The childless royal couple, Creusa and her foreign born husband Xuthus, have come to Delphi for an oracle. Unknown to Xuthus, Creusa was raped in her youth by the god Apollo, bore his child in secret, and exposed the newborn in the cave below the Acropolis where the god had violated her. Apollo arranged for Hermes to bring the baby to Delphi where he has grown up and works as a temple attendant, ignorant of his future as founder of the Ionian race. Hermes' review of these events is filled with proper names and places (well over 40 in 80 lines), and the god concludes his monologue by formally assigning the name 'Ion' to the young man who follows him on-stage: 'First of all the gods, I / name Apollo's son Ion, his name and destiny' (*Ion* 80–81).

Concern with naming and identity proves to be a driving force in the play, propelling the action towards clarification and disclosure much as in *Oedipus Tyrannns*. However, in Sophocles' tragedy the truth exists outside the action, an unseen but omnipresent order that Oedipus finally uncovers when he finds the murderer of Laius. In *Ion*, the wilful covering-up of the truth by Apollo, the god responsible for the confusions of the play, never admits full disclosure, leaving the characters – and the audience – to wonder how stable the underlying order is.

As Apollo's mouthpiece, Hermes outlines the action to come, but his dramatic map for the audience proves faulty: 'Xuthus will enter the shrine, the god will give him / the boy, his own child, saying he is / the king's true son. His mother will not know he is really hers / until they get home to Athens' (69–73). The god promises a neat scenario, but the action of the play proves far less tidy. Terrible crimes are countenanced and nearly committed, and events refuse to adhere to the hermetic plot arranged in advance, in no small part because the instruments of Apollo's plans are human beings. The very points at which they fail to operate as expected provide the audience with the moments of greatest emotional engagement. In particular, the qualitative difference between the god's eye view of key events in Creusa's past and the way she herself remembers and relives them on-stage helps ensure that we experience *Ion* as a tragedy.

Consider Hermes' first mention of Apollo's rape of Creusa: 'The daughter of Erechtheus the bright-god Apollo yoked in marriage / by force.' (*Ion* 10–11). The line-end suggests a proper wedding (the phrase 'yoked in marriage' was an Athenian commonplace), but the new line highlights it violent nature. A seemingly formal union turns, with the line-break, into rape. Similarly, a pattern of conflicting images reveals more uncertainty and ambiguity in Apollo's master plan than Hermes admits. A shimmering brightness dominates the language of the prologue (indeed the whole play), and Apollo, the sun god, is named nine times, frequently by his epithet 'Phoebus' ('bright one'). Working against the language of light and clarity, however, are images of darkness and secrecy. Apollo assaulted Creusa in a dark cave under the Acropolis, where she returned to abandon her baby, all kept secret from her family (11–17). The priestess who discovers the baby at Delphi assumes it was the 'secret birth' (45) of some local girl, and Apollo works overtime to keep it 'hidden' (73). At the end of the prologue, the verbal tension between brightness and clarity on the one hand and darkness and secrecy on the other generates its corresponding stage action. As Ion enters to 'make the temple steps shine / with his laurel broom' (79–80), Hermes sneaks off to hide in the laurel bushes and watch the story unfold.[2]

Ion brings with him a lyrical purity and innocence as lovely as it is unaware, manifest in his opening description of the sunrise over Parnassus:

Dawn's shimmering chariot bends over the earth,
lifting the blazing sun through the fiery air,
and routing the remnant stars
back into holy night.
The un-walked peaks of Parnassus
gleam with light, accepting for us
this day's gift of the sun.
The smoke of desert myrrh rises
to the rooftop of the bright god's shrine.

(*Ion* 82–90)

Everything appears luminous to Ion, even the expressive form he adopts when he shifts from anapaests to a lyric monody. He sings a strophe to his broom and an antistrophe to the Olympian god he serves, praising the twin realms of earth and sky, of work and worship, that define his innocent life.

The sudden appearance of a flock of birds prompts Ion to draw his bow and drive them from the sanctuary. He feels a twinge, however, for the eagles from Parnassus bring omens from Zeus, and the swans provide inspiration for Apollo's own music. Even so, Ion threatens to slay 'the red-footed swans' (162–63) and 'drown their beautiful song in blood' (168–69). The tone remains light, for the birds hardly pose a serious danger – they build their nests in the rafters, and their droppings pollute the shrine. Nevertheless, their song, like Ion's own monody, must cease, for 'the sound of the bow will end it' (173). The audience glimpse, in brief, the trajectory of the play – a movement from almost comic innocence at the start to near-tragic experience at the end, the conversion of Ion from broom-sweeping lad to bloodthirsty adult.

The invasion of birds is one thing, the arrival of the chorus quite another. Ion puts down his bow and shares the audience's bemusement at this group of Athenian maidens who have come to admire the sights of Delphi. Critics bound by the conventions of theatrical realism imagine an array of architectural and scenic elements that provoke the chorus's wonder. However, the abundance of deictic endings (Greek suffixes that indicate something is pointed at), the imperatives 'look!' and 'see!', the fact that the *parodos* is not sung in unison but broken up into individual and specific utterances, all suggest that the chorus create the sights from their words and gestures, and the spectators follow the verbal cues to project the sculptured images onto the conventional skene façade.[3]

Specific details spark the interest of the Athenian chorus, particularly the mythic battle between the Olympian gods and the earth-born giants (206–18). Their patron goddess Athena played a crucial role in the victory, using her gorgon-shield against the giant Enceladus. They learn from Ion that gorgons also are carved on the *omphalos* that lies at the centre of Apollo's temple (223–25), establishing an important imagistic link between Delphi and Athens. But the chorus' thoughts go no further than the surface: 'What we see outside is enough; it charms the eye' (231). By the end of the play, Ion will grow to challenge that attitude and attempt to look behind the temple façade, past its shimmering exterior to uncover a less charming story.

That story finds its central character in the figure that now arrives on-stage, the Athenian queen Creusa. Euripides develops the scene through the longest section of stichomythia in tragedy (105 lines), a novel way to intro-duce background information and advance the narrative. The dialogue draws unrecognized mother and son closer and closer together as each identifies with the other's situation (a childless mother and a motherless child), but it stops well short of full recognition. Creusa weeps at the sight of Apollo's temple, and her thoughts keep returning to the dark moments in her past, to the cave on the Acropolis where Apollo ravished her and where she later exposed her child. Ion's innocent curiosity about Athens and the Acropolis leads Creusa back to that dark place, and she deflects his questions or chooses silence. That pattern occurs several times, transforming the dialogue into a narrative exposition whose stops and starts convey its underlying meaning.

When Creusa introduces her 'fictional other', the third party for whom she ostensibly consults the oracle, the direction of the stichomythia changes for the last time. Ion learns that Apollo has fathered this woman's child. Although he dismisses the claim as incredible, he comes to sympathize with the unfortunate woman, recognizing the mirror image of his own mother-less upbringing:

> *Ion*:   But what if Apollo took the child and raised him in secret?
> *Creusa*: No right to act alone! He should share that joy.
> *Ion*:   Your story sings with my own grief.
>
> (357–59)

The dialogue leaves us with a very different Ion from the one we first met. Unlike the birds that flutter down to foul the shrine, the threat to Ion's peace of mind cannot be driven off with bow and arrow. Could the god he serves act unjustly? Can a mortal consult Apollo's oracle with questions that incriminate the god himself?

These doubts lead Ion to break out of stichomythia and deliver his first full speech (369–80), counselling Creusa to abandon the quest on behalf of her friend. No one can force the gods to divulge what they do not wish to. Creusa counters with her own request for secrecy, begging Ion not to tell her husband, Xuthus, what has passed between them. As if on cue, Xuthus arrives full of excitement, having received a preliminary prophecy that his wife will leave the sanctuary with a child, answering their need for a son and heir to the Athenian throne. This transitional scene brings together Ion, Creusa, and Xuthus, only to have them go their separate ways, unaware of the complex weave that binds them together. When her husband enters the temple to consult the Delphic oracle, Creusa is once again an outsider, forced to hear of Apollo's word indirectly, and she exits via an *eisodos*.

Left alone on-stage, Ion delivers a soliloquy that challenges the god he serves. That Apollo should rape women and not take responsibility for the results leads the young man to cry out: 'Since you have power, / do what is right' (439–40). For Ion, the possession of a god's might requires its virtuous application. Otherwise one has only rape and injustice, a world where evil cannot be condemned because men are simply following the example of the Olympian gods (*Ion* 442–51).

As we know from Thucydides, the relationship between power and moral responsibility provoked heated debate in Athens during the Peloponnesian War. His account of Athenian dealings with the neutral island of Melos, the famous Melian dialogue, encapsulates the issue. The Athenian envoys argue that the Melians must capitulate: 'For you know as well as we do that right, as the world goes, is in question only between equals in power, while the strong do what they can and the weak suffer what they must.'[4] Athens uses the might-makes-right argument to justify subjugating the island, putting the grown males to death, and selling the women and children into slavery. The audience in the theatre of Dionysus may not have recognized in Ion's moral imperatives a reference to this specific debate, but they would have perceived an image of innocence troubled by a question of great importance. The Ion who leaves the stage after these reflections has changed from the young man who, 300 lines earlier, was singing to his broom. The world of Apollo's shrine can never again be cleaned and purified so easily.

The significant action now takes place off-stage in the temple's inner sanctum, where Xuthus receives his prophecy about children. To set that event in its broadest context, the chorus organize their first stasimon around the issue of offspring, appealing to the virgin goddesses Athena and Artemis to help guarantee children for the Athenian house of Erechtheus. The women focus on Athena's birth without labour pains (delivered fully formed from the head of Zeus), and on the role of Artemis who traditionally helped women in childbirth. Perhaps we are meant to see in these goddesses the counter-image of Creusa, a mortal raped by a god, abandoned while pregnant, and forced to give birth alone and in secret.

In the antistrophe the chorus raise a paean to the joys of offspring, in which they pray for 'the beloved raising of our own children' (487). The choice of words is precise – the women ask not simply for children, but for the *raising* of children, and not any children but sons and daughters of *their own* (that is, not adopted). The first request has been denied Creusa completely, as she herself tells Ion earlier. As for the second, Hermes has informed us that Apollo plans to present Ion as Xuthus' offspring, not hers. Only later, in Athens, is Creusa to learn the truth. The contrast between the chorus's wishes for themselves and the reality that faces Creusa highlights their mistress' anguish.

In the epode, the chorus describe a strange scene on the Acropolis involving the mythical first family of Athens. The daughters of Cecrops and Aglauros dance in the meadow before the temple of Athena (the Erechtheum) to the music of Pan, the beast-god associated with rampant sexuality. These spectral daughters had leapt off the Acropolis to their deaths, after opening a crib and seeing the snake-baby Erichthonius, part of the myth of Athenian autochthony that Creusa shares with Ion in their first meeting (265–74). Into this strange atmosphere, the chorus introduce the woman (Creusa's 'third party') who gave birth to Apollo's child in a sunless hollow not far from Pan's cave. Imagining that the child's exposure led to a feast for the birds and wild beasts (503–05), the chorus conclude that they never heard a story in which there was happiness for children born between gods and mortals. At that very moment, Ion – the child of the god Apollo and mortal Creusa – enters to discover whether Xuthus has received an oracular response regarding a son.

From the paean for children to a rejection of divine-mortal offspring, the chorus call into question precisely the situation the play plans to celebrate. The lyric forces the audience to make a series of troubling connections, holding together ideas or images of virgin goddesses, families strengthened by legitimate children, licentious sexuality represented by Pan, the myth of Athenian autochthony, the ghosts of dead maidens, an exposed child, the unhappiness fated for the mortal offspring of a god, and the figure of Ion himself. The inherent contradictions disturb our faith in Apollonian beneficence, bringing to the surface the potentially deadly undercurrents that flow inexorably back to the crimes committed in a sunless cave.

Euripides prepares for the oracular pronouncement in dramatic fashion, bringing Ion back to the stage just in time for Xuthus' entrance through the temple doors. We know that the 'recognition' between father and son must fit into Apollo's plan to cover up his own paternity, and we understand Xuthus' joy at finding the son the oracle has promised him. To Ion, however, the affection of the older man seems like the homosexual advances of a pederast, advances that he forcefully – and humorously – repulses.[5] That Ion feels he must threaten Xuthus with his bow – till now reserved for dispersing birds from the temple precinct – marks his lack of preparation for the world that will press upon him with increasing insistence.

The two men deliver their exchange in trochaic tetrametre catalectic, a fast and lively dialogue rhythm that Euripides reintroduced into tragedy after it fell out of favour with the death of Aeschylus. We meet this metre in the virulent closing exchange between the chorus and Aegisthus in *Agamemnon*, discussed in Chapter 6. Here, however, Euripides uses it for comic ends. Ion finds Xuthus' claim to paternity a bad joke, until he comes to understand what the oracle proclaimed: the first person that Xuthus meets coming out of the temple is his son. The tempo of the scene quickens, shifting from line-for-line to half-line stichomythia, overlapping the thoughts and responses of the two parties. Ion questions the identity of his mother, an issue that Xuthus in his excitement forgot to raise with Apollo's oracle. Together they work through Xuthus' pre-marital affairs, concluding that he must have impregnated a Delphian girl one drunken night at a Bacchic festival. The cavalier way in which Xuthus tosses off possible pregnancies provides the emotional antithesis for the trauma of Creusa's 'bitter wedding rape' (506).

By severely truncating their actual reunion, Euripides marks the ambivalence of the recognition of father and son, which culminates in a stiff and awkward embrace (560–62). Ion instinctively addresses his absent mother and not Xuthus who stands before him: 'Mother, wherever you are, I burn to see you / even more than before, to press you to me' (563–64). The chorus also think of Creusa, whose prayers for a child of her own have gone unanswered: 'We share your happiness, / but want our mistress to have the chance / for children, to brighten the house of Erechtheus' (566–68).

Returning to normal iambic trimetre dialogue, Xuthus proposes that Ion come back with him to Athens. The young man remains wary, and in his second major speech he pleads with his newfound father to let him stay in Delphi. Ion focuses on what awaits a 'bastard son of an imported father' in a city whose people pride themselves on being autochthonous and not an 'imported' race (589–92). He reveals an astute awareness of the problems with Athens and Athenians: xenophobia, jealousy and envy of success, possible ostracism for public figures, political infighting, power-games, and the cynics' ridicule of those who participate in the political process at all. Ion's analysis reflects the crisis that faced the city in the late fifth century, when second-rate politicians rose to power and good men were shunted aside, or simply chose not to participate in political life.[6] Athens is a 'city full of fear' (601), and Ion compares the sovereign rule that Xuthus offers him to a building with a lovely façade, hiding an interior full of pain and sorrow (621–23). Euripides presents a critique of his city through the words of a most disarming critic, an innocent temple attendant who will become the founder of the Ionian people, and as such the guarantor of the Athens of the future.

As if to confirm Ion's portrait of a city full of insensitive and selfish men, Xuthus brushes aside his speech with a single line: 'No more talk like that. Learn to be happy, son' (650). Xuthus plans bring Ion back to Athens, introducing him into the house as a guest or 'onlooker' (*theatês*, 656).[7] Before that, the proud father will honour his child with a feast in Delphi, combining the rituals of *genethlia* (birth celebration) and *dekate* (child-naming), performed on the fifth and then the tenth day following a child's birth.[8] Xuthus names the young man 'Ion', from the participle 'going' (*iôn*), because he met him first when going from the temple (662).[9] In his final two lines (he never reappears on-stage), Xuthus threatens the chorus with death if they divulge his plans to their mistress (666–67). Even as Xuthus denies speech to the chorus, Ion prays that his mother turn out to be an Athenian, so that *he* will inherit the right to free speech as a citizen born of Athenian parents.[10] In this scene, as elsewhere, issues of disclosure and secrecy, expression and silence, power and resistance inform the dialogue.

For the second time the stage clears, and the chorus perform a countersong (primarily in dochmiacs) to the joyful reunion that Xuthus and Ion go off to celebrate. They sympathize with Creusa, who remains barren while her husband has found a child. Focusing on the fact that the boy's mother is unknown and that Xuthus himself is foreign born, the Athenian women betray the xenophobia that Ion associated with his new city. In the antistrophe they interpret Xuthus' actions as a deliberate attempt to disenfranchise their mistress and the ancient house of Erechtheus. The tone of the concluding epode shifts radically, beginning with an address to Parnassus and the uplands above Delphi where Bacchic revels take place, the very circumstance during which Xuthus ostensibly conceived Ion (comparing lines 550–54 with 714–18). Sharing in the wild dance of the Bacchantes, the women invoke the forces of nature and Dionysus to keep Ion away from Athens, praying that this first day of his new life might be his last. They answer Xuthus' threat to murder them if they divulge the truth to Creusa by praying for his son's death.

Following the lyric describing the Bacchantes with 'their slender feet leaping nimbly through the night' (718), Creusa re-enters down an *eisodos* propping up the old Tutor of her father. Euripides dwells on the physical difficulties of the old man's entrance, and his rejoinders sound like Attic versions of comic one-liners: 'The foot is slow but the mind is quick' (742, more freely, 'The spirit is willing but the legs are weak'); 'What good is an old man's stick when I can't see where to put it?' (744); and in response to Creusa's encouragement to keep up his strength, 'I'm with you. But I can't control what I no longer have!' (746).

Critics tend to view this odd entrance as a piece of protracted, and failed, dramatic realism. We would do better to take our critical cue from a statement of the old Tutor himself: 'The ways of prophecy are certainly steep' (739). Part pun on the precipitous climb to the temple of Delphi (as tourists still can attest), part reference to the false prophecies in the play, the old man's comment is humorously on target. Faced with twisted words of the gods, mortals turn to one another for help and support, given visual form with the old Tutor physically leaning on Creusa, and expressed in other ways during the scene. Creusa addresses the chorus more as confidantes than as servants, and the women in turn draw the Tutor and their mistress into a shared lyric *kommos*. For the first time someone with the choice to speak out or remain silent opts for disclosure. The chorus risk Xuthus' death sentence and divulge the prophecy that Creusa will have no child but that her husband has found a son. At the news, Creusa sings of her wish to fly from Greece beyond the Western stars (795–99) – an escape to death – and then falls silent for sixty lines.

Leaving the lyric, the old Tutor tries to reconstruct the past out of the fragmentary details presented by the chorus. Discovering Creusa to be barren, Xuthus fathered a bastard son, sent him to Delphi to be raised, arranged the ruse of seeking oracular help for infertility, plans to take the grown boy back from Delphi, and will set him up as the ruler of Athens. The Tutor's analysis is reasonable, but (almost) dead wrong. He offers to help Creusa murder both father and son, and the chorus add their voice, eager to join the plot. In their readiness to take violent action, Euripides presents a perverse manifestation of the mutual co-operation with which the scene began.

If the play to this point consists of scenes pressing towards disclosure that always stop short, then Creusa's monody shatters the barriers to secrecy. She hears the Tutor's accusations against Xuthus as a pale imitation of the charges she has levelled against Apollo, and against herself. Breaking her silence, Creusa sings an ode of unparalleled beauty and power, revealing fully the betrayal she has suffered at the hands of the god (859–922). She re-creates Apollo's epiphany before her, combining images of song, shimmering light, and the beauty of the natural world. But this splendid manifestation turns dark when the god drags her into a cave as she screams for her mother, and then shamelessly takes his pleasure. Creusa imagines the birth of Apollo on Delos, where Zeus created a palm and laurel bower to shade the goddess Leto in her labour – an idyllic counter-world to the sunless cave where Creusa was ravaged, gave birth in secret, and exposed her child.

In the details of her monody, the audience recognize the outlines of another myth of female abduction, Hades' rape of Persephone and the anguish of her mother Demeter.[11] Like Persephone, Creusa is swept away by a god while in the fields gathering flowers, and then she is raped in the underworld setting of the cavern in the Acropolis. Creusa invokes the myth again when she finally discovers that Ion is her son: 'I never dreamed I'd find you, but thought you shared / the earth and darkness with Persephone' (1441–42). Over the course of the play, Creusa comes to embody *both* female roles in the myth – the innocent victim of a god's rape, and the grieving mother whose child has been taken from her.

From the expressive but private mode of Creusa's monody, Euripides shifts to a series of questions and answers that clarify past events, the second longest stichomythic passage in Euripides (934–1028), surpassed only by the earlier dialogue between Creusa and Ion (264–369). The Tutor's interrogation of Creusa moves the play in a new, and deadly, direction. Unlike the earlier rapid-fire conversation that revealed a sympathetic bond between unrecognized mother and son, this extended stichomythic exchange focuses on Xuthus' betrayal and on the Tutor's plan to kill the young man who once had seemed so caring and solicitous.

Creusa drives the murder plot forward by stepping back into the mythic past. She relates the aetiology of Athena's famed shield-like 'aegis', made from the gorgon that the goddess slew in the battle with the giants, described earlier in the *parodos*. Two drops of the slain gorgon's blood were given to Creusa by her grandfather – one drop cures, and the other kills (1013–15). Creusa now gives the poisoned drop to the old Tutor to use against Ion. When he asks if she keeps the drops separate or together, Creusa responds 'Always apart. Evil and good do not mix' (1017). Euripides' play demonstrates the impossibility of maintaining such simple distinctions. By conjoining humour and pathos, the ludicrous and the deadly serious, *Ion* reveals an instability below the surface that demands scrutiny. Euripides does not blend the opposites in a palatable mix to be swallowed whole, but rather juxtaposes one mood against the other so surprisingly that we view their alternation as a form of critical re-evaluation, a call to think anew the gods, myths, politics, and social mores that inform the play.

With the murder plot in train, the clarity of Creusa's monody vanishes as the characters revert to secrecy, duplicity, and concealment. The Tutor exhorts his body (which barely could carry him onstage) to do its part, and he finds that old limbs grow young at the prospect of vengeance (1041–47). As he hastens off under his own power, we see the reverse image of the opening entrance when Creusa helped him into the orchestra. Rejuvenated by desire for Ion's blood, the Tutor leaves to poison the only party in the play (to this point) innocent of wrongdoing.

Left alone in the orchestra for the last time, the chorus begin their third stasimon with a prayer to Persephone/Hecate for success. Eager to ensure that no bastard outlander ever rules their city, the chorus again exhibit the xenophobia that Ion has associated with Athens. The tone of their closing antistrophe changes abruptly when they call for poets to represent women more fairly, ending the slander that finds females sexually culpable when men really are the seducers and adulterers. Reminiscent of the first stasimon of *Medea*, the chorus take on the sexism of their society, revealing Euripidean sophistication about the politics of representation: Who composes the song? Who sings it? In whose interest is it sung? The chorus's reflections take us back to the prologue, where Hermes explains that Apollo controls the 'song' of the play and has composed it to cover up his rape of Creusa.

A Messenger races on-stage to report that the murder plan has failed and that the Delphians have condemned Creusa to death. In an extended messenger speech (over 100 lines), he recounts the strange events that took place at Ion's birthday feast, including a long description of the tent that Ion erects for the guests, 'carefully guarding against / the rays of the sun, the midday / and the dying beams of light' (1134–36). Just as Creusa was raped and delivered her child in a sunless cave (500–02), so Ion's 'rebirth' will take place in a sunless tent, the golden rays shut out by a celestial cosmos woven into the ceiling and walls of the canopy. The artistic equipoise of the tapestry-heavens provides a counter-image to the world of human passion, violence, and deception that breaks out beneath it.

The Messenger abruptly cuts off his description of the tent to attend to the community of banqueters who have gathered in its shade. Creusa's Tutor ingratiates himself with the guests, claiming the office of wine steward and lacing Ion's cup with the gorgon poison. At the crucial moment of a ritual libation, one of the crowd utters an ill-omened word and Ion commands that the wine be poured out onto the ground, and a new libation prepared. In a play filled with lies and verbal duplicity, it is a wonderful touch that a wrongly placed word should save Ion.

Invading the artificial world of the banquet tent, a flock of doves suddenly flutters in and they drink the wine from the ground. Only the bird
that lands at Ion's feet suffers, and the Messenger compares its death-cries
to a garbled, impenetrable oracle: 'The bird screeched words / impossible to
interpret' (1204–05). The comparison to an enigmatic oracle is apt, given
the Delphic setting and Apollo's twisted prophecy that gave Ion to a false
father, and led his real mother try to kill him.

The dove's death also recalls a time in Ion's life – only that morning –
when the sole cloud on the horizon was a riot of birds in the sanctuary.
Then he only threatened the 'red-footed swans' (163) with his bow, but now
earth-bred Athenian poison kills the 'red-footed dove' (1207–08). The bird's
miniature passion symbolizes the death of innocence in the young man, a
process that began when Ion first questioned Apollo's morals (429–51) and
took root when he protested going to Athens (585–647). Now reborn as a
man of action and violence, Ion leaps over the banquet table and forces the
old man's confession. He then rushes to the Pythian elders and conducts the
swiftest prosecution in dramatic history (two lines of direct speech, 1220–21),
and within another three and a half lines the court has condemned Creusa
to death by stoning (1222–25).

The shotgun verdict, the abrupt departure of the Messenger, and the
brevity of the chorus's subsequent ode set up Creusa's wild entrance pursued by angry Delphians. She shares a short exchange with the chorus in
trochaic tetrametres (1250–60), the same metre used when Xuthus left the
temple and embraced his unwilling son (517–62). If that recognition scene
seemed strained, the forthcoming reunion appears even more so, beginning
with Creusa running for her life from her own child. To complicate matters
further, the chorus advise her to cling as a suppliant to the altar of Apollo
(1255–56), and Creusa finds herself appealing to the god who has plagued
her life to save it.

Sword drawn for murder, the 'new born' Ion who arrives on-stage is
a far cry from the concerned young man the audience last saw some 600
lines earlier, and almost unrecognizable when compared to the youth who
greeted the dawn light with a work song and a hymn of praise. In place
of the sympathetic woman he found in their first dialogue, Ion now sees
an earth-born Athenian monster, at one with the gorgon-blood she tried
to use on him. Each attempts to outdo the other in establishing a special
relationship with Apollo (1282–93), particularly unsettling given what we
know about the god. Ion wonders how Creusa could possibly cling to his
altar, and Creusa surrenders her body to Apollo for protection. When Ion
calls himself Apollo's son, Creusa claims an even closer connection to the
god. Ion argues he has a right to an Athenian inheritance through Xuthus,
and Creusa responds by telling him to go instruct his mother (whoever she
is), but to leave her alone. For all the verbal jostling, the failed connection
between mother and son has reached a crisis. With his sword raised, the
unknowing Ion is on the verge of matricide.

Euripides' *coup de théâtre* comes with the opening of the doors of the temple, closed for the last 800 lines, and the sudden appearance of the Pythia. An earth-bound *dea ex machina*, she speaks not in the oracular voice of Apollo's priestess but as Ion's surrogate mother. First, she stops him from spilling Creusa's blood at the altar. Then the Pythia presents the wicker cradle in which she found him as a baby so many years before, and she urges Ion to take it with him to Athens to help track down his real mother. The priestess gives Ion a maternal kiss and re-enters the temple, her touching farewell a prelude to the recognition that will follow between true mother and son.

The prospect of discovering his past leads Ion to forget the suppliant at the altar, as the story darts off in a new direction, ending in a reunion guided by the objects in the crib. Uniting more than mother and son, the tokens bring together a complex set of images as carefully patterned as any in tragedy. Each object in the crib – the garland of undying olive leaves, the golden snake-clasp for the child, Creusa's unfinished weaving of gorgons fringed with snakes – forges a symbolic link between the abandoned baby and the foundation myths of Athens. The snake-clasp 'retells the tale of Erichthonius' (1427), an important myth of Athenian autochthony and prototype of Ion's own story. As told to Ion in his first dialogue with Creusa (265–74) and later referred to by the chorus (492–502), Athena entrusted the young Erichthonius to the care of the daughters of Cecrops and Aglaurus, the mythical king and queen of Athens. The goddess commanded the maidens not to look inside the cradle, but they disobeyed. The sight of the snake-child proved so terrifying that the girls leapt from the Acropolis to their deaths. Ion hesitates before opening his crib, fearful he may discover that he was born a slave, and again the play teeters on the brink of concealment and secrecy. But the voice of the past no longer can be silenced, and Ion repeats the mythical action of the Aglaurids. He opens the crib and finds a snake-image, but one that provides a clue to his identity rather than a spectre that leads to his death.

Abandoning Apollo's altar, Creusa forces herself back into the scene to claim her son. Through stichomythic question and answer, she predicts the contents of the cradle in order to prove her maternity to the incredulous Ion. Their recognition unfolds as a kind of *ekphrasis*, or verbal description of a work of art. Earlier in the play, the chorus describe the sculptural programme carved on the temple, and the Messenger details the heavenly scenes woven into the banquet tent. The final *ekphrasis* involves the unfinished embroidery on the swaddling clothes for the newborn baby, and these modest traces of the young Creusa's hand prove to be the most important in the play. The snakes and gorgon she describes establish Ion's connection to her and to Athens, and Ion equates the presence of the predicted image with finding an oracle (1424). *This* is the prophecy that the play was looking for, not the false revelation that Apollo arranged with

Xuthus and Ion. Creusa needed no consultation with the Delphic oracle, only the chance to break through the secrecy and deception that had kept her from her own past.

In the joy of recognition that follows, Creusa shifts into lyric while Ion remains in dialogue metre. Given their earlier solo-songs, a shared monody was well within the capabilities of the actors playing Ion and Creusa, but Euripides denies Ion a lyric celebration. While feeling his mother's joy, he wonders who his father is. When he hears that Xuthus is not that man, Ion again feels disconcerting doubts about his parents, doubts that eventually lead him to challenge Apollo in his prophetic shrine.

Creusa, too, cannot suppress an under-song against Apollo: 'No [nuptial] torchlight streamed me to my bed, / no wedding hymns or dance / swept me kindly to your birth' (1476–78). When she refers to the tokens in the crib, they evoke only the hardships of the past:

> Girlish things, my loom's wanderings,
> that did a mother's work.
> I never put you to my breast,
> never washed you with my hands,
> but in a desolate cave
> I left you for the claws of birds,
> their blood feast ...

> (1489–95)

Ion himself abandons his initial enthusiasm at the prospect of a divine father, emphasizing instead the death he nearly suffered from his mother and that he himself nearly inflicted on her.

Ion begins to wonder whether Creusa has concocted the story of Apollo's paternity in order to cover up a youthful indiscretion. He attempts to save his mother public shame by drawing her away from the chorus, so that she can confess the truth only to his ears. Critics invariably point to these lines as evidence that Euripides found the chorus an obstacle to dramatic realism. They fail to consider the play's ongoing concern with openness and disclosure. By taking Creusa aside and promising to 'bury all of it [her past affairs] in darkness' (1522), Ion re-enacts the processes of secrecy that the play has shown to be ultimately futile, and potentially fatal.

Although Creusa swears by Athena that Apollo is his father, Ion remains unconvinced, and he vows to cross the threshold of the temple to ask the god point blank (1547–48). Earlier in the play Ion warned Creusa that 'No one should ask / questions that oppose the god' (372–73), but now he finds himself ready to do just that. As Gilbert Norwood observed some 75 years ago, the young man's challenge goes to the heart of the play:

> Apollo has said both that he himself, and Xuthus, is the father of Ion. Which of these statements is true matters comparatively little. One of

them must be a lie. The god who gives oracles to Greece is a trickster, and no celestial consolations or Athenian throne can compensate the youth for the loss of what filled his heart only this morning.[12]

The sudden appearance of Athena on the *theologeion* stops Ion in his tracks. Sent by Apollo, the goddess explains that he thought it best 'not to reveal himself in person, lest he be blamed / in public for all that has happened' (1556–57). Assuring Ion that Apollo is his father, Athena outlines the glories awaiting the young man as founder of the Ionian race. Far from providing a clean dramatic conclusion, however, Athena herself adopts the discredited mode of secrecy and concealment, commanding Creusa to keep her real relationship with Ion from her husband: 'Absolute silence! Not a word about how you got your child. / Let Xuthus cherish his sweet illusion' (1601–02).

The ending of the play remains purposefully equivocal. After the appearance of Athena, Creusa clings to the ring knockers on the temple door, in sudden rapture at recovering her son (1612–13). Have the wild emotional swings of the play disoriented her? Does she want to stay in Delphi? Whatever her gesture signifies, it calls attention to the simple fact that the temple doors remain shut to Creusa, as they have been throughout the play. For his part, Ion does not enter the temple, but he does remain sceptical of Apollo's role in his birth. Twice he responds to Athena's assurances of the god's paternity by stating that it is 'not unbelievable' (1606, 1608). The use of litotes (affirming by negating the contrary) here and elsewhere at the end of the play suggests that the basic uncertainties remain.[13]

On the other hand, the ending holds out great promise, both for Ion and for his new city. Athena proclaims that the young man will found the Ionian race, and his half-brothers (future sons of Creusa and Xuthus) will play a similar role as the founders of the Dorians and Achaeans, ancestors of the Spartans. Although the date of *Ion* is in question, it probably was produced several years after the resumption of the Peloponnesian War between Athens and Sparta in 418 BC. The fact that both the Athenians and their Spartan enemies stem from the same heroic stock suggests that Euripides has transformed the myth of autochthony from a parochial symbol of Athenian chauvinism to an image of common Greek origin and brotherhood. All Greeks have their roots in violent, earth-bound nature, but as ancestral brothers they also share a common lineage that makes war between them fratricidal.

Leaving for Athens to father the Ionian race (the basis of the later Athenian empire), Ion represents the future of the city that most of the audience knew as their own. In his troubled reflections on life in Athens earlier in the play, and in the fate he nearly suffers at the hands of Athenians, Ion discovers a people moving between introspective xenophobia and outward-reaching power. Euripides' anachronisms convert the mythical Ion into a potential victim of the very empire he is destined to found, as well as a symbol of its best hopes. Emerging from the cloistered world of Delphi into the full contingency of adult life, Ion displays to the audience the humorous and deadly, the tragic and the transcendental, proclivities of their own nature. A *Bildungsdrama* of individual growth, discovery, and reunion, *Ion* is also a masterpiece of cultural self-inquiry, a tragedy that explores the boundaries of the genre and the critical (and self-critical) capacities of its audience.

Notes

1 See D.J. Conacher, 'Some Profane Variations on a Tragic Theme', *Phoenix* 23, 1979, pp. 26–38. Lowe, op. cit. (Chapter 5, n. 5), pp. 182–84 analyses the two plays in terms of what he calls 'cross-purposes' plots.
2 In a modern theatre a director might have Hermes exit into the audience and take a seat. Gods as both scene-setters and audience are as old as the *Iliad*, where Athena and Apollo arrange the single combat between Hector and Ajax and then, disguised as birds, perch in a nearby tree and watch (*Il.* 7.17–45, 57–62).
3 See K.H. Lee, intro, trans, and comm., *Euripides, 'Ion'*, Warminster, Aris & Phillips, 1977, pp. 177–81.
4 Thucydides 5.89. The translation is Crawley's, *The Peloponnesian War, Thucydides*, rev. by T.E. Wick, New York, Random House, 1982, p. 351.
5 B.M.W. Knox, 'Euripidean Comedy' (org. 1970), in op. cit. (Chapter 5, n. 30), p. 260.
6 On this development in late fifth-century Athens, see Carter op. cit. (Chapter 8, n. 2).
7 The word also is used for 'theatre spectator'. Perhaps Euripides is reminding the audience that the process of 'looking on' in the theatre also implies looking 'into', as Ion does in his soliloquy challenging Apollo (*Ion* 429–51) and here in his speech about Athens.
8 Lee, op. cit. (above n. 3), p. 233 on *Ion* 653; also J.D. Denniston, ed. and comm., *Euripides: Electra*, Oxford, Clarendon Press, 1939, pp. 131–32 on *El.* 654.
9 Characters frequently pun on Ion's name. Hermes proclaims the name when Ion makes his first entrance (81); the chorus tell Ion that Xuthus is coming out (*exionta* 516) of the temple; Xuthus tells Ion of the oracle pronouncing the first one he meets coming out (*exionti* 535) as his son; and the Tutor convinces Creusa that the name (*Iôn, ionti* 831) is a blatant cover-up for Xuthus' long-standing plan to foist his bastard son onto the Athenian throne.
10 Other Euripidean passages involving freedom of speech include *El.* 1049–57, *Phoen.* 391–92, *Or.* 905, *Ba.* 668–69, and *Hipp.* 421–23, discussed by W.S. Barrett ed. and comm., *Euripides: Hippolytos*, Oxford, Clarendon Press, 1964, p. 236. See also H.M. Roisman, 'Women's Free Speech in Greek Tragedy', in *Free Speech in Classical Antiquity*, eds I. Sluiter and R. Rosen, Leiden, Brill, 2004, pp. 91–114.
11 See the Homeric *Hymn to Demeter*, 1–32, 417–33, and discussion in Chapter 8.
12 G. Norwood, *Greek Tragedy*, 3rd edn, London, Methuen, 1942, p. 238.
13 A reading of the play handsomely presented by K. Zacharia, *Converging Truths: Euripides' Ion and the Athenian Quest for Self-Definition*, Leiden, Brill, 2003.

Select bibliography

For invaluable bibliography (with index) and summaries of most published scholarship dealing with the ancient theatre, see J.R. Green, 'Theatre Production: 1971–86', *Lustrum* 31, 1989, pp. 7–71, 273–278; 'Theatre Production: 1987–1995', *Lustrum* 37, 1995, pp. 7–139, 309–318; and 'Theatre Production: 1996–2006', *Lustrum* 50, 2008, pp. 7–200, 367–391.

In addition to the books and articles cited in the endnotes to each chapter, the following works are worth consulting.

Aristotle's Poetics: A Translation and Commentary for Students of Literature (1968), L. Golden (trans.) and O.B. Hardison (comm.), Englewood Cliffs, NJ, Prentice-Hall.

Bacon, H. (1982) 'Aeschylus', in T.J. Luce (ed.), *Ancient Writers, Greece and Rome*, vol. 1, New York, Scribners, pp. 99–155.

Barlow, S. (2008) *The Imagery of Euripides*, 3rd edn, Bristol, Bristol Classical Press.

Cambridge Companion to Greek and Roman Theatre (2007), M. McDonald and J.M. Walton (eds), Cambridge, Cambridge University Press.

Conacher, D.J. (1967) *Euripidean Drama*, Toronto, University of Toronto Press.

Dover, K.J. (1974) *Greek Popular Morality in the Time of Plato and Aristotle*, Berkeley, University of California Press.

Encyclopedia of Greek Tragedy (2014), H.M. Roisman (ed.), Chichester, Wiley-Blackwell.

Foley, H.P. (2001) *Female Acts in Greek Tragedy*, Princeton, NJ, Princeton University Press.

Goldhill, S. (1986) *Reading Greek Tragedy*, Cambridge, Cambridge University Press.

Gould, J. (2001) *Myth, Ritual, Memory, and Exchange: Essays in Greek Literature and Culture*, Oxford, Oxford University Press.

Green, J.R. (1994) *Theatre in Ancient Greek Society*, London, Routledge.

Hall, E. (2010) *Greek Tragedy: Suffering Under the Sun*, Oxford and New York, Oxford University Press.

Harrison, G.W.M. and V. Liapis (eds) (2013) *Performance in Greek and Roman Theatre*, Leiden and Boston, MA, Brill.

Lattimore, R. (1969) *Story Patterns in Greek Tragedy*, Ann Arbor, University of Michigan Press.

Lebeck, A. (1971) *The Oresteia: A Study in Language and Structure*, Washington, D.C., The Center for Hellenic Studies.

Lesky, A. (1983) *Greek Tragic Poetry*, M. Dillon (trans.), New Haven, CT, Yale University Press.

March, J. (1998) *Dictionary of Classical Mythology*, London, Cassell.

Oxford Readings in Greek Tragedy, (1987), E. Segal (ed.), Oxford, Blackwell.

Parker, R. (1996) *Athenian Religion: A History*, Oxford, Clarendon Press.

Rose, P.W. (1992) *Sons of the Gods, Children of the Earth: Ideology and Literary Form in Ancient Greece*, Ithaca, NY, Cornell University Press.

Rosenmeyer, T.G. (1982) *The Art of Aeschylus*, Berkeley, University of California Press.

Schmidt, D.J. (2001) *On Germans and Other Greeks: Tragedy and Ethical Life*, Bloomington, Indiana University Press.

Segal, C. (1981) *Tragedy and Civilization: An Interpretation of Sophocles*, Cambridge, MA, Harvard University Press.

Vernant, J.P. and P. Vidal-Naquet (1990) *Myth and Tragedy in Ancient Greece*, trans. J. Lloyd, New York, Zone Books.

Whitman, C.H. (1951) *Sophocles, A Study of Heroic Humanism*, Cambridge, MA, Harvard University Press.

Wolff, C. (1982) 'Euripides', in T.J. Luce (ed.), *Ancient Writers, Greece and Rome*, vol. 1, New York, Scribners, pp. 233–66.

Zeitlin, F.I. (1996) *Playing the Other: Gender and Society in Classical Greek Literature*, Chicago, IL, University of Chicago Press.

Index

Printed in the USA
CPSIA information can be obtained
at www.ICGtesting.com
LVHW020231230823
756039LV00009B/354

9 781138 812628